STAFF DEVELOPMENT IN HUMAN SERVICE ORGANIZATIONS

HARVEY J. BERTCHER

University of Michigan

PRENTICE HALL, Englewood Cliffs, New Jersey 07632

Library of Congress Cataloging-in-Publication Data

BERTCHER, HARVEY J.
    Staff development in human service organizations.

    Bibliography: p. 206
    Includes index.
    1. Social workers—In-service training—United
States.   2.   Social work administration—United States.
I. Title.
HV40.5.B47   1988   361.3'07   87-18687
ISBN   0-13-840273-6

Editorial/production supervision and
    interior design: Rob DeGeorge
Cover design: Wanda Lubelska
Cover photo: Burgoyne, Inc.
Manufacturing buyer: Ray Keating

 ©1988 by Prentice Hall
A Division of Simon & Schuster
Englewood Cliffs, New Jersey 07632

Printed in the United States of America

10   9   8   7   6   5   4   3   2   1

ISBN   0-13-840273-6   01

PRENTICE-HALL INTERNATIONAL (UK) LIMITED, *London*
PRENTICE-HALL OF AUSTRALIA PTY. LIMITED, *Sydney*
PRENTICE-HALL CANADA INC., *Toronto*
PRENTICE-HALL HISPANOAMERICANA, S.A., *Mexico*
PRENTICE-HALL OF INDIA PRIVATE LIMITED, *New Delhi*
PRENTICE-HALL OF JAPAN, INC., *Tokyo*
SIMON & SCHUSTER ASIA PTE. LTD., *Singapore*
EDITORA PRENTICE-HALL DO BRASIL, LTDA., *Rio de Janeiro*

CONTENTS

PREFACE

This book was written to supplement a course I have been teaching on staff development at the University of Michigan's School of Social Work. I had a special interest in the course because I helped to create it, in cooperation with my colleague, Charles Garvin. We had come to believe that such a course was needed in our School. We remembered having major staff development responsibilities in the jobs we held after receiving our Masters of Social Work degree; jobs which entailed training and supervising staff, making use of consultants, conducting problem-solving staff meetings, and so forth. We thought that Michigan MSW graduates should be prepared for similar responsibilities. Initially, we co-taught the course, but in subsequent semesters, we each taught a section of what turned out to be a popular subject for many students. Over the years I tried several texts, but never found one that proved satisfactory. Meanwhile, I was teaching the course by adding this, changing that, and learning from my students' attempts to apply what I was teaching, in a wide variety of human service organizations. This book is a distillation of those experiences.

To create this course, we first organized a Special Studies seminar and recruited four graduate social work students to help us design the course: Harold Craft, Shalini Damle, Joseph LaRosa, and Marie Sandoli. Subsequently, we used the outcome of that seminar as the basis for a four-day summer institute on staff development: thirteen social work practitioners registered for the institute, and our colleague, Frank

Maple, joined us as a resource person. Thanks to the generous support of Dean Fedele Fauri, we were able to employ one of the School's graduates, Judith Braver, to serve as recorder for these sessions. With her help, we produced a slender volume of 106 pages, entitled *Staff Development in Social Welfare Agencies,* published by our School in 1969 as a set of institute proceedings. That volume became our first course text. With this experience in hand, we guided the course through our School's curriculum committee, and then to its final approval by the governing faculty.

What I have tried to write is a practical guide rather than a scholarly text, but I have attempted to build this guide on relevant social science knowledge and research. Today's world is perhaps more cost-conscious than ever, and human service organizations must continually fight the battle of the budget, seeking adequate resources to undertake impossible tasks. Faced with being under-funded and under-staffed, human service organizations have to try to make their staff as efficient and effective as possible. Good staff development can play a vital role in the achievement of these twin goals. Hopefully, this book can play a part in the development of well-planned and well-managed staff development programs.

Many people helped me to complete this text. Pauline Bush typed several of the chapters, and when she retired, Dan Madaj took over, with skill and good humor. Several graduate students graciously allowed me to quote at length from the project reports they wrote for the course; they include Cheryl Bader, Wendy Gunther, Suzanne Orr, Douglas Spaight, and Karen Stiger. These projects were carried out in a variety of human service organizations in which the students were either doing an internship or were employed at the time they took the course. Two of my faculty colleagues, Jack Rothman and Bill Lawrence, read portions of the manuscript and offered constructive feedback. As indicated above, Charles Garvin collaborated with me on the development of the course and stimulated my thinking on the subject. Another colleague, Jesse Gordon, invited me to participate in a number of innovation-diffusion-staff-development projects for the U.S. Department of Labor and we learned together from these experiences. I want to thank Philip MacBride for asking me to serve on his doctoral dissertation committee; this proved most helpful when I was working on issues pertaining to the evaluation of staff development. In addition to Dean Fauri's support of our efforts to create the staff development course, Deans Phillip Fellin and Harold Johnson have provided the necessary assistance and encouragement to complete this text.

Finally, the support given to me by my family has made it possible for me to persevere whenever I faltered. Writing a book is not an easy task when a host of other work demands continually interfere. The family put up with frequent bouts of, "Dad's working on his book." Without their patience and understanding, I doubt that I would have finished. The shortcomings of this book can all be laid at my door, but that it did get written is due in no small measure to the tender loving care I received from my wife, Gloria, my children, Quincey and Corey, and a houseful of pets, including Pumpkin the cat, our dogs Shane and Natasha, and Monty the (what else?) python.

H.J.B.

chapter 1

INTRODUCING THIS BOOK

- For whom was this book written?
- How should you use this book?
- How will *staff development* be defined in this book?
- What staff development is not.
- What activities in organizations are *staff development activities?*
- What kinds of problems and obstacles should be addressed through staff development?
- Who should do staff development?
- Where does staff development fit into your organization?
- How is this book organized?
- What should you be able to do as a result of reading this book?

FOR WHOM WAS THIS BOOK WRITTEN?

You, the reader, might fit into any of these categories:

1. You might be an *administrator* in a human service organization who has been assigned the responsibility for creating, managing, or improving staff development in your organization.

2. You might be a *staff member* in a human service organization who has volunteered for or been assigned to a staff development committee—a committee that has some responsibility to create, manage, or improve staff development in the organization.
3. You might be a *student* in an undergraduate or graduate program in the human services, such as social work, nursing, education, counseling, recreation, occupational therapy, or child care, who anticipates having responsibility, after graduation, for the creation, management, or improvement of staff development.
4. You might be a *faculty member* in an undergraduate or graduate program in the human services who wants a text for a course devoted wholly or in part to staff development.
5. You might be a layperson who is simply interested in the subject of staff development.

HOW SHOULD THIS BOOK BE USED?

This book will help you to identify one or more important *needs* of the staff in your organization and to arrive at a resolution of the need(s). Reading about staff development is one thing, but doing it is another. As Mark Twain (n.d.) said:

> But you cannot forget that experience is the best way to find out about something. A fellow who takes a hold of a bull by the tail once is getting sixty or seventy times as much information as the fellow who hasn't. Anybody who starts in to carry a cat home by the tail is getting knowledge that's always going to be useful. He's never likely to grow dim or doubtful. . . .Chances are he won't carry the cat that way again. . . .

Accordingly, you will find that the chapters are organized sequentially to help you carry out and evaluate staff development projects in a human service organization. Each chapter contains explanatory text, sometimes including examples of staff development projects, and a set of guidelines to help you carry out your own projects.

HOW WILL *STAFF DEVELOPMENT* BE DEFINED IN THIS BOOK?

Here is a dictionary definition of the word *staff:*

> a body of assistants to a superintendent or manager: the group of officers and aides-de-camp appointed to attend upon, or serve as escort to a civil executive, esp. a president or governor, . . .an establishment of officers not having a command, as the officers of the supply, medical, chaplains, etc.; officers detailed to serve on the staff of the commander of a fleet or lesser unit. . .(*Webster's Seventh New Collegiate Dictionary,* 1961, p. 851)

An appropriate modern counterpart might be *upper-middle management,* for the emphasis in the foregoing definition is on those with the key to the executive washroom—not line supervisors—or upper-echelon commissioned officers—not just any commissioned officers. Clearly this definition does not include assembly-line workers, people offering a service, or front-line troops. Modern usage is somewhat more inclusive, using *staff* to refer to people on the line, as contrasted with *management*. For example, one state department of social services' training division has been called Staff Training and Management Development.[1]

In human service organizations, the term *staff* can refer to those persons directly engaged in delivering the organization's services to its community. It can also include support service personnel, such as secretaries and maintenance workers, who make it possible for the organization to deliver those services. It is also common to speak of the staff of a hospital as including doctors, nurses, technicians, researchers, and the like. Some organizations consider volunteers to be part of staff; others do not, but cast them in a distinct category. The members of an organization's board of directors may think that *everyone* who works for the organization, including the executive director, is a member of "our staff," but the director may not see himself or herself as a staff member. Most people probably do not think of members of the board of directors themselves as staff, although they certainly are volunteers who work on behalf of—if not for—the organization.

Defining the positions to be included under the heading *staff* determines the appropriate target of staff development activities. For purposes of clarity then, I will define *staff* as follows:

Staff: All those who work for or on behalf of the organization. This includes people in the following kinds of positions:[2]

> Board members
> Administrators
> Middle management
> Supervisors
> Line workers
> Secretaries
> Clerks
> Paraprofessionals
> Volunteers
> Maintenance personnel

Clearly, the role expectations for each of these positions vary widely, as do their staff development needs. Nevertheless, an effective staff development program should target each of these positions in terms of its own development needs—which leads us to the *development* portion of the term *staff development.*

---

[1]The idea that staff are to be "trained" but management is to be "developed" suggests a number of humorous possibilities, but I shall forgo the pleasure of pursuing them in these pages.

[2]The one exception to this definition is those specialists who work for (that is, are paid by) the organization, but are not staff—consultants, plumbers, and the like.

Turning again to the dictionary, one finds the following definition of *development:*

> to unfold more completely; to evolve the possibilities of; to make active (something latent); advance; further; to promote the growth of. . . . (*Webster's Seventh New Collegiate Dictionary,* 1961, p. 227)

Thus, *development* in the term *staff development* can refer to (1) the growth of staff members—either as individuals, as subgroups, or as a total staff group—in relation to their knowledge about their job, their attitudes toward their job, and/or their skills in doing their job; to (2) enhancing the knowledge, attitudes, or skills of staff members in relation to movement within the organization—including promotion—to other positions; or to (3) the professional development of staff members in relation to their life career, some of which might well be played out as staff members in other organizations. Like human growth, development can be a natural process, unfolding over time; conditions in a human service organization, however, can sometimes serve to discourage or limit the growth of staff members, maintaining some valued status quo. Then again, growth can occur haphazardly unless there is some planning to give it direction.

With these comments as background, a definition of *staff development* can now be presented:

> *Staff development*: A planned process designed to improve the ability of staff members to do their jobs in such a way that they and their organization achieve their goals for clients, and that staff members find their work personally rewarding.

The term *staff development* is often used interchangeably with *in-service training,* but in-service training is only one of many activities that fall within the broad category of staff development. Given the broad definition of staff development used in this book, the following are activities that include staff development as a primary purpose:

1. Orientation to the organization
2. Supervision (individual and group)
3. Consultation (individual and group)
4. In-service training
5. Out-service training (for example, attendance at conferences, institutes, workshops, and courses that are external to the organization)
6. Full-time educational leave
7. Field trips to cooperating agency
8. Problem-solving staff meetings
9. Participation in the development and implementation of an accountability system
10. Participation in research focused on service delivery or organizational operation
11. Serving as a field training site for students
12. Operation of an organization library

13.   Informal social activities
14.   Periodic individual evaluation

WHAT STAFF DEVELOPMENT IS NOT

Another way to define a term is to state what is does *not* mean. There are many factors in an organization that affect the ability of staff to do their jobs well and to their own satisfaction that I have not listed: They fall into the general category of personnel management, which includes such activities as:

Recruitment and hiring processes
Establishment of pay levels
Management of an affirmative action program
Union–management relations
Promotional procedures
Personnel practices
Termination procedures

My reason for excluding them is to limit and focus the content of this book. In addition, they have to do with the internal management of the organization in which staff work. No doubt they have an impact on staff members' activities, but that impact is indirect. This distinction, I realize, is not precise or clear-cut. Supervision, for example, has both a staff development and a personnel management function (see, for example, Milkovich and Glueck, 1985; Sayles and Strauss, 1980).

STAFF DEVELOPMENT ACTIVITIES: A RATIONALE

In each instance, the criterion for including each of the activities listed earlier under the umbrella term *staff development* was that the activity had, as a major reason for being performed, the improvement of staff members' abilities to do their jobs well so that the organization could achieve its goals and the staff members would find their work more rewarding.

Orientation to the organization.   Socializing new staff members to the formal policies, procedures, and belief systems of the organization—as well as to its informal systems—is basic to helping them do their jobs. Brim and Wheeler (1966) indicate that an adult who occupies a new position and is expected to perform effectively in the role attendant to that position requires (1) knowledge of what is expected in that position; (2) the skills necessary to meet these expectations acceptably well; and (3) the motivation to do so. Orientation is designed to provide needed information about the job, to help the new staff mobilize needed skills (or recognize skill deficits that need to be made up), and to strengthen the motivation to do the job well that the individual had when first hired.

Supervision.   Individual or group supervision has been defined as:

> an administrative process for getting the work done and maintaining organizational accountability... supervision... [is] the... method by which knowledge and skill are transmitted from the experienced to the inexperienced.... (Miller, 1971, p. 1496).

Emphasis on the administrative aspects of supervision is designed to make a staff member's job performance more predictable and more in conformity with the organization's policies and procedures. This, in turn, is meant to facilitate coordination of individual staff members' actions, leading—one hopes—to a consistently high quality of service to clients. The educational aspects of supervision are designed to help staff members learn new techniques, engage in self-assessment, and introduce an objective third-party perspective into a review of service delivery and organizational issues. Individual supervision can be based on needs of individual staff members; group supervision adds group thinking to the process of helping individual staff with work problems. Group supervision differs from in-service training in its focus on specific day-to-day service delivery issues; in-service training focuses on more general issues of concern to everyone in a staff group. In reality, however, the boundary between group supervision and in-service training may, at times, be difficult to discern.

Consultation.   Individual or group consultation has been defined as:

> a way of giving advice and counsel to a person (or group of persons) on a specific problem in a defined area—advice and counsel which this person is free to accept or reject. Its purpose is to add to and enhance the knowledge and understanding of... the person (or persons) seeking the help in order to resolve the problem. The consultant does not have ongoing responsibility for the client(s) being consulted about or for the evaluation of the consultee, or for the development of the program being discussed. (Hamovitch, 1963)

Consultation differs from supervision in two ways: First, the consultant is usually someone from the outside—either an individual or a group totally separate from the organization, or a person or group from an administratively separate unit of the organization. Second, the consultant has no administrative control over any staff member's job performance. Like supervision, individual consultation is paced according to the needs of individual staff members, whereas group consultation is targeted more toward the common needs of that staff group. One notable exception to these specifications is *peer group supervision,* in which a group of staff peers meet to help one another with job-related problems that individual staff members present to the group. Since none of the members of such groups have administrative control over any of the other members—that is, each person is free to accept or reject the counsel and advice of the others in the group—it is, in fact, a form of group *consultation,* not group supervision (although the term *group supervision* is often used to describe such an arrangement).

In-service training.   Many people use the terms *in-service training* and *staff development* interchangeably. I do not. It should be clear by now that in-service training is only one of many staff development activities. This book will make the point that training that is based on the assessed needs of the staff members toward whom it is directed has the greatest probability of success.

Out-service training.   Attendance at conferences, institutes, workshops, and so forth that are external to the organization could be classified as *out-service training*. Their inclusion as staff development activities has the same rationale as does in-service training or full-time educational leave. The emphasis here is on the attachment of staff to outside instructional and inspirational resources that the organization does not possess, concurrent with—and preferably related to— their work. An important aspect of out-service training is the broadened perspective it affords the individual staff member through interaction with staff members from other organizations who are engaged in similar tasks.

Full-time educational leave.   In the relatively plush postwar era of the 1950s and 1960s, many organizations would select promising staff and send them to school for undergraduate or graduate education, with the clear understanding that the individuals were committed to return to the organization that had financed their education, so as to bring into the organization what they had learned in school. Here, the staff members' development took place outside of the organization; when they returned, they could spread to other staff the knowledge, attitudes, and skills that they had acquired.

Field trips to cooperating agency.   As the old saying goes, seeing is believing. Field trips improve staff members' ability to do their jobs in several ways, not least through the benefits derived from meeting, face to face, people from other agencies who have previously been disembodied telephone voices, and then seeing the physical plant in which they operate. In addition to the knowledge gained, the informal social aspects of traveling together and being guests together in another organization can have a beneficial effect on staff members' feelings about themselves as a cohesive group.

Problem-solving staff meetings.   Assembling staff members periodically is a common administrative device for disseminating information efficiently. Staff meetings may also be held to formalize, through a rubber-stamp voting process, decisions that have been worked through by staff committees or administrators. The more democratically managed such meetings are—that is, the more staff participate in attempting to work out consensually based decisions on a broad range of job-related issues—the more staff learn from one another about the complexities of their work. Because learning about the job to be done is an important aspect of staff's ability to do their jobs, these problem-solving staff meetings can be thought of as a significant staff development activity.

If staff development is well done, one important outcome is the creation of good staff morale. The organizational literature has consistently indicated that good staff morale is positively associated with staff's participation in decision making (Gouldner, 1965; Pawlack, 1976). It would seem logical to suggest that much of the "burnout" phenomenon (Maslach, 1976) can be traced to staff's feelings that they have been excluded from the decision-making process. Staff members who are burned out are likely to have little enthusiasm for staff development in any form, except when it offers a questionable excuse to escape the daily pressures of work. Staff meetings provide the opportunity for joint problem solving and decision making by staff, as a group, in a way that can reduce burnout.

Participation in the development and implementation of accountability systems. In this time of increasing costs and decreasing resources, human service organizations are faced with increased pressure for accountability, to justify their demands for their "piece of the pie." The internal development of an accountability system forces staff to ask themselves such questions as: Just what are we trying to accomplish, and how can we measure our accomplishments? What do we believe is a feasible success rate (assuming we've defined *success*)? How long should it take us to accomplish at least some "success"? Once an accountability system is in place, staff have a means of reviewing their efforts and—where they prove deficient—working to improve their own job performance, readjust the accountability system to a more realistic level, or both. As with problem-solving staff meetings, widespread participation in the development and implementation of an accountability system increases the likelihood that it will be put to good use rather than being subverted.

Participation in research focused on service delivery or organizational operation. In one sense, accountability measures represent a form of research, although a major purpose of such research is to justify the community's continued support of the organization. But just as in the creation of an accountability system staff members inevitably learn more about their jobs, so too research, whether on general issues or focused on single subjects, is bound to increase staff members' understanding of their work. This understanding should lead to improved job performance and increased job satisfaction.

Service as a field training site for students. Those who teach find that they never know their subject as well as when they have to communicate their knowledge, attitudes, and skills to others. When you teach something to someone, you are forced to clarify fuzzy concepts, reinvestigate the process by which you acquired a skill, or question your own most cherished opinions. Students also bring the latest knowledge from the campus to the organization, along with their enthusiasm, their confusion, and their fears. Accordingly, staff members who supervise these students learn more about their *own* jobs as they teach, as well as learning from their pupils.

Operation of an organization library.   Books, journals, unpublished reports, abstracts, audio- and videotapes and so forth contain the accumulated knowledge available to a jobholder who wants information, and who is not interested in reinventing the wheel. It is usually impossible for an individual staff member to know about all the literature and resources that are available from the past, or to keep up with the avalanche of potentially useful new information on their own. Organization libraries make such resources easily available (and therefore more likely to be used) and act as a screen to select the most relevant resources. They can also be a major resource in enhancing the continuing education of staff who may never again be able to devote themselves to the luxury of full-time education.

Participation in informal social functions for staff members.   The point has been made that good staff morale has a beneficial effect on job performance. Another way to improve morale is through attention to the small social niceties—for example, recognizing a staff member's birthday with a simple in-house party. (Experience suggests a note of caution here: Staff parties held off the premises that involve too much unaccustomed frivolity may have a negative impact on work-site relationships the morning after.) Social events must be planned, if only to make sure, for example, that no one's birthday is overlooked. Although social events do not directly increase a staff member's ability to do his or her job, they can create a work environment in which people want to do their best because they enjoy working together.

Periodic individual evalution.   There are several reasons for evaluating the job performance of individual staff members. Evaluations, of course, are linked to decisions about increases in pay, promotion, or employment termination. But evaluation can also be used to improve an individual's job performance by recognizing areas of strength on the job and identifying areas where improvement is needed. The evaluation process provides an opportunity for staff members to see where they are in relation to their immediate job goals as well as their long-range career goals. Where deficits or performance problems are noted, the evaluation process can be used as an occasion for making plans to deal with the difficulty—plans that may involve any of the staff development activities already mentioned.

AN ORGANIZING FRAMEWORK FOR STAFF DEVELOPMENT: PROBLEMS AND OBSTACLES

The organizing framework that follows indicates which of the staff development activities described in the preceding section would be most appropriate for resolving problems or surmounting obstacles faced by individual staff, staff units, or the organization as a whole. The accompanying diagrams are used to present these ideas graphically, using the following key:

○

represents the individual staff member.

represents the individual staff member's goal-
directed behavior—that is, doing one's job.

represents a situation in which the staff member
is blocked from goal achievement by some problem
or obstacle.[3]

Category 1: Individual-Unique Problems or Obstacles

An individual staff member encounters some problem or obstacle that is unique to that individual—for example, poor use of time (problem) or insufficient space in the agency to conduct a group meeting for clients (obstacle). Since many human service organizations use an independent case load approach in the delivery of services, individual workers are often functionally independent of other staff. Success or failure in their case load has little or no effect on the case loads of other workers. In the *individual-unique* category, the following staff development activities seem most appropriate:

- *Individual supervision,* focused specifically on the staff member's needs
- *Individual consultation,* which can go beyond supervision in two ways: The consultant may have particular expertise that the supervisor lacks and, because the consultant is not part of the organization, he or she can provide confidential help. (This latter fact may be particularly important if part of the staff member's difficulty involves a strained relationship with a supervisor.)
- *Out-service training,* such as attending conferences or workshops, taking courses at a college or university, or even *full-time educational leave,* each option chosen because it is particularly appropriate for this staff member

[3]*Problem* refers to a difficulty located *within* the individual, such as a lack of knowledge, a skill deficit, or a bias. *Obstacle* refers to something *outside* the staff member, such as a lack of resources, uncooperative fellow staff, or assignment overload. Problems and obstacles can be dealt with in several ways—for example, by hiring more staff or hiring better prepared staff; attention here is focused on the uses of staff development to solve the problem or remove the obstacle.

- *Periodic individual evaluation,* designed (as indicated previously) to help the individual take stock and plan for dealing with problems and obstacles
- *Orientation procedures,* used to help new staff members cope with being new so that they can begin to make an effective and self-satisfying contribution to the organization as soon as possible

Category 2: Individual–Common Problems or Obstacles

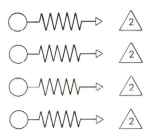

Several individuals—for example, members of the same work unit—encounter a similar problem (for example, a new category of client population about whom they know little), or obstacle (for example, a reduction in clerical staff on whom they all depend, as part of organizational cost cutting). Although it is true that each staff member experiences this difficulty as an individual, the similarity of these difficulties as experienced by each member suggests the use of the following staff development activities:

- *In-service training* for clusters of staff, designed to improve the ability of staff members to handle their jobs more effectively
- *Problem-solving staff meetings,* which provide a way for staff to identify a common problem or obstacle and develop a group approach to a solution
- *Group consultation,* which provides expertise not available within the organization, from someone who is not affiliated with or enmeshed in the organization and who can therefore provide a staff group with objective information with no strings attached
- *Field trips to cooperating agencies,* so as to provide face-to-face contact with a previously unknown situation
- *Group supervision,* used to provide feedback and support from fellow staff with regard to problems and obstacles faced by individual staff members
- *Development of a staff library,* as a way of keeping individual staff members current with the literature, so that they can keep pace with current professional developments and innovations
- *Research,* undertaken to find a solution to a commonly experienced problem or obstacle

Category 3: Group-Internal Problems or Obstacles

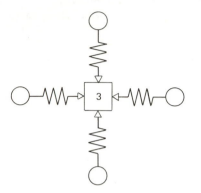

Work units (departments, teams, and the like) are groups of staff who, to some degree, are interdependent around the accomplishment of work tasks. Such groups have *common* goals, which differ from *similar* goals. (A *common goal* would be the creation of a ward atmosphere that facilitates patient recovery, whereas *similar goals* might include the successful management of his or her own job by each individual staff member.) Although interdependence is essential for the achievement of common goals, it is not easy for a staff unit to achieve effective interdependence. Needs of individual staff and of staff subgroups often interfere. Organizational politics can create obstacles to teamwork. Work units must expend considerable energy and expertise to achieve effective interdependence, characterized by open communication, a division of labor that is acceptable to all, and agreement on the group's common goals.

Staff development activities that can help to achieve these conditions of effective interdependence include the following:

- *Problem-solving staff meetings,* in which members of the work unit identify the difficulties that are internal to the group and develop ways of handling them. This may involve the use of sensitivity-training-like group exercises, designed to improve communication, clarify role expectations, or create new sets of expectations to deal with changing conditions that have caused a dysfunction in the existing division of labor.

- *Individual or group consultation,* occasionally used by staff groups who are experiencing internal difficulties within their work unit, since consultants can be asked to work for the well-being of the team as a unit, rather than limiting their activity to one individual or faction. Schmuck, Runkel, Saturen, Martell, and Derr (1972) have noted that staff who wish to improve an organization's ability to achieve its goals invariably discover that they first must improve their own interpersonal behaviors before setting out to solve their organization's problems.

- *Informal social activities,* another way to achieve good group morale by smoothing the communication channels and making people feel they are a welcome and important part of the unit. After all, a birthday party is fun for everyone, not just the person whose brithday it is—and fun, within limits, is an important morale booster.

Category 4: Group-External Problems or Obstacles

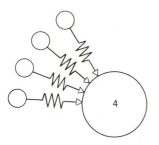

Often the problems or obstacles with which a work unit must cope are found in the unit's environment rather than within the unit itself. Experience indicates that units are better able to handle this last category of difficulties if they have first learned to manage *group-internal* difficulties, but it takes more than good morale to manage a stormy or restrictive environment. Staff development activities that seem appropriate here include the following:

- *Problem-solving staff meetings* in which the unit as a whole develops a consensus around strategy for dealing with an environmental issue
- *Development of an accountability system* to provide the basis for decisions by the organization about the provision of resources needed by the unit.[4] When funds are in short supply, an accountability system could serve to justify continued support of a work unit, or point to those things the unit should do to retain or increase support from the organization.
- *Doing research* on practice. This may not justify continued support to the unit, but it can enhance the status of the unit and thereby give the organization another reason to continue supporting the unit
- *Field trips,* which could be used to bring staff into contact with people or organizations that are viewed as obstacles, so that communication can take place in the interest of removing the obstacle.

To summarize, staff development can be used to resolve various problems or obstacles encountered by staff.

---

[4]A spin-off from such a system could also involve the development of greater clarity and consensus about unit goals, thus helping in the management of current or potential difficulties in the Category 3, *group-internal,* area.

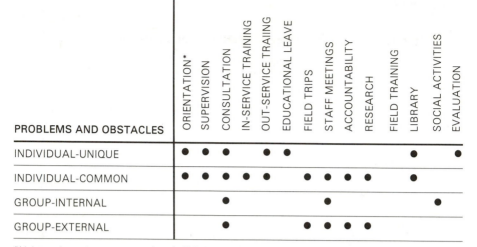

PROBLEMS AND OBSTACLES	ORIENTATION*	SUPERVISION	CONSULTATION	IN-SERVICE TRAINING	OUT-SERVICE TRAINING	EDUCATIONAL LEAVE	FIELD TRIPS	STAFF MEETINGS	ACCOUNTABILITY	RESEARCH	FIELD TRAINING	LIBRARY	SOCIAL ACTIVITIES	EVALUATION
INDIVIDUAL-UNIQUE	●	●	●		●	●						●		●
INDIVIDUAL-COMMON	●	●	●	●	●			●	●	●	●	●		
GROUP-INTERNAL			●					●					●	
GROUP-EXTERNAL			●					●	●	●	●			

STAFF DEVELOPMENT ACTIVITIES

*Using orientation to respond to *individual–common* problems or obstacles is appropriate when (a) several individuals are starting work in the same or similar units of the organization, in the same or similar jobs, or (b) a new work unit with an entirely new staff is getting started.

WHO SHOULD DO STAFF DEVELOPMENT?

Given the broad definition of staff development used in this book, staff development, in one sense, is everyone's responsibility. The initiation, coordination, and management of staff development, however, cannot be left up to everyone: It is necessary to assign this responsibility to one or more staff members, who then attempt to involve a wide range of staff in the process. The larger the agency, the more likely it is that staff development will become the full-time responsibility of particular individuals. Large state agencies often have whole departments responsible for staff development, with individuals in branch offices responsible for staff development at the local level. Such agencies often bring staff to the agency's central office for in-service training but leave some of the other activities, such as ongoing supervision and consultation, for the local office.

There is no generally accepted college or university program that prepares individuals to manage staff development programs. As a result, the people who manage staff development in the human services range all the way from paraprofessionals with "street knowledge" to administrators with master's degrees in social work, guidance and counseling, education, and psychology. In smaller agencies, the director or assistant director is often responsible for whatever staff development goes on. Other agencies rely on a representative staff commitee to plan staff development activities, with membership on the committee rotating from year to year so that the responsibility is shared. In some cases the chief preparation for managing staff development seems to be longevity; that is, individuals who have been with the agency a long time (even though they have little or no preparation for the position) are asked to manage staff development.

If all this sounds chaotic, it nevertheless reflects the way staff development is often managed. Although some organizations implement some of the staff development activities just described, few implement them all or view them as an entity called *staff development* that needs coordination to make sure that all four types of difficulties presented here are addressed. Students have talked about some agencies that have one in-service day a year and others that do not have even that. Some agencies make no use of consultation or limit the availability of consultants to certain staff components. Many agencies do no research, have no students, do not create their own accountability system, and provide only administrative supervision (which focuses primarily on people who make noticeable mistakes).

Ideally, people interested in taking up staff development as a major professional interest should know something about their organization and the way it does its business, as well as having some formal preparation in adult education. Practice experience in human service settings is important but not sufficient preparation for the staff developer if he or she is going to be involved in needs assessment, evaluation, selection of educational methods, and other aspects of staff development.

WHERE DOES STAFF DEVELOPMENT FIT INTO THE ORGANIZATION?

There is no way to understand staff development fully without understanding the organization in which it takes place. More fundamentally, one must understand *organizations* in order to learn how the attributes of an organization affect staff development, and how staff development, in turn, can affect these attributes.

We begin by defining the term *organization*:

> An organization is a collectivity with a relatively identifiable boundary, a normative order, authority ranks, communications systems, and membership coordinating systems; this collectivity exists on a relatively continuous basis in an environment and engages in activities that are usually related to a goal or set of goals. (Hall, 1972, p. 9)

Human service organizations are organizations:

> whose primary function is to define or alter the person's behavior, attributes and social status in order to enhance his well-being. . . . These organizations are differentiated from other bureaucracies by two fundamental characteristics: (a) their input of raw materials are human beings with specific attributes, and their production output are persons processed or changed in a predetermined manner, and (b) their general mandate is that of "service," that is, to maintain or improve the general well-being and functioning of people. . . . Examples of such organizations are the public

schools, hospitals, welfare agencies, employment placement offices, and police departments. (Hasenfeld & English, 1974, p. 1)

One view of human service organizations divides them into two major types—people-changing, and people-processing. *People changing* is defined as follows:

> ...the major functions of people-changing organizations are socialization and social control. In each instance a specific population is dealt with in ways calculated to insure the preservation of dominant values and patterns...the university and military academy, guidance clinic and mental hospital, probation and correctional institution are all examples of organizations in this class. (Vinter, 1963, p. 3)

People processing is defined in this way:

> ...[the] explicit function [of people processing organizations] is not to change the behavior of people directly, but to process them and confer public statuses on them. Examples of such organizations are a diagnostic clinic, a university admission office, an employment placement office, a credit bureau or a juvenile court. (Hasenfeld, 1974, p. 60)

Organizations have been studied by a great many scholars (see, for example, Weber, 1947; March and Simon, 1958; Hall, 1972). A number of fascinating case studies have focused attention on human service organizations, beginning with Clemmer's classic study of the prison (Clemmer, 1940) and including several studies of psychiatric hospitals (see, for example, Stanton and Schwartz, 1954; Caudill, 1958). A particularly useful review of studies of people-changing organizations can be found in Chapter 1 of Moos's book on the evaluation of treatment environments (Moos, 1974). All this work has made clear that human service organizations have a powerful effect on *all* the people who make them up—staff *and* clients (or "residents," "patients," "inmates"—depending on the kind of organization being discussed). These studies make clear that to understand these organizations fully, it is important to recognize that clients and staff in human service organizations affect each other's attitudes and behaviors in many ways.

In order to survive and to achieve their goals, organizations develop policies and procedures, create divisions of labor, develop authority and communication structures, and devise a number of ways to maintain and improve efficiency and effectiveness. One of these ways is staff development. Whether or not it is an *effective* way depends on the interplay between the staff development enterprise and a number of organizational variables, including the organization's size, complexity, formalization, power, and politics.

Size.   According to Hall (1972) *size* refers to the number of staff who work for the organization, including full-time and part-time paid staff, and volunteers. For staff development purposes, measuring the size of a human service organization must also include a measurement of the client population. For example, the operation of a staff development program can be powerfully affected by the fact that the staff/client ratio is low—that is, there are too many clients per staff—so that there is simply no time for most staff development activities to occur. It has been found that there is a positive association between the size of an organization's membership (staff plus clients) and the size of its resources (Hall, 1972). Size has also been found to be correlated with the number of levels (hierarchical) and divisions (horizontal) within the organization (Hall, 1972). For the staff developer, the size–resource relationship can mean that as the organization grows larger, more resources may be available to staff developers to get the job done, but the job that must be done will be made more complicated by the diverse range of needs that can be expected from a larger number of divisions. In addition, the fact that there are more layers in the bureaucracy can increase the difficulty of locating and securing administrative support at the appropriate level.

As an organization grows larger, a division of labor is likely to occur. A staff development division may even be created to give full-time attention to this function. Although this can be beneficial in terms of recruiting individuals with some expertise in managing staff development, and giving these individuals time to do it well, it can also lead to a situation in which the staff developer is too far from the firing line, with the result that staff development activities may become unrelated to the felt needs of staff. (See Chapter 3 for a more thorough discussion of staff's felt needs and their relationship to staff development.)

On the other hand, as an organization grows smaller, staff development responsibilities are likely to be assigned to staff members who have other responsibilities as well—who "wear many hats"—with the result that they will have less time to give and, perhaps, less specialized training in managing staff development activities. On the other hand, they are likely to be closer to the day-to-day operation of the organization and thus in a better position to develop activities that are relevant to the staff's needs.

According to Hall (1972, p. 128), the effects of organizational size on individuals has not been systematically studied. Studies have been done, however, that relate indirectly to this issue. For example, Rothman (1974, p. 457) reports that as the number of *professionals* employed by organizations goes up, the adoption rate of innovations increases. He also reports on a number of studies pertaining to organizational size and its impact on the organization (and thus on its staff); for example, as size increases, "formal surveillance and formal rules will increase, relative to informal, personal surveillance" (Rothman, 1974, p. 144). Hall notes that size and morale appear to be linked; larger organizations often create situations, based on size alone, that cause stress and lowered morale, although other variables also affect stress and morale. For example, students coming to a large university are less likely to feel overwhelmed by the sheer size of the place if they have attended a large metropolitan high school (Hall, 1972).

Complexity. The simplest organization can be seen as complex. All organizations are made up of subparts requiring coodination and control, and each of these subparts can vary from the others in its degree of complexity. Certainly size, as already noted, can compound complexity. Three elements of complexity have been studied frequently: (1) *horizontal differentiation* (the way tasks performed by the organization are subdivided among its members); (2) *vertical or hierarchical differentiation* (roughly the number of job levels between the boss and front-line staff); and (3) *spatial dispersion* (the way in which activities and staff are spread around in geographical space—for example, several satellite offices, versus one central location) (Hall, 1972). In some organizations, changes in any one of these variables can take place independent of changes in another, whereas in others, a change in one has a direct effect on the other two.

Staff developers are likely to find that the degree of complexity of their organization affects their activities. Hall reports on several studies of complexity: For example, Hage and Aiken (1967) found that concentration of authority at the top of the organization was associated with a decrease in the rate of program change and a weakening of the role of professionals in decision making; further, as horizontal and vertical differentiation increased, much of the information flowing in the system contained conflicting ideas and proposals. "Organizations that are complex in this way face the problem of integrating the diverse occupations and ideas deriving from the different organizational members" (Hall, 1972, p. 152). Certainly a number of the staff development activities described earlier could be used to deal with the problems involved in integrating diverse occupational groups— for example, problem-solving staff meetings involving team members from various occupations can provide an opportunity for sharing and comparing each occupation's approach to an issue, or in-service training can be used to familiarize staff from one occupation with the work of staff from another occupation.

Formalization.   Hage and Aiken define formalization as "the use of rules in an organization" (Hage and Aiken, 1967, p. 79). Rules can exist in the form of job codification (written descriptions of what job occupants are expected and allowed to do), policies and procedures (often encoded in an agency manual), and more informal day-to-day expectations about job performance. Pugh, Hickson, Hinings, and Turner (1968, p. 75) define formalization in terms of "the extent to which rules, procedures, instructions and communications are written." The degree of formalization in an organization is of direct concern to staff developers. Any organization is concerned that its staff get the job done, effectively and efficiently. But, as Hall notes:

> It is exactly at this point that the organization faces a dilemma. If it allows too little freedom for its members, they are likely to feel oppressed, alienated and "bureaucratic," and to engage in rule following for its own sake. If, on the other hand, it allows more freedom, behavior is apt to become erratic and organizationally irrelevant. A basic factor here appears to be the kind of guidelines for behavior that the individual brings to the organization. The more work standards he brings with him, the less the need for organizationally based standards. (Hall, 1972, p. 190)

In Hall's view, such standards are more likely to be present in professionally prepared staff. From the staff developer's point of view, however, this is only part of the story; many of the job-specific standards that can make for a high-quality operation can be fostered by good staff development, regardless of the professional training of each staff member, thus lessening the need for the kind and degree of formalization that staff can find oppressive.

Power and politics.   In general, organizations want to be able to predict how staff will perform in their jobs, so that they can facilitate coordination, cooperation, and appropriate staff utilization of whatever technology seems likely to achieve the organization's goals. To guarantee this predictability, an organization distributes power—the ability of one person or group to control the behavior of another person or group—in some planned way. In the traditional Weberian view of bureaucracy, power flows from the top down, thus ensuring an orderly and rational operation. As indicated before, however, professionals who are not at the top level of an organization tend to resent the use of power over them when it interferes, in their opinion, with the exercise of their professional expertise. The dilemma for human service organizations, often characterized by a preponderance of professionally trained staff, is to strike a balance between useful coordination and intrusive displays of power.

One way to achieve this balance of power is through the use of staff development activities that aim to meet individually felt staff needs while also meeting organizational needs. That, of course, is easier said than done. The subparts of any organization can become little fiefdoms in which power is held very tightly by members of that particular unit, and attempts to control their behavior by other components of the organization are strongly resisted.

The realities of power distribution in any organization make it essential that staff developers recognize the universality of intraorganizational political activity. Robbins defines *politics* in organizations as "any behavior by an organizational member that is self-serving. This in itself is not power, but it requires power to attain its end" (Robbins, 1976, p. 64). The term *self-serving,* as used by Robbins, refers to such things as promotion, enhanced personal status, or an increase in personal income. This view of politics seems unnecessarily narrow, although he makes it clear that political activity can be either functional or dysfunctional for the organization. A definition of politics that makes better sense to me is *any behavior by an organizational member that is designed to achieve a change in the existing power arrangements.*

The approach to staff development presented in this book is aimed at a greater democratization of power arrangements, whereby staff have greater control over their own circumstances. In this effort, the staff developer must continuously assess the existing power structure in the organization, and, where it appears likely that it will impede the staff development process, seek ways to open the structure up to change. In some organizations, the act of involving staff in the kinds of needs assessment described later can be a potentially powerful political act that may threaten the status quo in terms of who controls staff performance. Given a political understanding of the organization, staff developers will need tact, patience, a sense of humor, good timing, and political alliances to move staff development forward.

HOW IS THE BOOK ORGANIZED?

Ideally, the process of staff development unfolds in a logical order. It is this logical sequence of events that has been used as the framework for this book: Chapter 2, "Contracting for Staff Development"; Chapter 3, "Assessing Needs"; Chapter 4, "Specifying Objectives and Evaluating Outcomes"; Chapter 5, "Making Use of Theories of Learning and Change as the Bases of Staff Development"; Chapter 6, "The Skillful 'Doing' of Staff Development Activities"; Chapter 7, "Managing Staff Development"; and Chapter 8, "Keeping Staff Development Alive and Well." Several chapters include examples of how the ideas from the text worked out in some actual staff development projects. Most of these examples are taken from a few hundred projects developed by graduate students as a major requirement of the staff development course I have taught over the years. Many of these students were employed full time in human service organizations at the time they took the course—as part-time students—through the University of Michigan's Extension Service. Consequently, their projects were directly related to their jobs rather than academic exercises primarily undertaken to meet a course requirement. Each chapter concludes with a set of guidelines that should help you, in the role of staff developer, to carry out your own project and assess your own progress at each step in the staff development process. Here is a brief summary of each chapter's contents.

Contracting

A *contract* is an explicit agreement between individuals that defines the goals each wishes to achieve and the roles each will play in their interactions. Staff development, whether done to problem-solve, instruct, or innovate, cannot proceed without a contract for administrative support and staff willingness to participate. Chapter 2 describes the process of negotiating a contract (and, if necessary, renegotiating a contract) to provide a solid foundation for staff development.

Assessing Needs

Too many staff development activities are planned *for* people regardless of what they themselves think they need. This chapter will distinguish between felt needs of staff, needs attributed to staff, and organizational needs, and will discuss and describe procedures for involving staff in assessing and determining priorities of needs—procedures that are likely to attract the voluntary support of staff for staff development activities.

Specifying Objectives and Evaluating Outcomes

Once needs have been identified and a priority of needs agreed on, objectives must be specified to provide both the staff developer and the participant with a sense of direction. As Mager (1962, p. vii) says, "if you're not sure where you're going, you're liable to end up someplace else—and not even know it." This chapter describes the use of objectives and teaches you how to create measurable ones, which in turn become the basis for designing and evaluating staff development activities both during their implementation and once they have been completed. The chapter also reviews the literature on the evaluation of staff development and includes a discussion of methods you can use to evaluate your own staff development activities.

Using Theories of Learning and Change

Staff development activities are often conducted with little attention to what is known about the ways in which people learn and the ways in which organizations change. This chapter reviews some theories and research that pertain to learning and change, demonstrates their relevance to staff development activities, and serves as a basis for selecting and implementing staff development activities.

The Skillful "Doing" of Staff Development Activities

People who work in human service organizations need many different skills, but there is no guarantee that a good interviewer will also be a good trainer, a good line worker will also be a good supervisor. This chapter describes many of the specific skills needed by someone doing staff development, and offers guidelines for using these skills effectively. It includes sections dealing with the lecture, discussion leading, role playing and simulation games, audiovisual approaches, programmed instruction, use of resource persons, and the like.

Managing Staff Development

Successful staff development usually requires that a complex array of tasks be completed in some logical order, by some particular time, in a way that achieves the greatest benefits while using up the fewest resources. This chapter presents ideas about the location and use of resources as well as several planning techniques designed to increase the efficiency with which staff development is done.

Keeping Staff Development Alive and Well

For many organizations, what has been described so far is an approach to staff development that differs from the one they have been using. In some cases, or so I have been told, organizations do not believe in staff development at all—they use *no* approach. Then, as mentioned earlier, there are the organizations that designate one day a year as the "in-service day" and provide little supervision, no consultation, and only a cursory orientation. Such organizations have almost no planned staff development; the only way to go is up, since their "staff development" is unplanned, haphazard, and probably counterproductive in terms of staff morale, effectiveness, and turnover. But once a staff development program has been developed, what must be done to keep it flexible and responsive to changing needs and circumstances? This chapter discusses issues in the maturation of a staff development program, and examines organizational and environmental conditions (including budget) that affect and may even impede staff development; it then offers guidelines for maintaining a creative staff development process.

WHAT ARE THE INSTRUCTIONAL OBJECTIVES OF THIS BOOK?

After reading this book, you should be able to do the following:

1. Negotiate contracts for staff development that are likely to be complied with voluntarily so that the goals of the contract are achieved and all parties are satisfied with both process and results.
2. With such contracts as the foundation for action, conduct a needs assessment of the organization and of the individuals in it.
3. On the basis of that assessment, you should be able to describe (verbally or in writing) the functions that a staff development program could serve in your agency, or in that portion of it for which you are responsible. You should be able to describe staff development objectives in the kinds of action terms I am using here.
4. You should be able to negotiate a consensus on these staff development functions and objectives with all relevant levels of staff, such that administrative support will be forthcoming and at least a majority of potential participants in these programs will want to participate.
5. You should be able to create, design, or locate resources for staff development in such a way that a majority of the participants agree that the nature and objectives of these experiences are appropriate to one or more of the functions mentioned earlier, and also meet their particular needs.
6. You should be able to serve as, or recruit and supervise, the resource person(s) for the staff development experiences, in such a way that you obtain staff members' high, voluntary participation throughout, and so that at least half of the staff group achieve preselected objectives.
7. Where the staff development experiences continue for some time, you should be able to design and use procedures for evaluating and then modifying these experiences in midstream in order to maintain or improve staff members' satisfaction with their learning from the staff development activities.
8. Where staff development experiences have been used at least once (and are to be used with other staff groups later on), you should be able to develop procedures for evaluating and modifying these experiences in order to achieve as good or better levels of participation, satisfaction, and achievement for later staff groups, when compared with earlier groups.

Now that I have given you an overview of how this book is organized and what I hope you will get from reading it, let's get started with the first step in the process—negotiating a working contract, the launching platform for your staff development activities.

chapter 2

CONTRACTING FOR STAFF DEVELOPMENT

- Some introductory remarks.
- What is a contract?
- How should you negotiate a contract for staff development? The DSS example.
- What are some problems in contracting?
- What guidelines should you follow when contracting for staff development?

SOME INTRODUCTORY REMARKS

Role clarity and consensus among actors (in particular between the practitioner and his relevant superordinates) facilitates effective role performance. (Rothman, 1974, p. 68)

The idea that a *contract*—an explicit, negotiated agreement between a helping person and a client—is an essential part of social work practice emerged in the social work literature in the 1960s. Until then it was usually assumed that all parties to a social work transaction understood what was expected of them and what they could expect of the others involved. The reasons behind this naive assumption are obscure. Certainly, the idea of a legal contract is an old one:

> Historically, the concept of contract was a primary part of the beginnings of law as a recognized and viable institution. According to Corbin (1963), "That portion of the field of law that is classified and described as the law of contracts attempts the realization of reasonable expectations that have been induced by the making of a promise." (Croxton, 1974, p. 169)

Perhaps the problem has always lain in the fact that most social relationships simply happen without formal negotiation. For example, suppose you receive the following invitation in the mail:

> We're having some folks over Saturday night. Why don't you and your wife join us. Say about 8:30? R.S.V.P. regrets only.

Experience has taught me (sometimes to my sorrow) that where you *live* suggests what the host or hostess means—and even then you can't be 100 percent sure. When I lived in Los Angeles, such an invitation usually meant you were being invited for dinner—and *don't* show up before 9:00 P.M.! In Ann Arbor, however, on one occasion, it meant: Be there at 8:30, but eat first, because all you'll get are drinks and snacks.

Studies in role theory make it eminently clear that role consensus is not easily achieved (Biddle, 1979). Sometimes semantic issues get in the way. Suppose your boss says: "We need to set up a better way to orient new staff. Why don't you draw up a plan and let me see it?" Is this request clear? Why is a "better" way needed? What did the boss think was wrong with the old approach? If orientation has been done in different ways, was one way better than the others in the boss's opinion? By what deadline does the boss want this plan? Does the boss want a brief tentative outline or a detailed final design? Is the staff member allowed or expected to discuss the plan with anyone else? Probably you, the reader, could come up with a host of other clarifying questions regarding this apparently simple assignment.

Role consensus may be difficult to achieve for other reasons. One problem concerns the spoken word versus the unspoken word. Maybe what the boss is really saying in this example is: "My assistant director ran last month's orientation. He'll be expecting to do it for the next group of new staff, and we have to figure out a way to box him out of it. He does a lot of things well, but he scares the hell out of new staff!" Wouldn't it be a challenge trying to design a terrific plan for orientation without knowing the boss's hidden agenda? An explicit statement of the assignment, along *with* the answers to all these questions, could facilitate getting the job done correctly.

Trying to do good staff development without an explicit contract seems likely to lead to a host of problems that can effectively destroy the best designed and best managed activity. For that reason, I will begin my discussion of staff development by focusing on the contract.

WHAT IS A CONTRACT?

In this book I will use the term *contract* to refer to an explicit agreement negotiated between two or more persons—an agreement that makes clear to all parties what specific goals are to be sought, what each person's role is to be in working toward the goals, what resources can or cannot be used in working toward these goals, and how the contract itself can be renegotiated. Let me try to make my own terms clear:

1. *explicit agreement:* By *agreement,* I mean a freely given consent to the deal, task, or assignment, by all concerned. By *explicit* I mean that the words used to achieve this agreement have the same meaning for all concerned, insofar as possible. This often involves the process of checking things out: "When you say *X,* do you mean...?" or "Based on what you've just said, can I assume that thus-and-so is what you're talking about?" Written contracts are often best since they provide a point of reference both during negotiation and later, when parts of the agreement need to be recalled.

2. *negotiated: Negotiated* refers to free give and take—a chance to speak your mind without fear that what you say will cause trouble for you or others. The ideal outcome of a negotiated agreement is that all parties believe the agreement has some important payoff for them, even when compromise is involved. Even when the boss says, "I'm sorry—my hands are tied on this one by the board (or the legislature)—you're just going to have to do it!" there may be room for negotiation around other issues: Do it how? Do it when? Do it where? Do it for how many people? This gives participants a sense of some control over the situation—and some control is better than none.

3. *two or more persons:* In the example given at the beginning of this chapter, two people were involved. Certainly, such an assignment could be given to a group of staff, not just one individual, in which case the contract is best negotiated with the entire group. Or the boss may give such an assignment to the supervisor, who in turn contracts with his or her staff group. When this happens, the group may decide that the task, as assigned, needs further negotiation before they understand or feel good about the assignment. They may ask to speak directly to the boss, or ask the supervisor to renegotiate on their behalf. But even when such an agreement with the group is reached, another step remains in the contracting process: the further negotiation of the contract with those staff members who are to be participants in the staff development activity, if they are part of a different group. Returning to the new orientation program, new staff could be asked about the kinds of information and experiences regarding orientation they would find helpful, given some options about the amount of information they would find useful in a given time span, asked if and when they want to tour the agency, and so forth. In other words, contracting is needed sooner or later for everyone involved in the activity, although the roles of the various participants will necessarily differ.

One might argue that in training (as in school) trainees (or students) are told what they must learn and are simply expected to learn it. But this is exactly my point: When people are told what they must do and are faced with the threat of real punishment if they don't do it, they will do it—*and no more*. Students, for example, will learn just enough to pass the course and then promptly forget it all after the final exam; they will perform only as long as they believe their performance is being checked. Think back to your own schooling and what you took away from it. Chances are you retained best—and used most—what you wanted to learn and/or were allowed to negotiate for.

Let me go one step further. By "what you *wanted* to learn," I mean that a learner's *motivation* is a key factor in the learning process. The issue of motivation in relation to felt needs is discussed more fully in Chapter 3 on assessing needs, but in developing a contract, the motivation of participants must be addressed. For example, agency directors will be *less* cheerful in negotiating a contract for staff development that ignores *their* motivations for such things as control of staff behavior, achievement of cost-effectiveness, simple procedures for conducting staff development that do not interfere with organizational routines, and the like. One could argue that staff do not have a right to such a contract negotiation process. As staff, they are obligated to do their jobs as directed. Perhaps. But I would assert—as part of my own values, which might disagree with yours—that they do have this right I think I can make a convincing argument that a freely negotiated contract is an effective tool for facilitating communication and enhancing motivation for all parties involved.

4. *specific goals. . . to be sought:* Chapter 4 is devoted to a fuller discussion of goals. Here, however, it should suffice to say that I am referring to *measurable* goals for this contract—measurable so that they provide direction for effort, as well as criteria by which success can be determined. Ideally, the goals should be ones that can reasonably be attained and are desired by as many participants in the activity as possible.

5. *what resources can or cannot be used:* Staff development activities usually require some resources—time from staff members' schedules, space or equipment for the activity, money for expenses, and so forth. The most crucial problem may be finding the time for staff members to participate in a staff development activity. The old question, "Who's minding the store?" applies: Staff development takes time, which often has to be taken away from service delivery activities. In contracting, it's essential to know what resources will be needed, and who controls them. Without *their* informed approval, the resources may be withheld or taken away at any point in the staff development process.

6. *renegotiation of the contract:* A contract needs to be reexamined from time to time to make sure it's working. All kinds of realities can intrude on staff development that necessitate a change in plans, and it should be clear how these changes can be made. The ideal contract is freely negotiated by all parties; thus, it ought to be equally possible for any and all parties to participate in its renegotiation. In in-service training, for example, the trainer should actively solicit midstream evaluations from trainees to make sure they feel the training is working for them; if not, there should be a chance to renegotiate the process or the content of the training.

It's generally a good idea to build in a chance for participants to renegotiate. Otherwise, people may hesitate to voice their concerns because they are afraid that these concerns will meet a negative response from the powers that be.

CONTRACTING FOR STAFF DEVELOPMENT: THE DSS EXAMPLE

To demonstrate the contracting process, I will present a portion of a report by a staff developer pertaining to a work unit in a local office of a state department of social services (DSS). Note that this is an example of *successful* contracting. I will also provide examples of staff development projects that were less than successful. Too many social work texts make the mistake of providing only success stories as examples, giving the reader the impression that success is always easy to achieve. Remember that the greatest hitters in baseball can do no better than bat .400—just four successful hits out of every ten tries. Set yourself realistic goals, and remain undaunted even when you don't bat 1.000!

EXAMPLE 1: THE DSS EXAMPLE

The A_____ County Department of Social Services is one of a large number of county offices in the state whose function it is to provide social services and/or financial assistance to individuals and/or families, within its geographical boundaries, who are deemed to be in need. At the present time, this local office comprises thirty-two employees who are assigned to one of four units: Services, Assistance Payments, Clerical or Volunteer Services. Each unit is directed by a first-line supervisor who reports to the local office director. The local office director heads the agency and is responsible for and accountable to upper administration for the overall functioning and operation of the department as a whole. . . .

As the services supervisor for the Services Unit, I am responsible for the overall functioning and performance of the unit, which comprises seven workers. As a member of the supervisory staff, I have been delegated the responsibility for the operation of this unit, and expectations have been set by the director in terms of unit performance and staff development within the unit.

Contracting for Staff Development

I arranged a conference with my supervisor, the local office director, during which time I advised him of some of the staff development activities I had in mind. He was very supportive of my ideas and presented me with some of his own suggestions, from a management perspective, of staff development activities he thought needed doing. Some of the suggestions offered were:

1. Annual planning process, a reemphasis on the nature of and reasons for planning, and objective setting
2. Training in organizing, planning work, effective use of time because of case load increase, and increased demands on workers
3. Development of plans for increases in office space to allow each worker an individual office

4. Improvements in workers' communication skills
5. Introduction of workers to the budgetary process
6. Discussion of subsidized housing and more nutrition centers for senior citizens
7. Local involvement in the policy formation process
8. Public relations training

During the conference, the director acknowledged that some of his suggestions and ideas were areas that would be difficult to deal with from a supervisory level. However, some areas, such as work organization, objective setting, and improving communication skills, were areas he felt could be realistically addressed. Although he offered many suggestions, he really felt that whatever was done should be based on what the workers perceived as their needs. Basically, he felt that the unit was functioning adequately except in the areas of redeterminations and in quarterly narratives, where performance was noted to be deteriorating. He expressed a desire that the activity address something that would be beneficial to the workers in terms of the responsibilities and the performance requirements of their positions.

Following a discussion of suggestions and ideas, we moved on to a discussion of possible methods of doing an effective needs assessment. Again, he offered many helpful suggestions and advised me of potential resources that might be utilized in establishing and developing the project.

Prior to the termination of the conference, the director indicated an interest in having progress reports on the status of my efforts. I sensed that he would not hesitate to stop me if he thought I was creating a disaster.

Basically, the reception of and reaction to the staff development project was well received. Support was provided, and assistance was offered. I was left with suggestions to ponder and yet was given free rein to develop an activity that would benefit the staff as a whole.

The supervisor's position made it easy and natural for her to negotiate a contract for a staff development program with her director. Note that she initiated the request to do the program, whereas in many organizations it is the administrator who initiates the contract process. In either case, you should assume that there is always room for negotiation, although it is sometimes easier said than done. The director was responsive and indicated several areas in which he saw a need for additional staff development. He made it clear, however, that the final choice of a staff development program should be up to the supervisor, in consultation with her unit staff. It was further agreed that it was her role to provide periodic progress reports.

Note that contracting proceeds in a series of steps: The contract here only gave the supervisor permission to start the ball rolling and made it clear that she was not to make final plans without first touching base with him. In Chapter 3 on assessing needs, we will return to the DSS example to find out how she managed that step in the contracting process.

SOME PROBLEMS IN CONTRACTING

Thomas and Feldman (1967, p. 20) define *role* in relation to *position* as follows:

Position is a collectively recognized category of persons who are similar in some respect. . . . *Role* is the set of role expectations held by relevant others concerning how the rights and duties of a position should be carried out. . . . [a] role expectation is an idea held by a relevant individual concerning how the occupant of a position should perform the rights and duties of that position.

Knowing when and how to make role expectations clearly understood and acceptable to all involved is not easy, but it is essential to any contract. In most cases the staff developer wants to negotiate a clear contract; this usually involves gaining administrative clearance to proceed with a staff development plan. Occasionally, however, you may want to negotiate a contract that purposely allows for role ambiguity, as a way of allowing some leeway in the development of a new idea. *Role ambiguity* has been defined as "a lack of clarity of role expectations about the rights and duties of a position" (Thomas and Feldman, 1967). It is often a cause of *role strain*—anxiety about whether or not you are meeting expectations for your role acceptably well. Ambiguity, however, can also give you the freedom to experiment with a role—something that can be useful when you're in a new position.

Experience has shown that a number of problems can arise when someone thinks it might be a good idea to negotiate a contract for a staff development activity or to modify an existing activity. What follows is a discussion of some of these problems, with some possible solutions.

Problem 1: Territory and Dominance

Students of animal societies have made us aware of the concepts of *territory* (anything an animal will fight to protect) and *dominance* (the rank accorded to different animals within a particular territory, with one animal having attained dominance—supreme power—often by having superior fighting ability and by others' acceptance of their place in the hierarchy) (see, for example, Scott, 1958). These concepts aptly describe what goes on within complex organizations, especially in the subspecies of such organizations that we are discussing—human service organizations. Suppose, for example, that a comparatively new social group worker wanted to initiate staff development in a residential institution for emotionally disturbed and disturbing children. She offered to conduct an in-service training session for houseparents and negotiated a contract for this activity with the agency's director. In this contract the director gave her permission to assess the needs of the houseparent staff and then proceed with a relevant in-service training session. Through the needs assessment process, she learned that there was a widespread felt need for help with discipline problems, so she began to plan a training session on discipline. Before the group worker could go any further with her plans, however, the supervisor of houseparents returned from sick leave, and, learning of the plans, simply refused to allow her to proceed. As the social worker tried to find out what had gone wrong, she learned that she had trespassed on the supervisor's territory, a territory in which he insisted on remaining dominant. He viewed the proposed training as a threat, and squashed it.

Out of experiences like this comes a fairly straightforward principle: *Before proposing a contract, study the terrain and identify organizational territories and the dominant persons in the contract negotiation process. If they refuse to become involved in this process, and if you want to start your staff development program with a success, back off and look for a more receptive territory.* In the example just given, the social group worker might have appealed to the director to override the supervisor's objections; she might even have gotten the director's support (an unlikely event, but still conceivable). Or she might have attempted to work around the supervisor by holding the session at a time when he was off grounds. From a *practical* point of view this would certainly have backfired; from an *ethical* point of view it would be unacceptable. It would still be best to back off, because the in-service session would be designed to teach ways of handling children that eventually would have to be implemented under the supervisor's direction, once the actual in-service training on discipline had taken place, and it seems likely that he would sabotage such an effort.

Problem 2: Assessing Needs

Chapter 3 presents reasons for basing staff development on a comprehensive needs assessment of the particular staff who are to be "developed." Administrators, however, are more likely to be willing to negotiate contracts for staff development if they can clearly see some payoff in response to *their own need* to manage effectively. For example, the manager of a state-supported employment program for youth was willing to allow his counseling staff to be trained in the use of group approaches by central office trainers when he learned that the training would include instructions on the development of individualized measurable objectives for each client member of the groups. He had been trying for some time to develop a way of measuring the effectiveness of the counselors' daily work, and he hoped the behaviorally specific objectives used in the group approach would give him a way to assess the effectiveness of their activities. Since he was under considerable pressure from *his* superiors to show that his counseling program was effective, he was willing to contract for this particular training—because it could meet *his* needs.

From experience like this we can derive a second principle: *When negotiating a contract with an administrator, it is wise to base the negotiations on the relevance of the activity to that administrator's needs.* Inherent in this principle, however, is a dilemma: Activities that may meet the needs of administrators often do not meet those of staff at lower levels. Again, experience suggests that when starting a staff development program, one must first gain the trust of administrators by being sure to meet their needs; this means selecting a project that appears likely to meet both the needs of administrators and those of other staff, as in the case of group work at the employment program just mentioned. Administrators who come to trust staff developers are more likely to accept other activities later on that are not primarily directed at meeting the administrator's immediate needs.

Problem 3: Limited Resources

"For want of a nail, the shoe was lost; for want of a shoe, the horse was lost..." Inattention to small details can indeed doom large-scale efforts. For the staff developer, no resource is more problematic than time—the time to engage in staff development. This is particularly true when an activity involves assembling groups of staff. But even activities that can be pursued individually (such as reading a journal article or listening to an audio cassette tape) can conflict with the immediate demand to see clients, complete paperwork, return telephone calls, and so forth. When negotiating a contract, one must be able to show that the activity is cost-effective.

Proving that a staff development activity or set of activities is cost-effective is not easy. As a staff developer you have to ask yourself: Is there something tangible that can be shown to have been gained or saved as a result of this activity? Can we, for example, cut the error rate in our paperwork? Can we show that we can save time and expense by training staff to use a group orientation procedure that helps people learn how to play the client role more quickly and effectively? Would it pay us (either in time or in dollars and cents) to hire a consultant? How can we measure staff productivity? Can we show a link between productivity and staff development?

These questions suggest another principle of contract negotiation: *When negotiating a contract, the staff developer should be aware of the cost factors involved and should include in the negotiations some means of measuring the cost-effectiveness of the activity.* One further way to promote acceptance of the contract is to identify in advance specific high-priority organizational needs regarding resource deficits or ways of making more efficient use of already available resources, and then to select staff development activities that seem likely to address those needs.

Here is an example of how the issue of time was handled during contracting. This staff developer was employed full-time as an occupational therapist at a 600-bed regional state hospital for the developmentally disabled. Her contracting process might be described as "sneaky": First she assessed the needs of her colleagues in the occupational and physical therapy departments, where there were only two therapists other than herself. She discovered a common concern about physicians who confused occupational therapy with physical therapy, leading to inappropriate referrals. She then contacted the four staff physicians and asked if it would be helpful to learn (that is, did they feel a need to learn) about the difference between these two therapy services; she received an affirmative response. Only then did she approach the medical director to negotiate a formal contract for her project.

EXAMPLE 2: THE OCCUPATIONAL THERAPY EXAMPLE

. . . Permission to pursue my staff development project was obtained by talking to the medical director, Dr. B. He was the last physician I interviewed, as I wanted the support of the other doctors behind me. I explained the whole process of my needs assessment and the results of talking with the other physicians. I explained I came to him last because there would have been no need to come at all if the other doctors were not interested. I then asked Dr. B if he felt an in-service on the differences between occupational and physical therapy would benefit his staff. He seemed receptive and stated the project would be beneficial. We discussed a time frame—how long would the in-service take. I wanted an hour and fifty minutes; he suggested fifteen minutes. This led me to the conclusion that he and I were not placing the same emphasis on the need for my in-service. Dr. B said that each doctor has a heavy patient load and that it is difficult to get them all together at one time. However, they did meet monthly at the administration building and were all required to attend this meeting. I said I would be willing to use that time and reminded him that the doctors all carried beepers and have easy access to a telephone in case of an emergency. I stated that I felt we really could not do an adequate job in fifteen minutes. Dr. B reconsidered and said we could have an hour and fifty minutes.

The occupational therapist got her contract, with the additional resource she needed—time. Subsequently, she gave the director a report on the degree to which the project had cut down on the inefficiencies of inappropriate referrals, thereby enhancing the likelihood that the director would receive future proposals enthusiastically.

Problem 4: Staff Development as Innovation

Rothman (1974, p. 420) defines an *innovation* as "any idea perceived as new by a population, group or organization...." Some staff development is so much a part of the organizational fabric that it could not be called an innovation: Examples would include a standardized orientation procedure for new staff, the organization's system of providing supervision, or the staff library already in operation. In general, however, the best staff development program is the one that is most responsive to the needs of staff members—needs that are likely to change as staff turn over, as the organization encounters new demands and pressures in its environment, and as new technologies appropriate to this organization are developed elsewhere. In other words, staff development, because it attempts to respond to changing needs, is often innovative by definition.

Contract negotiation, therefore, is often used to initiate an agreement about introducing an innovation. Hence, guidelines from the literature on the innovation process should apply.

In his review of the literature, Rothman (1974) found that certain organizations are more innovative than others, and that innovative organizations tend to have certain attributes in common: They adhere less to traditional norms; they are composed of individuals from a higher socioeconomic status; they have previously had good experiences with innovation; they feel a need to change; they are characterized by value systems that are compatible with liberalism, a belief in science, and nonauthoritarianism; and they have members who are socially active. The relative speed with which an innovation is likely to be adopted, Rothman found, was influenced by (among other factors) the degree to which: (1) the innovation is perceived as compatible with the existing values of the organization; (2) it can be broken into parts and tried out on a partial basis; (3) it can be explained easily in terms familiar to the organization's members; (4) it is reversible and can be eliminated once tried, even if only on a small scale; and (5) it is supported by some of the opinion leaders within the organization (Rothman, 1974, pp. 422–457).

The recognition that some contract proposals represent an important step in the attempt to achieve adoption of an innovation should guide a staff developer to propose—at least initially—the kind of contract that has the best chance of being accepted. Based on the foregoing, here are a number of interrelated principles regarding contracting for staff development when the proposal represents an innovation:

1. Select goals that are compatible with existing agency values.
2. Contract in such a way that the innovation can be tried out on a limited basis and withdrawn if it does not work.
3. Choose an innovation that can be easily explained to staff.
4. Select an innovation that is acceptable to at least some of the opinion leaders within the organization.

GUIDELINES FOR CONTRACTING

This section of the chapter is designed to help you develop the kind of contract that will help you carry out your own staff development project. In addition, the questions you are asked to answer should provide an expansion of the chapter's main points, whether or not you apply them to a specific project.

Note: Your answers to the following questions will depend on your position in the organization; an agency director would address these questions differently than would a unit supervisor or the chair of a staff development committee.

1. *To whom must you speak first, before you get started, if you want administrative support for your project?* If you don't know, find out. If the project covers more than one territory, you may have to gain the approval of several people. The person may be your superior, who will decide which tasks you should or may undertake. The person may control a staff group you want involved or a resource you believe you will need. Finally, the person's lack of support or open resistance may doom the project.

   a. First I would seek the approval of _____

   b. I need this person's approval because _____
   _____

   c. I would also seek the approval of the following person(s) before I get started, for the following reasons:

   Name _____   Reason _____

   Name _____   Reason _____

   Name _____   Reason _____

2. *What need(s) of the above person(s) do you think this project is likely to resolve? Why do you think this project could resolve the need(s)?*

   a. The need(s) to be resolved are _____

   _____

   _____

   b. The project should resolve the need(s) because _____

   _____

   _____

3. *Based on your experience in this organization, how do you plan to approach the person(s)?* It is often best to follow agency procedures here, at least until you develop the kind of rapport with administrators or other staff members that permits a less formal approach (unless, of course, the norm in *your* organization *is* to initiate projects informally). In some settings it might help to present your ideas in the form of a one-page memo, including some tentative notions about your goals and the resources you are requesting. Depending on procedures where you work, it might be better to send that memo to the administrator or other staff person before you see him or her, to pave the way for your proposal; in other cases, it might be better to go into a meeting prepared to produce a copy of such a statement on the spot—but to produce it only if it seems appropriate to do so.

   My approach will involve: _____

   _____

   _____

4. *Who in your organization is likely to be* negatively *affected by your proposal?* Always assume that there may be someone who will experience your project as a threat to the *status quo,* or to his or her power, or to some program that may suffer as a result of your project. (A major factor in the downfall of some attempts to improve an organization is the well-documented observation that the inadvertent consequences of the change attempt may act to defeat the desired change in the long run. See, for example, Gall, 1975.) Accordingly, you should speculate about any negative side effects your project may generate.

   a. The person(s) who may be negatively affected by the proposed project

   include: _____

   _____

   b. The program(s) that may be negatively affected by the proposed project

   include: _____

   _____

5. *What do you propose to do about:*

    a. The people (who might be negatively affected)? _____

    _____

    For example, you might try to involve them, early on, in the planning process; if this seems too formidable a task, you might choose another project that is less likely to engender their resistance—a project that might even directly respond to *their* needs in such a way that they would be more likely to trust you when other projects are proposed. Or, before you talk with them, you might do some informal organizing, so that someone *they* trust presents the project idea to them, on your behalf.

    b. The program(s) (that might be negatively affected)? _____

    _____

    If a staff development project is *designed* to replace an existing program, you will want to be sure there is a general consensus that the program should be eliminated. But if, for example, staff decide through some problem-solving activity that a new intake procedure is to be introduced, you should notify staff other than those providing the new service (for example, secretaries who must explain some aspects of the new procedure to new clients, the person in charge of office supplies who must obtain multiple copies of the new intake forms, the maintenance people who should know whether different patterns of agency space utilization are called for) about the new procedure.

6. *What are your specific expectations for this contract?* When you negotiate a contract for this project, you may want, initially, to be free to explore a range of possibilities. At this point you would prefer that the situation remain fluid, with no firm expectations established (other than an O.K. to explore a range of options). Eventually, however, you will want an explicit agreement about (a) the roles that will be played by different participants in the project, (b) the goals the project will be designed to attain, (c) the resources that will be available for this project, and (d) the ways in which these resources will be controlled and used.

    a. *Roles: Who will do what?*
        What will your role be? (I should be expected to do the following):

    _____

    _____

    Who else will play a role in this project, and what kinds of roles will they play? (What will *they* actually do?) _____

    _____

    _____

(Have you included the administrator? The participants? The people who will help to develop the project? The people who will help to implement the project? Be as inclusive as possible, recognizing that one aspect of contract renegotiations will be the addition of new people, as needed.)

b. *Goals.* It's often hard to state goals in measurable terms, but without measurable goals you can't be sure where you want to go, or how you'll know whether or not you've "arrived." Goals are so important that I've devoted all of Chapter 4 to the subject. At this point, your contract should attempt to address the following questions:

By the end of your project,

who (person or persons) _____

should be able to do *what* _____

how well? _____

(For example:

who (person or persons)   *intake workers*

should be able to do *what*   *complete, in writing, the new intake form, during an intake interview*

how well   *during the inverview, lasting no more than thirty minutes, with all blanks filled in correctly*

c. *Resources.* This could include time, space, equipment, money, the participation of a number of staff members, previously duplicated handouts, secretarial support, refreshments, and the like.

What resources will you need? _____

_____

How will you get these resources? _____

Who will be in charge of the resources? _____

How will the resource be used? _____

_____

(In many cases you won't know what resources you'll need until plans for the project develop. At that time, you will probably need to submit a proposal for the needed resources.)

7. *Renegotiation.* Throughout this outline, I have indicated possible points at which *further* negotiation—discussion of new or developing ideas—or *renegotiation*—a change in direction or specific items—might take place. It helps to set up renegotiation in the contract as a normal part of the process— for example, "I'll be getting back to you for your approval when I have a clearer idea of what we're going to need." What plans have you made—as part of

the contract—for renegotiation of this contract? _____

_____

8. *Innovation.* If your project represents a new way of doing something, you should answer these additional questions:

    a. As you review this process, can you be sure that you have used language that was clear to all involved? How can you tell it was clear?

    _____

    _____

    _____

    b. What have you done to keep the project small? _____

    _____

    c. If the project doesn't work, what can be done to get rid of it?

    _____

    d. How does the project fit in with the way you usually do things?

    _____

    (If the project is too different from the ways things are now, it may not be the best project to use when *starting* a *new* staff development program).

9. *Formality.* A written contract—for example, a memo describing the project—is useful in clarifying and making concrete the plans that have been discussed. However, it can also make plans too defined and inflexible, and provide a target for those who do not fully support the plan. I would/would not use

    a written contract because _____

    _____

10. *The written contract.* If you decide to use a written contract, the following outline is suggested. You will probably want to develop your own form, based on your own realities and your own experience. The use of a *written* contract is strongly recommended. It forces attention to crucial questions that need to be addressed in the contract negotiation process, and provides a written record as a hedge against fuzzy memories of what was agreed on. (You can, if you wish, write some ambiguity into the contract—for example, "Prior to the commencement of the contract, there will be an exploratory period, not to exceed one month, during which a number of options can be considered."

SUGGESTED CONTRACT OUTLINE

I. Identifying Information
    Agency name, subunit (if appropriate), staff developer's name(s):
II. Activity
    The projected staff development activity can be described as follows:

III.   Goals
    The goal(s) of this activity is/are:
      Under what circumstances:
      Will who:
      Be able to do what:
      How well:
IV.   Why?
    Why is this activity being undertaken at this time? How will it benefit the organization? the staff? the clients?
V.   Responsibility
    To carry out this activity, the following persons will be responsible for the following activities:
VI.   Who will be affected?
    Which staff members are expected to benefit directly from this activity?
    What problems might staff (participants and/or nonparticipants) experience as a result of this activity?
    How will these problems be addressed?
VII.   Resources
    What resources (space, funds, time, and so forth) will be needed, and how will they be secured?
VIII.   Renegotiation
    What are the plans for monitoring this contract, and for modifying it, if that is needed?
IX.   Approval
    I have read this contract and agree to its provisions.

    Signed:
    Date:
    Copies sent to:

WHAT'S NEXT?

One purpose of contracting is to garner administrative support to engage in an assessment of staff and organizational needs. In the next chapter, the process of assessing needs will be discussed.

chapter 3

ASSESSING NEEDS

- What is meant by *needs?*
- What dilemmas and conflicts exist in the concept of *needs* as it relates to staff development?
- What is a need assessment in staff development?
- Whose needs should you assess when doing staff development?
- How does role theory pertain to needs assessment?
- What needs assessment techniques will be presented?
- What guideline should you follow when assessing needs for staff development?

WHAT IS MEANT BY *NEEDS*?

The process of staff development follows a typical problem-solving model that can be stated in terms of *need*: recognition of a need, a decision to do something about the need, an analysis of factors causing the need, generation of a strategy to reduce the need, implementation of that strategy, and finally evaluation of the degree to which the strategy has reduced the need. Central to this process is the concept of *need*. The purpose of this chapter is to define the concept, establish a theoretical basis for its use, describe a number of techniques that can be used to assess needs, and discuss problems in employing these techniques.

After completing this chapter, you should be able to conduct a needs assessment in a way that is relevant to your organization—a needs assessment that could provide the basis for a staff development program. First, however, it is essential that the concept of *need* be clearly defined.

Defining Need

You can first clarify your own understanding of *need* by writing your definition here and then comparing it with several other definitions. How would you define *need*? (If you want to get the most out of this book, *don't fall prey to the temptation to skip this small task. Writing* your answer to this question forces you to think in a precise way about something you may have taken for granted. Writing

a definition is never easy, but neither is any real learning.) _____

_____

_____

_____

First, a dictionary definition of *need*: "pressing want, lack or absence of something required for the welfare or success of a person or thing or something useful or satisfying" (*The World Book Dictionary,* 1971, p. 1376). Next, from a psychology text: "a condition of unstable or disturbed equilibrium in any organism's behavior appearing typically as increased or protracted activity or tension" (Cameron, 1947).

Need is discussed in relation to *motive* by Cofer and Appley (1964):

> When the hypothetical man on the street asks, "What motivates behavior?" he is asking to have identified one or a combination of three kinds of things: (1) an environmental determinant which precipitated the behavior in question, the application of some irresistable force which of necessity led to this action; (2) the internal *urge, wish, feeling, emotion, drive, instinct, want, desire, demand, purpose, interest, aspiration, need,* or *motive* which gave rise to the action; or (3) the *incentive, goal,* or *object value* which attracted or repelled the organism [emphasis in original].

Maslow's theory of human personality is centered around his notion that humans have a

> tendency to seek personal goal states that make life rewarding and meaningful. . .that human desires (i.e. motives) are innate and are arranged in an ascending order of priority or potency. . .These needs are, in order of potency (1) basic physiological needs; (2) safety needs; (3) belongingness and love needs; (4) self-esteem needs; and (5) self-actualization needs, or the needs for personal fulfillment. (Hjelle and Ziegler, 1981)

According to this theory, higher-order needs cannot emerge and become operative until lower-order needs are satisfied. Maslow recognized that some creative individuals pursue high-level needs despite physical deprivation and insecurity. In general, however, Maslow saw human motivation as flowing out of the attempt to satisfy needs in this hierarchical order. In staff development terms, staff who believe that their jobs may be wiped out by a funding cut (a threat to the need for safety) are not likely to be motivated to participate in staff development activities (which could fill higher-order belongingness, self-esteem, or self-actualization needs).

In a less technical vein, I would define *need* as the difference between where one is and where one wants to be. The greater the difference, the greater the need.

People concerned about staff development are often unaware of the different ways in which the word *need* is used. First, there is the situation in which individuals sense the absence of something important to them in doing their job; this has been called a *felt need*. Felt needs refer to people's feelings, attitudes, and aspirations for their work that cause them to perform on the job as they do. Staff members' felt needs might include such things as wanting to feel that they are being successful in their work, and that their success is being recognized and rewarded by other staff, including administrators; that they are growing in professional competence; that their time and energy are being well spent; that other people at work are friendly, supportive, and caring; and that the problems they experience in their work are similar to the problems others experience, and can—in time—be resolved. There seems to be an association between variables here: The more that staff believe that their felt needs are met, the better their morale; the better their morale, the better staff efficiency and effectiveness are likely to be. The opposite appears to be equally valid: The more that felt needs are ignored, the lower the morale; the lower the morale, the poorer the quality of work.

Attention to felt needs is particularly crucial if staff development is to be effective. After all, staff development activities are designed to foster the processes of growth, learning, or change that will help the organization both achieve its goals and maintain good staff morale. These processes are more likely to occur when staff members involved in these activities believe that their felt needs are being addressed. This commonsense assertion has considerable support in the literature. For example, Rothman (1974, p. 433), writing to community organization practitioners, states:

> The innovativeness of a target system is directly linked to the extent to which it feels a need for change...this concept of "felt needs" has become institutionalized in the community-development literature. The social work precept "start where the client is" has a similar connotation.

Bass and Vaughn (1966, p. 56), writing for the industrial trainer, state:

> The individual must be psychologically ready in order for effective learning to occur. He must *want* to learn, or *want* to satisfy an existing drive state [emphasis in original].

Similarly, McKeachie (1969, p. 183), writing for beginning college instructors, says:

Students will learn what they want to learn and will have great difficulty in learning material in which they are not interested.

Clearly there is more to staff development than simply providing activities that meet the identified felt needs of staff members, just as there is more to school than only working on those things that a student wants to learn. For one thing, there are some things all students are required to learn; for another, efforts can be made to change a student's motivation so he or she will *want* to learn something not previously experienced as a felt need. But continued inattention to staffs' felt needs, or failure to help them see and value the connection between what they *must* be able to do (organizational needs) and what they *want* to do (their own felt needs) inevitably leads to lowered motivation—and motivation appears to be an essential ingredient to growth, change, and effective job performance.

Then there is the situation in which someone *other* than staff members believes or guesses that staff members have particular needs. Let's call these *attributed needs*. Administrators attribute needs to their staff for at least two reasons: Either in their opinion, staff *need* to do better—that is, need to learn how to do something without so many mistakes, or need to acquire a new set of skills and understandings to respond to an unmet client need, or need to do something they are supposed to do but have failed to do at all; or, out of their interaction with staff, administrators make what they consider to be informed guesses about the felt needs of staff. In the former case, the administrators may be quite correct in their assessment: Staff may be performing below par. The reason for poor staff performance, however, is often not—as some administrators believe—the laziness of staff members. Rather, poor performance sometimes occurs when the felt needs of staff are unaddressed. In attributing certain needs to staff, administrators are often indirectly expressing their own felt need to have greater control over staff performance. In this latter case there seems to be a clear relationship between the accuracy of their guesses and the size of the staff group: As staff size increases, the accuracy of their guesses is likely to decrease. When administrators find that their responsibilities take them further and further away from regular interaction, both formal and informal, with their staff, they may be deprived of knowledge about current staff needs. Experience has shown that the attribution of needs to others, without checking on those others' views of their own needs, can lead to inaccurate assessments; and, further, that administrative activity based solely on attributed needs can lead to staff resistance. The distinction between felt needs and attributed needs is not a trifling matter: Too often, the choice of a staff development activity is based on someone's incorrect attribution of need to one or more staff members, without asking them to describe (or paying attention to) their own felt needs. For example:

The resource person in a three-day university-sponsored workshop was unnerved to notice that about half of the forty participants in his workshop were unresponsive to his best efforts, looking bored or disgusted. At the mid-morning break, two of these scowling participants approached him and apologized for their demeanor.

They, along with twenty other staff members from the same state-sponsored agency, had been told to go to *this* institute, and to *no other* (in spite of their expressed desire to attend some of the other forty-five human service oriented workshops and institutes being offered by the School of Social Work that summer). Then they complimented him on the delivery of the material, informing him that they knew it pretty well because they had already had two in-service training seminars on the same topic at their agency, using the same source material! Apparently, administrators in their agency believed that the content had not been adequately learned, and was essential, if an effective job was to be done.

In addition to felt needs and attributed needs, there are also *organizational needs*. Organizational needs are those things the organization must have or must do to continue to exist and to fulfill its mandate. Under *must have* are such things as funds, staff, facilities, equipment, and—for human service organizations—clients. Under *must do* category are providing designated services, demonstrating to a funding source a reason for continued existence and perhaps growth, developing cooperative linkages with a network of other organizations, managing tensions within the organization, and establishing and maintaining organizational boundaries. Still another category includes the *should do's*—carrying out research, training students, and conducting an active staff development program: Usually these receive priority to the extent that they are seen as helping to reduce *must have* or *must do* needs. It is hard to think of a staff development activity that does not serve organizational needs, but if there is one, it is not likely to last long. Trying to develop a contract for a staff development activity that doesn't serve organizational needs is not likely to work; on the other hand, one way to sell a staff development activity is to make sure that everyone involved is aware of the ways in which the activity does serve organizational needs. The trick, of course, is to set up the activity in such a way as to respond to *both* organizational and felt needs. When that happens, the results can be very satisfying:

EXAMPLE 3: LEARNING A NEW PROCEDURE

Supervisors in one office of the State Department of Social Services were informed of a new federally mandated procedure which had to be followed by all staff. The procedure was not self-explanatory: An in-service training session was called for. Rather than use the traditional (and boring) lecture method, one of the supervisors introduced the new procedure with a role play demonstrating the use of the procedure with a simulated client. For this particular office, this approach was quite novel, creating a lot of discussion and interest in the topic. Staff who participated gave the session a high rating: Given that they had no choice to ignore the new procedure, the session met two felt needs, which were (1) to avoid being bored, and (2) to avoid wasting time, time that might be otherwise devoted to management of their work load. In addition, they learned the new procedure, and learned it well, thus meeting the organization's needs.

Dilemmas and Conflict in the Concept of *Need*

Not only is there confusion in the use of the word *need*—sometimes to mean *felt* need, sometimes *attributed* need, sometimes *organizational* need—there are also inherent dilemmas within and between the subcategories of felt need and organizational need that further complicate the use of *need*.

As indicated earlier, one felt need of most human service professionals is to feel successful in their attempts to help other human beings. Yet, as Bernard notes, their chances of regular success are slim:

> A reasonable statement about services is that they can help some, the best prepared, upwardly mobile minority among the disadvantaged to achieve substantial improvement in their personal or social condition. The lives of others will be improved somewhat, but not dramatically so. And services may be harmful to some.... (Bernard, 1975, p. 206)

Whether a lower than desired success rate is a result of ineffective technology (Perrow, 1970), of poor selection by graduate schools of fledgling professional helpers and, subsequently, ineffective schooling (Carkhuff, 1969), of inadequate resources to get the job done well, or, as Bernard suggests, of the fact that "social services . . . will not eliminate poverty, divorce, child abuse, or any other major social problem" (1975, p. 206), it is likely that this need will seldom be satisfied. Indeed, as Cherniss notes, this unsatisfied felt need seems to be associated with staff burn out:

> Looking at the individual, Herbert Freudenberger (1974) who was the first to use the term burnout in an article, argued that the dedicated and committed are most prone to burnout. . . . In our own research, we have found that the professional group most prone to burnout also tends at first to be the most idealistic and committed; these are poverty lawyers working in legal aid and public defender offices. (Cherniss, n.d., p. 8)

Organizational needs also face an inherent dilemma; goal displacement. Etzioni (1964) discusses the way in which organizations that are created to achieve specific goals soon acquire their own needs in relation to maintenance and survival of the organization itself; in time, these organizational needs can become preeminent. Other organizations select a major goal but find that in time they are actually operating so as to achieve a very different goal. For example, prisons that were established to rehabilitate inmates may find themselves locked into the goal of maintaining custodial control of prisoners in a way that makes rehabilitation impossible (Vinter, 1963). Gall writes of this phenomenon with tongue in cheek: "Systems in general work poorly or not at all" (Gall, 1975, p. 4) and, further, "Systems tend to oppose their own proper functions" (Gall, 1975, p. 23). Just two examples should suffice to illustrate this point:

> *Item:* The Aswan Dam, built at enormous expense to improve the lot of the Egyptian peasant, has caused the Nile to deposit its fertilizing sediment in Lake Nasser, where it is unavailable. Egyptian fields must now be fertilized artificially. Gigantic fertilizer plants have been built to meet the new need. The plants require enormous amounts of electricity. The dam must operate at capacity merely to supply the increased need for electricity which was created by the builiding of the dam. (Gall, 1975, p. 18)

Item: The Ann Arbor School bus system was created to make it easier for children to reach school on time. Due to monetary limitations there are not enough buses to go around; accordingly, each bus must make three runs in the morning; first for high school youngsters, then junior high kids, and finally elementary school students. In winter, this means that high school students are picked up so early that they are driven to school by moonlight, while elementary school children arrive at school at 9:20 A.M., long after their parents have left for work. The school bus schedule now controls the starting and closing time of the entire school system, much to the consternation of the community!

To confound this picture, there exists an inherent tension, if not a direct conflict, between the felt needs of individual staff members and the organization's needs. Because the organization's needs are usually the first order of responsibility for administrators, and because administrators have the power to control formal staff development activities, I often find that the felt needs of staff are overlooked. For example:

I recently taught an off-campus university extension service course in staff development. All of the sixteen students in the class were human service workers, some with a fair amount of administrative power; for example, two were directors of hospital social services departments. All students were required to do a staff development project of their own choosing, in their agency, as the major assignment for the course. I was struck by the almost unanimous feedback that staff in these agencies were delighted and astonished that anyone would think of asking them what *they* wanted in terms of staff development. This novelty, which I had assumed was nothing new, was actually a major innovation in almost every agency represented by the students in my class.

Examples of conflict between felt needs and organizational needs abound:

Line workers need a lower job load so that each can provide more intensive, high-quality service, but the organization needs to serve as many people as possible to justify its existence. Or an entire staff unit needs to be relieved of regularly scheduled service-delivery duties so they can participate in problem-solving staff meetings, as a unit, with regard to issues that concern them as a unit, but the organization lacks the resources to replace them while they meet; that is, it needs them to deliver services and cannot afford to pay others to fill in for them while they meet, or to pay them extra to attend staff development activities immediately before or after their assigned work times. And so on.

This tension is also evident in the decision of some administrators *not* to assess staff's felt needs. Aside from the familiar notion of attributed needs (in which administrators decide that *they* know best what type of staff development their staff needs), there is also the concern that, once asked, staff might request something that the organization cannot or will not supply. For example:

Item: One work unit of the State Department of Social Welfare decided that they were having trouble, as a unit, with internal communication. A member of the unit happened to be taking my course, on campus, in staff development. Using the required course project as justification, he recruited (at no cost) a human relations trainer from a local mental health agency to conduct some T-group sessions with the unit. The members of the unit found their sessions extremely useful, and the trainer was willing to work with them again, for no fee. In addition, a second unit, hearing of this experience, requested similar training, focusing on improved communication within their unit. Administration, however, said *absolutely no.* No reasons were given, but the student's sense was that administrators were afraid that the group training would give the units too much sense of their own latent power with regard to administrative decision making. He was also made to feel (by his supervisor) that pursuing this matter could create problems for him.

Item: In addition, I am continually surprised by the number of students who report that administrators will not allow *any* in-service training to go on in their agencies (not just student-initiated projects). There appears to be a significant minority of administrators who want no staff development at all (beyond the most basic orientation), viewing it as costly, unnecessary, nonproductive, and—perhaps most important—a threat to their authority. Under these conditions, the administrator does not allow a needs assessment to occur because there is no intention of attempting to meet assessed needs. (In every case that I have heard of, this stance by an administrator creates considerable tension between staff and administrator, making the administrator's job even more difficult.)

Summary on Needs

In summary, when using the term *need* in relation to staff development, it is important to clarify whether the term is being used in relation to felt needs, organizational needs, or attributed needs. Further, it is important to note the dilemmas inherent in trying to satisfy needs—dilemmas that lead to burnout for individuals and/or goal displacement for the organization. Finally, some administrators may not be too interested in the felt needs of staff, but may believe that they know their staff's needs or that inquiring into them will only raise expectations that cannot or should not be met.

WHAT IS A NEEDS ASSESSMENT?

Needs assessment refers to a process in which

1. The felt needs of staff members are determined.
2. Needs of the organization that pertain to staff development are determined.
3. An attempt is made to achieve consensus among staff on a priority of needs that blends felt needs and organizational needs.

One further point: The needs assessment techniques that will be described all have a spin-off value for the staff developer that should not be ignored: publicity. The needs of a staff development program itself must compete with the needs of other programs for the organization's limited resources, and the possibility of securing some of these resources is helped by a visibly productive staff development program. Involving people in needs assessment makes them aware that something is happening; when that *something* assumes a specific form that staff members have helped to shape, they are more likely to remain interested in and supportive of such programs. At each step of the way, then, needs assessment techniques provide a way of calling attention to the process—announcing first what will be done in the ways of needs assessment, then involving individuals in the assessment process itself, then informing staff of what was learned from the needs assessment, then making clear to potential participants the link between a staff development activity and the needs assessment process that produced it, and so forth.

Of course, there are many aspects of staff development that are better done without publicity—private consultation, the formations of informal coalitions, discussions of alternative staff development strategies until one or more are selected, and so forth. The point here is that several needs assessment techniques openly involve staff and therefore can be used to draw attention to the staff development process where that is useful.

WHOSE NEEDS ARE ASSESSED?

When employing a needs assessment technique, you need to decide whom to assess. A supervisor who wishes to assess the staff development needs of his or her work unit will limit the use of needs assessment to the members of that unit. Defining who qualifies as a *member,* however, is not always easy. Should secretaries who work for social workers in the medical social work unit of a hospital be considered members of the social work unit? How about program volunteers who assist a recreation department in a large institution? This question has no simple answer, but my own inclination is to include all the people whose primary job responsibilities involve them directly and actively in the unit's day-to-day operation. I would tend to include the secretaries and the volunteers in the needs assessment process.

In the same vein, an organizationwide needs assessment would do well, in my view, to include support personnel—secretaries, maintenance personnel, and the like—in any effort to determine the organization's high-priority needs. Such an inclusive effort in no way precludes a separate assessment of the needs of people in specific job categories, such as supervisors, secretaries, or line staff. The criteria for deciding who to include in the needs assessment process are (1) purpose and (2) feasibility—*purpose,* in relation to what the staff development is designed to achieve, and for whom, and *feasibility,* in relation to what can be accomplished efficiently given limitations of time and personnel. For example, if staff development is aimed at improving the operation of a hospital ward, then everyone who works on that ward should be involved in needs assessment: doctors, nurses, social workers, specialty therapists, ward clerks, attendants, and so forth. Questions of feasibility enter here: Will doctors who follow a few patients on a ward be willing to participate? Will hospital administrators allow the involvement of attendants in decision making, on a par with professionally trained staff? There is no pat answer here, except to note that the more people are excluded from the needs assessment process, the greater the probability of operating on the basis of attributed (and therefore probably inaccurate or incompletely assessed) needs.

ROLE THEORY: ONE FRAMEWORK FOR NEEDS ASSESSMENT

Role theory can provide the basis of focus—on a grand scale—in the process of needs assessment. In the lexicon of this theory, a *position* is "a collectively recognized category of persons who are similar in some respects," and *role* is defined as "the set of role expectations held by relevant others concerning how the rights and duties of a position should be carried out" (Thomas and Feldman, 1967, p. 20). Studies of complex organizations suggest that position occupants—people in particular jobs—are likely to encounter problems that are inherent in the positions themselves rather than a function of the attributes any individual brings to the job (see, for example, Katz and Kahn, 1966). For example, someone who is new on a job is likely to experience role discontinuity and an associated felt need to reduce that role discontinuity. Thomas and Feldman have identified three problems, in role theory terms, that are likely to produce felt needs: role discontinuity, role ambiguity, and role conflict. Needs assessment techniques can be used to determine typical needs associated with each position in a human service organization in relation to predictable role problems so that plans can be made to anticipate the need, thereby reducing role strain.[1] *Role discontinuity* is defined as "a lack of correspondence between the role expectations of one position that an individual has held and the role expectations associated with a different position he now holds or has held" (Thomas and Feldman, 1967, p. 28) and is likely to occur when an individual first joins the organization's staff, when he or she moves into a different position within the organization (for example, through promotion), or when he or she is leaving the organization.

Role ambiguity, defined as "a lack of clarity of role expectations about the rights and duties of a given position" (Thomas and Feldman, 1967, p. 27), is likely to accompany role discontinuity but is also likely to occur when circumstances within or outside the organization impose new or unclear demands on a particular position, and thus any person in that position.

Role conflict is defined as "the opposition of role expectations such that a position member cannot perform in terms of all of them at the same time" (Thomas and Feldman, 1967, p. 27). Role conflict may occur because the position occupants'

---

[1] "*Role strain* is the experienced difficulty of a position member in performing in that position." (Thomas and Feldman, 1967, p. 28)

own standards for job performance conflict with the expectations of others, or because two sets of significant others have differing expectations for occupants of that position. In either case, position occupants need to experience a consensus of expectations if they are to do their job without role strain.

Using role theory as a framework, the needs assessment process can proceed as follows: First, the predictable benchmarks and crisis points in the career of a particular position need to be identified. *Benchmarks* could include (1) being newly hired or just assigned to a position; (2) completing a probationary period; (3) completing one year (typically a point of evaluation); and (4) reaching some point in time whose significance is established by the organization's operation, such as the opening or closing of school. Predictable *crisis points* occur (1) just before certain benchmarks; (2) when the occupants of key administrative positions change (since this may threaten the existence of role consensus that had been generally accepted); and (3) when conditions in the organization's environment threaten to block the flow of needed resources to the organization or place new and perhaps conflicting demands on the organization and on the role performance of its staff.

Role theory, then, can be used by those responsible for staff development to heighten their awareness of recurring and predictable felt needs of staff in relation to the problems and obstacles discussed in Chapter 1.[2]

TECHNIQUES OF NEEDS ASSESSMENT

Needs that pertain to the various categories of problems and obstacles—*individual-common, group-internal,* and *group-external*—can be determined in a number of ways that involve group problem solving. These include brainstorming, Delphi, nominal group technique, time machine, interviewing, questionnaires, and informal observing. Needs that pertain to the first category of problems and obstacles, *individual-unique,* can be determined using the techniques of personal competency assessment and task analysis.

You will learn this material best if you select the assessment technique best suited to your current situation and use it—once you have negotiated a contract to do so—to build a staff development program, using this text as your guide.

Brainstorming

Brainstorming is a well-known technique designed to produce the longest list of items possible in relation to a given subject—for example, the longest list of possible solutions to a given problem, the longest list of positive aspects of a particular organization, or the longest list of problems faced by one unit in an organization. Not only is the list meant to be long, but it is also hoped that the very freedom of the brainstorming process will produce previously unthought-of items. In other

[2]Such heightened awareness *still needs to be tested by involving staff in the needs assessment process,* lest the perspective of role theory be used to attribute needs to staff that they may not feel.

words, the emphasis is on *quantity* of items: The hoped-for product is *creativity*—new ideas, or novel blendings of items previously seen as unrelated. To achieve this outcome, the following rules should be observed:

1. State the topic in the form of a key question in terms familiar to participants; then make sure (by asking) that the topic is clear. When brainstorming is used for needs assessment, it may be a good idea first to ask the participants to list as many things as they can about their jobs that they *like* and want retained (to avoid creating an overriding negative tone to the process), then a separate list of things they *dislike* about their jobs and want to see changed. This second list represents the felt needs of staff—the difference between the way things are and the way they would like them to be.

2. Set a time limit, such as fifteen minutes, so that the participants feel some urgency to respond without too much introspection.

3. Announce that no criticism or evaluation of verbalized ideas will be allowed, although participants can add to another person's ideas. Also, participants cannot ask for clarification in a way that prompts members to discuss and evaluate an expressed idea.

4. Encourage participants to express ideas they think are so ridiculous or implausible that they are sure others would think something was wrong with them for stating the idea. The motto here is "Think *big,* and feel free to think *silly!*" Making this experience funny—almost giddy—helps the creative juices flow.

5. Publicly display ideas by writing them on a large newsprint pad with a thick felt pen, or on a chalk board.[3]

6. Reward participation, not content—for example, "Good, good," "More," "Time's running out," "Let's see if we can get at least twenty-five ideas."

7. Give a two-minute warning. Then, call "time" on time.

8. Next, involve the group in reviewing their list so as to:
   a. Combine items that may say the same thing in different ways. Try hard to pare the list down.
   b. Eliminate totally impossible (illegal, immoral, or otherwise unacceptable) ideas.

9. Rewrite your list using precise language so that the list is ready for use. Most people have participated in brainstorming, but if your group has not, here's a simple practice exercise that will set the proper atmosphere: Take a common object, such as a coffee cup, and ask the group to create a list of twenty-five uses for the object in five minutes. Give this a "contest" atmosphere, and make it fun.

Delphi

Brainstorming can be used to create a list of needs; Delphi provides a way of achieving consensus among staff on which needs should have high priority

[3]*Note:* writing ideas (with chalk or felt pen) for public display can be tiring—get at least one volunteer scribe to assist you. If you do this, you'll need two pieces of chalk, or two felt pens, etc. Then each scribe can write out items on an alternating basis—"You take #1, I'll get #2, you get #3 . . ." and so on. In a large group, I find that three scribes works best.

(Linstone and Murray, 1975). Delphi is best used when a staff group is large (more than ten) and would experience difficulty in participating together in a priority-setting group meeting. In addition, Delphi protects individuals who are timid about speaking up in a group meeting, or who have little power in a group, by giving each staff person one vote and keeping that vote secret. The Delphi is fairly simple to administer, but does involve asking staff to vote, privately, at least *twice* on the list of needs, to indicate which they think are most important. Here's how it works:

1. A list of needs (such as one generated by brainstorming) is duplicated and circulated to all staff considered relevant with a covering memo that explains the Delphi process. Whenever possible, this memo should go out over the key administrator's name as evidence of administrative support for this process. The memo should urge prompt return—and appear to be something fairly easy to do. It could also include a statement that recognizes the large amount of paperwork staff are continually asked to "fill out and return immediately," pointing out that the Delphi will be used to identify the needs *they* feel are important (including "too much paperwork"), so that something can be done about them. Voting is to be done privately, and staff are *not* to sign their name to their form.

2. The Delphi form looks something like this (I have written in some items that might appear on such a form in the "Needs" column):

| | Importance to *Me* | | | |
NEEDS	GREAT IMPORTANCE	FAIRLY IMPORTANT	SOME IMPORTANCE	NO IMPORTANCE
1. Reduce paperwork				
2. More time for supervision				
3. More privacy for interviews				
4. Etc.				

The cover memo and the Delphi form itself should make it clear that each item is to be voted on in terms of its importance to the staff member. In other words, given a list of twelve items, a staff member could rate three of these as having "great importance," four as "fairly important," two as having "some importance," and three as being of "no importance." (They are *not* being asked to rank those twelve items with only one as "most important.") In the column marked "Needs," each need should be listed, using as few words as possible, but making the meaning of each item quite clear—for example, "Reduce paperwork."

Sometimes, only a *portion* of staff participate in creating the original Delphi list. For this reason, the rest of the staff should be encouraged to add items to the form. Space should be left on the form for individuals to add items and to explain (in writing) their reason for adding the item(s).

3. When forms are returned, the results should be tabulated. (I usually use an extra Delphi sheet on which to tally scores.) Every "great importance" answer is multiplied by 3, every "fairly important" is multiplied by 2, and every "some importance" counts as 1 vote. I have filled in a hypothetical vote on lines 1, 2, and 3 to demonstrate the simple arithmetic involved. The total for each cell is shown in parentheses.

Importance to Me

NEEDS	GREAT IMPORTANCE (×3)	FAIRLY IMPORTANT (×2)	SOME IMPORTANCE (×1)	NO IMPORTANCE (×0)	TOTAL SCORE
1. Reduce paperwork	(//////) (15)	(///// ///) (16)	(//) (2)	(///) (0)	33
2. More time for supervision	(/) (3)	(///// ///// ///// /) (32)	(/) (1)	(0)	36
3. More privacy for interviews	(///// ///// /) (33)	(//) (4)	(///) (3)	(//) (0)	40
4.					

For Need #1	For Need #2	For Need #3
most 3×5 = 15	3× 1 = 3	3×11 = 33
very 2×8 = 16	2×16 = 32	2× 2 = 4
fairly 1×2 = 2	1× 1 = 1	1× 3 = 3
none 0×3 = 0	0× 0 = 0	0× 3 = 0
Total = 34	Total = 36	Total = 40

When the totals for each need have been computed, a *second* Delphi form should be prepared. This time, however, the first need on the list should be the need that received the *largest total score,* the second need the one that received the next largest score, and so on. The total score for each item should be displayed next to that item. This form notifies all those who voted how the total staff group voted, including the total score each need received; this information may cause staff members to shift their votes but does not force them to change their votes in response to group pressure, as a public group discussion might. In this way, staff can vote their preferences free of group pressure, but informed of group opinion.

4. The second Delphi should be circulated, clearly labeled "Delphi #2" with a cover memo explaining this step in the process. This time, however, staff are to choose a limited number of items—for example, 3 of 12, or 5 of 20. If it's 3 of 12, choose only *one* "great importance," *one* "fairly important," and *one* "some importance."

If items were added to the first Delphi form, they should be shown on Delphi #2, including whatever explanations were written on Delphi #1.

5. When Delphi #2 is returned, the results should be tabulated and a memo prepared (and sent to all who participated) that displays the voting results. Again, each "great importance" vote should be awarded 3 points, each "fairly important" vote, 2 points, and each "some importance" vote, 1 point. Usually staff members' priorities concerning felt needs should have emerged at this point. If a few items are about equal in "popularity," you should select the item(s) that are both (1) most feasible to do, and (2) most likely to be successful. Beginning a staff development program with a success makes it that much easier to build future programs.

Nominal Group Technique (NGT)

The prohibition in brainstorming against criticizing or evaluating each other's suggestions serves two purposes: First, you avoid getting stuck on a particular issue during a time-limited period in which the goal is to produce a large quantity of ideas in a freewheeling atmosphere. Second, you encourage individuals to speak out, expressing ideas that may appear deviant, outrageous, or downright weird. Human beings depend heavily on social approval, but in many staff groups, factors of power, subgroupings, office politics, and strongly established norms can combine to muzzle individual creativity, whether or not it is the group's intention to do so. The nominal group technique (NGT) is designed, like brainstorming, to encourage novel or apparently unacceptable ideas while protecting creative individuals from the censure of their peers. Because this is inherent in its design, it should create an atmosphere in which participants will think more freely, conjuring ideas that they might otherwise keep to themselves or might not even try to dream up. Unlike brainstorming, however, it also provides a procedure for reaching consensus on a priority of needs *in one meeting* where staff are assembled. By definition, then, it is most useful when staff can be assembled in order to achieve consensus on a priority of needs. *Nominal* here means that the "group" is noninteracting; as will be seen from the instructions that follow, the process allows for joint decision making but keeps *interaction* to a minimum.

The nominal group technique proceeds as follows:

1. The group should be no smaller than 5 and no larger than 15. If the group is larger than 15, it should be broken into separate groups; for example, a group of 18 would be broken into two groups of 9. This may necessitate the use of two rooms or one large room, with the groups far enough away from each other so that they can proceed without distraction.

2. An important consideration is group composition. NGT is most easily used by a fairly homogeneous work unit—for example, all of the child care staff in an

institution, or all of the teachers in one school. On the other hand, there may be occasions when a heterogeneous group is called for—for example, all staff in a medical hospital who work on a ward that focuses on a particular medical problem. (For a fuller discussion of group composition, see Bertcher and Maple, 1977).

3. Each participant is supplied with a number of 3×5 cards and a pencil. The actual number of cards will depend on the number of written responses being sought, as described next.

4. One or more questions is posed, and participants are asked to write their answers to the question(s) on the 3×5 cards. For example:

> Using two cards, print *strengths* at the top of one card, *weaknesses* at the top of the other. (1) List (on the *strengths* card) three major strengths of our work group. (2) List (on the *weaknesses* card) three major weaknesses of our work group.

Or, using another example:

> Print, at the tops of three different 3 × 5 cards, the words, *clients, our organization, the community;* on each card write what you consider to be the three most important problems you face in your daily work in regard to each of these areas (clients, our organization, the community).

5. All participants are to write their responses privately. A time limit is set. During this writing period, participants are asked not to communicate with one another.

6. There are two ways to proceed at this point. Both involve, as in brainstorming, publicly displaying what participants have written: (1) To preserve anonymity, cards are collected and one or more scribes copy—for all to see—what is on the cards, using a chalkboard and chalk or large newsprint pads and thick felt pens; or (2) each member reads one item from his or her list, and it is then copied for all to see. If anyone else has more or less the same item on their list, he or she can so indicate by raising his or her hand when asked to do so. One check is placed next to the item for each person so indicating.

The process continues around the group until all privately written items have been recorded. The advantage of (2) is that duplicate items need not be copied over again for all to see; the disadvantage is that anonymity is destroyed. Whether approach (1) or (2) is used, participants are asked not to comment, criticize, or in any way evaluate what has been written. Since method (1) takes time for copying all responses, participants who are not scribes can be given a short break until the copying is completed.

7. Participants can discuss the list, but only to *clarify* the meaning of words or phrases, to *synthesize,* or to *add* items.

8. Participants are now asked to vote secretly for the items they consider most important. Again, there are several ways to do this, depending on the number of items on the list(s). For example, they might be asked to select the three items they think are most important, and to indicate this vote on a 3×5 card. Or they could

be asked to rank the three (or four, or five—it's up to you) they think are most important, in order of importance. If this latter approach is used and participants rank, for example, three items, then each time a participant ranks an item "tops" it is given 3 points in the voting, the next is given 2, and the last is given 1. The item with the largest total score "wins."

9. Results of this vote are tallied and reported; they should represent what the component members regard as the most important needs to be addressed.

The Time Machine[4]

Here is another way to encourage creative thinking. Because it asks staff to devote some time in private to the needs assessment process, however, busy staff members who are uncommitted to participating in the planning of staff development may not respond well to it. My guess is that it would be better to use this approach with a staff that has good morale, good internal communication, and a generally positive attitude toward its existing administrative structrure. Where these conditions do not prevail, staff might too easily react negatively because of the "let's pretend" aspects of the technique.

Put most simply, you ask staff to imagine privately what the organization will be like ten years from now: At that time (they are to pretend) the major work problems facing each staff person will have been resolved. Each person is to write a brief description of his or her work situation at that time. In my own case, for example, I might pretend that—at that time—I will have the same secretary (who is perfection itself) but that the School of Social Work (where I work) will have moved to a building that would better facilitate faculty interaction (since we are currently scattered throughout various hallways in a four-story building, and often do not see one another for weeks). If you compare what I dream up as a good future situation with my present situation, a picture of my needs emerges. While writing this book, for example, I had no significant needs with regard to secretarial support, but I did have a need for closer associations with colleagues, something the physical structure of my building made quite difficult to achieve.

To give this technique greater structure, a written form can be used; a sample follows. Once the form is completed, staff could meet and allow each person to read one or more items to the group, or the forms could be submitted, unsigned, to a committee that would review them in search of commonly expressed needs. If need priorities do not emerge, brief descriptive phrases might be created that pick up major themes from each person's written submission, and the Delphi technique could be used to arrive at a consensus on priorities. Here's a sample form:

Sample "Time Machine" Form

Assume it's ten years from now, and you are still working here. Imagine that all the significant problems you face in your work have been resolved to your satisfac-

---

[4]Suggested by the work of Schmuck, Runkel, Saturen, Martell, and Derr (1972).

tion. Think about this a bit, and then answer the following questions in as specific a way as you can.

1. It's ten years from now, so it's 19____ .
2. The things that are working well with my clients include:

_____

_____

_____

_____

3. The things that are important to me that are working well within the organization include:

_____

_____

_____

_____

4. The things that are important to me in regard to our organization's environment that are working well include:

_____

_____

_____

_____

5. Looking back at my answers, and comparing them with the way I know things to be today, the things I'd most like to see improved around here include:

_____

_____

_____

_____

Please feel free to use more paper if you wish (end of Sample Form).

A cover memo could be attached describing briefly the way in which the form will be used.

The primary advantage of this technique is that it facilitates creative imagining in a novel way. The primary disadvantage is that some staff groups might reject its make-believe quality or the time it requires and simply not fill it out. The decision to use the time machine for assessing needs would, therefore, depend on your sense of staff members' willingness to participate in such a needs assessment process.

Interviews and Questionnaires

Interviews and questionnaires are two similar methods of gathering information for the purpose of needs assessment. The interview, as described here, is more structured than the counseling interview or job interview. That is, all the questions are prepared in advance and are read to each respondent. The difference between the information-gathering interview and the questionnaire is in the method of administration: The interview is verbal, either face to face or over the phone, and the interviewer records the answers. The questionnaire is written in advance and then self-administered by the respondent.

Length.   Questionnaires and interviews used with busy staff members should not be too long. For most purposes, an interview of fifteen minutes or a questionnaire of two to five pages should be more than adequate. Beyond these limits, the respondent may become tired or bored, and the questions toward the end may be rushed over and answered inaccurately, if at all.

Questionnaire or interview?   The main advantage of an inverview is the interviewer's flexibility to seek further information from the respondent and to follow up ideas. Its main disadvantages are: (1) the amount of time it takes to administer, (2) the lack of anonymity of the respondent, and (3) the fact that the interviewer's position in the organization is known to interviewees and may influence their responses.

The questionnarie has two main advantages: (1) Since no interviewer time is needed, more people can be surveyed, allowing for greater confidence in the results; that is, your results are not based on the opinions of a small percentage of staff; and (2) the self-administered nature of the questionnaire ensures that respondents remain anonymous, allowing them more freedom to express opinions honestly. The two disadvantages of the questionnaire lie in the possibility of (1) receiving incomplete answers that cannot be followed up and (2) having questions misunderstood.

Question type.   There are three types of questions: (1) fact, (2) perception, and (3) opinion or attitude. Questions of *fact* ask respondents to provide information about things of which they have a direct knowledge, such as age of clients served or number of phone calls received. These questions allow the respondents to be divided into groups in order to see if there are any differences between groups in the ways other questions are answered. For example, supervisors could be compared to counselors to see if they have different information on certain issues.

Questions of *perception* are designed to determine respondents' levels of information about various things of interest in the assessment—that is, to find out what the respondents *believe* to be the facts. Usually, respondents are asked to provide an estimate of something that can then be checked objectively.

For example:

About how many clients do you think fail to return after their first interview every month?

_____   0–9

_____   10–24

_____   25–49

_____   50–99

_____   more than 100

Questions of *opinion or attitude* ask respondents to make a value judgment about the issue.

For example:

How much are you in favor of, or opposed to, training on the nature of problems faced by physically handicapped clients?

_____   strongly in favor

_____   in favor

_____   neither for nor against

_____   opposed

_____   strongly opposed

Question Format.   There are two forms of questions: unstructured and structured.

Unstructured questions are also known as open-ended or free-response questions. In this form, respondents are free to answer in any way, rather than being asked to choose from a given set of answers.

For example:

What problems of communication do you see among staff members?

_____

_____

Unstructured questions are useful if: you don't know what type of answers to expect, so you can't list the possibilties in advance; if you expect a wide range of responses; if you want to preserve the flavor of the individual answers; or if you want the respondent to give specific examples. But there are disadvantages, too: First, unstructured questions are unwieldy, especially in an interview where the interviewer must record answers word for word. Similarly, in self-administered questionnaires this type of question is very time-consuming and bothersome for the respondent to fill out. The respondent may lose interest and may never fill out the questionnaire. Second, these questions take up a lot of space, especially if you want to leave ample room to write an extensive answer. Third, the answers are especially difficult to analyze since there are no specific criteria for similarity of answers, making it difficult to calculate percentages, averages, or majorities. Consequently, it is hard to draw conclusions from this type of question.

Structured questions give the respondent a fixed number of alternative answers from which to choose.

For example:

How effective do you think you are in working with people who are older than you are?

_____ very effective

_____ effective

_____ somewhat effective

_____ ineffective

_____ very ineffective

Structured questions have several advantages. Because every respondent chooses from among the same alternatives, comparisons of responses can be made. Structured questions are easy to administer, as only a check mark is needed to indicate the desired answer, rather than extensive writing by the interviewer or respondent. More questions can be asked in the same amount of time because the responses are faster and easier to make, so that respondent fatigue is avoided. Finally, the answers are easy to analyze because responses can be counted, grouped, and added. The main disadvantage is that the color or flavor of the response is lost; the personalities of the respondents and their feelings are hidden.

In general, if it is at all possible to anticipate the likely answers to questions before the assessment, structured questions are recommended. You will have more control and will end up with usable answers. Many different types of structuring are available so that you can choose the type that elicits the kind of information you want. Also, if you wish, unstructured and structured questions can be mixed in the same questionnaire.

Types of structured questions

1. *Dichotomous:* Only two choices are offered—yes–no, good–bad, true–false, agree–disagree.

2. *Multiple choice:* More than two choices are usually offered, but there does not have to be an underlying continuum as is implied in a dichotomous question.

For example:

Which of the following occupational classifications in our organization do you think has the *greatest* need for more training? (choose only one)

_____ managers

_____ supervisors

_____ counselors

_____ receptionists

Caution: It is important that the respondent choose only *one* answer to the question; thus, the wording is important in stressing that only one response is called for. Consider the previous question slightly reworded:

Which occupational classification in our organization do you think needs more training?

_____ managers

_____ supervisors

_____ counselors

_____ receptionists

It is conceivable that some people might check two, three, or all four choices to answer this question. Others might choose only one of the four—the one they feel has the *greatest* need. It is best to avoid situations like this one by being very specific, as was demonstrated in the previous example. Otherwise, you may find it difficult to make sense of the responses you receive.

To score this type of question, simply count the number of times each alternative is chosen. In this case, you can then make a judgment about the respondent's perception of the need for training.

For example:

Suppose the results for this question come out as follows after thirty questionnaires are returned:

"managers" checked by 3 respondents
"supervisors" checked by 5 respondents
"counselors" checked by 18 respondents
"receptionists" checked by 4 respondents

This type of response would indicate that a majority of the staff (60 percent) believes that counselors could use more training. A problem arises, however, concerning the *intensity* of the answer. You cannot tell how much importance the staff placed on the need for training. This is a disadvantage in using multiple choice questions, but it can be handled by asking respondents to make alternative choices.

For example:

How important is it to you to have a library that is available to all staff?

_____ very important

_____ important

_____ unimportant

_____ very unimportant

When all the responses to this type of question are counted, you will have some information about the intensity of the respondents' feelings about the issue.

A handy method of finding out how respondents feel about an issue, policy, action, or idea is to use what is called a Likert-type question in which a *scale* of choices is constructed. This type of question usually consists of a very positive or very negative *statement* followed by a standard set of *responses* asking the respondent to indicate how much he or she agrees or disagrees with the statement.

For example:

Our method of making policy changes is excellent:

_____ strongly agree

_____ agree

_____ ambivalent

_____ disagree

_____ strongly disagree

With this type of question, a series of statements about different issues can be written, each with the same set of responses: "strongly agree," "agree," and so on. The respondent can learn the overall pattern of expected responses and answer the questions more rapidly. In this type of format, positive and negative statements should be interspersed to reduce the possibility that respondents will fall into a pattern of response.

Other scales and weighting methods exist and may be effectively used. They tend, however, to be more complicated to construct and analyze. We suggest, therefore, that it is best to stick to the basic types described here.

In general, if your purpose in using the questionnaire is to gather information about topics of which you have no previous knowledge, the unstructured question will generate much information that can be used to generate more specific questions. Conversely, if you already have some previous information, the structured question allows for more accurate measurement and more definite conclusions.

Question wording problems.   Probably the most crucial element in interview or questionnaire design is the wording of questions in a way that will lead to accurate conclusions. To achieve this end, questions should be worded so that responses are not biased and so that questions are interpreted similarly by all respondents. Wording problems can be classified under three major headings: ambiguity, misperception, and bias. It is essential to deal with these problems when developing questions in order to have confidence in the results.

1. *Ambiguity:*   Questions that are exactly and precisely worded are easier to understand and to answer than ones that are incomplete, imprecise, or indefinite.

For example:

Are you in favor of or opposed to the changes that have taken place in this office? _____

The above is an example of an incomplete question. Its ambiguity makes it difficult for all respondents to interpret it in the same way. Respondents may ask themselves: What changes? Over what period of time? A person who is not aware that a change took place may have difficulty in answering at all. One person might think that *change* refers to a change in the color of filing cabinets and may favor the new color. Another may be opposed to a change in supervisors. Another may not consider the promotion of the assistant director to director a change because "he's been running the place all along." The point is: Ask about the specific change you have in mind.

For example:

Are you in favor of or opposed to the policy of flexible office hours proposed in last week's memo?

_____ strongly in favor

_____ in favor

_____ ambivalent

_____ opposed

_____ strongly opposed

Other sources of ambiguity arise from words that have more than one meaning. Sometimes even a word that is too simple can cause problems with ambiguity.

For example:

Do you think the waiting room is too cold?

_____ Yes

_____ No

Answers to this question could include:

- "Yes"—by a person who means that a few paintings on the wall and some plants would make the room seem warmer.
- "No"—by a person who thinks the receptionist is one of the friendliest people he knows.
- "No"—by a person who thinks that a room temperature of 66 degrees Fahrenheit is good because it conserves energy.

The way to avoid ambiguity is to be very specific in what you are asking. To ensure that your questions are understood in the way you want them understood, you should *pretest* the questions by asking them of some people (at least two, but preferably three to five) who will *not* be in your final survey, and seeing whether they all interpret the questions in the same way. It is best to use people from the same population you intend to survey; but if they are not available, friends or co-workers will do. After you finish the pretest, ask each person what he or she understood each question to mean. If different people saw different meanings in the same question, then the question is unclear and should be rewritten. If one of the pretest respondents asks you what a question means, then clearly a new question is needed.

2. *Misperception:* The second wording problem is misperception. Words that are not within the realm of the respondents' experience may have no meaning for them. Jargon and technical words should be avoided unless you are *sure* the respondents are familiar with the words. This problem is especially important in interviewing, for respondents tend to misinterpret words they hear that are unfamiliar to them. They are likely to answer the question they *think* they heard, which may include a word or phase with which they are familiar that sounds similar to the actual word used by the interviewer. For example, if some people working in an agency were asked if they would benefit from a "time and motion" study, they might well resent an implication that their "emotional" health is in question. Remember, the questionnaire or interview is an information-gathering tool, not an achievement test. Keep in mind who the respondents are and use language with which they are familiar. Use *their* words for things, even if these are different from your own.

3. *Bias:* This wording problem is, perhaps, the most difficult to overcome.

In order to gather accurate information, care should be taken to provide a neutral atmosphere that does not suggest to respondents that one answer is better than another. Questions can be biased in several ways, some obvious and others rather subtle. An obvious bias is introduced in multiple choice questions that do not provide adequate choices or are worded in such a way that the respondent is trapped.

For example:

Do you feel women are inferior because of:

_____ heredity

_____ family pressure

_____ peer pressure

No matter what answer you give, you are forced to agree that "women are inferior. "

Another type of bias is more subtle: an appeal to prominent figures, in which the emotional value associated with an important person can introduce bias.

For example:

The director has suggested having a staff meeting every week. Do you agree or disagree with this proposal?

_____ agree

_____ disagree

Depending on how the respondent feels about the director, he or she may agree or disagree *regardless* of the issue. Similarly, any type of emotionally charged words or value judgments can introduce bias into the question.

For example:

Are you in favor of or opposed to the hiring of an extra clerk to help with the tremendous problem of excessive paperwork?

_____ in favor

_____ opposed

In this example, words like "extra," "tremendous," and "excessive" tend to influence respondents to answer "in favor. " A more neutral way of asking the same question would not inlcude such emotionally laden words.

For example:

Are you in favor of or opposed to the hiring of another clerk to help with the paperwork?

_____ in favor

_____ opposed

In general, try to avoid bias by keeping questions neutral. This requires considerable effort as it quite often does not show up in a pretest. Since in an interview you read the questions from your questionnaire, be sure to read them in the same way to each interviewee. In that way, you'll avoid inadvertently biasing the response because of the way you ask the questions.

4. *Special wording problems:* There are certain problems that are best described in a list of "don't"'s:

    a.   Don't assume too much knowledge on the part of the respondents. Ask questions within their area of understanding.

    b.   Don't talk down to the respondents; they may get impatient or even antagonistic.

    c.   Don't use lengthy questions that can be difficult for a respondent to follow. Long questions also exhaust patience.

    d.   Don't use two-part questions. You won't know for sure which part is being answered.

    e.   Don't violate good grammar. Double negatives and illogical sentence structure can create problems.

Conclusion: interviews and questionnaires.   Writing good questions involves much thought and effort. But no amount of forethought and planning can prevent all errors. Always pretest the questions. You will end up with a much better questionnaire, and you will learn a lot from your mistakes.

In needs assessment, you are particularly interested in staff members' ideas about their own jobs, as well as about their work unit or the organization as a whole. As indicated earlier, seeking information only about felt needs, or only about organizational needs, can overfocus the needs assessment process and interfere with comprehensive planning for staff development. You also want some identifying information so that you can compare the responses of one work group (for example, line staff) with those of another (for example, supervisors). Obviously, this is easier to do in an interview, where you already know who the respondents are (although you may want to promise each respondent to report only *total* responses to a question, rather than what any one individual said). It is easier to maintain anonymity when your interview or questionnaire is directed at a fairly large staff group.

Why use an interview or questionnaire instead of brainstorming/Delphi, nominal group technique, or time machine? Use interviews or questionnaries when you want a great deal of individualized information and have the time to analyze the information you gather. Perhaps this approach is best used in an organization that wants to overhaul its entire staff development program, or in introducing a staff development program where there has been no significant program in the past.

It is also possible that either of these approaches is best for an extremely large organization in which it is only feasible to deal with a sample of staff.

Exit interviews and postemployment surveys.   A special category of interview or questionnaire has been suggested in a book published by the Hospital Continuing Education Project (Schecter and O'Farrell, 1970): exit interviews, which take place after a staff member has resigned but before he or she has left, or a postemployment survey, several weeks after a staff member has left the job, when he or she can look back on it with some detachment. Of course, the usefulness of this approach varies with the circumstances of the staff member's departure. Assuming, however, that in many cases people leave jobs in the normal course of events and would be willing to share their ideas about the organization, some extremely valuable insights could be gained. Thus, for example, a postemployment questionnaire could be created covering general work-related issues, and routinely sent to all employees once they have left the organization.

One approach to needs assessment that pertains to the categories of felt need and individual–common, group–internal, and group–external is referred to as *informal observation.*

EXAMPLE 4: INFORMAL OBSERVING

Several years ago I was participating in the development of an instructional package that would teach manpower agency staff how to work effectively with groups. As part of our preparation, we spent many hours observing the agency in operation, with particular attention to the work of employment counselors. In contacts with these counselors, individually or in twos and threes, we noted frequent reference to the following problem: Clients who were not job-ready were referred by job interviewers for counseling, but these clients incorrectly assumed that they were being sent to a specialist who had "just the right job referral" for them. This disturbed the counselors, who saw themselves as people who helped clients with the problems that prevented them from being job-ready, not as persons who referred clients to jobs. I was struck by the fact that, independent of one another, they always described this concern in the same way: Each one would pantomine opening an imaginary top right-hand desk drawer, and say plaintively, "They always act as if they expect me to have the perfect job card waiting for them in my desk drawer!"

When we thought we had a good feel of the organization, we called a meeting to discuss some ideas for next steps. At one point, I reported my observation of the pantomimed drawer opening. Apparently, this was the first time that they had discussed, as a total work unit, the fact that *each* of them felt the *need* to work with clients who had been given—by job interviewers (members of a different staff unit, who referred problematic clients to the counselors)—an inaccurate picture of what to expect and what not to expect from counseling. They were pessimistic about influencing interviewers: That staff group was composed of people who were older and more experienced that the counselors; yet the counselors, by virtue of the graduate degrees many of them held, earned more than the interviewers. This had led to tension between the two groups, which had not been resolved. Instead, the counselors decided to develop a one-time only, precounseling group meeting that would be offered periodically before newly referred clients saw their counselor. Its purpose would be to orient clients to the counseling process.

The counselors were uncertain of their ability to conduct these meetings effectively, so it was decided to create a brief videotape of five former counselees discussing the nature of their experience, good and bad, in counseling. The plan was to use the tape to kick off a discussion among a group of five to eight clients prior to their first interview with a counselor.

On the basis of informal observation, an individually felt need had been brought to the group's attention—a need that the counselors had not previously recognized as one that was common to all of them. This led to the creation of a plan for meeting this need. In carrying out the plan, the counselors learned how to use videotape for orientation purposes by making a tape and then using it. In time, their comfort with group meetings increased: They found that they did not need to use the tape to start a meeting. Their skill in managing a group meeting had been enhanced to the point that they looked back at the tape as a prop they had needed to help them move into a new technology: group work. We felt that we had achieved our objectives as trainers: Group work, a new method for this agency, had now gained a foothold among counselors because its use resolved a need each counselor had had.

To be effective, informal observation requires time for the gathering of impressions, followed by an opportunity to check out these observations with the observed parties. The observer(s) should be able to provide some fresh insights into staff needs. In the situation just described, the counselors' "Aha!" reaction (when confronted with their feelings about the pantomimed drawer opening) indicated that we had indeed recognized a strongly felt, but poorly expressed, need. Once the group became aware of it, they were highly motivated to do something about it.

We were less successful in dealing with the need for more accurate referrals by the job interviewers, perhaps because that issue was less central to our particular project. Efforts were subsequently undertaken to acquaint the supervisor of the interviewers with this particular concern, but that is another story. The point here is that the use of informal observation by impartial uninvolved observers, focused on the day-to-day operation of an organization, can bring to light needs that are only dimly felt or are not recognized as common to many staff members.

Assessing Individual–Unique Needs

I have left individual–unique needs for last because assessing such needs presents a particular kind of difficulty. It is one thing for a staff member to participate in the protected environment of brainstorming, or to complete—anonymously—a questionnaire or a Delphi rating form, or to be interviewed concerning his or her view of the staff development needs—in general terms—of the work unit or the organization as a whole. It's a very different matter for a staff member to admit that he or she is performing some job tasks poorly, or only adequately. Expressing a unique, individual need can, from the individual staff member's point of view, leave him or her open to an accusation of incompetence, with potentially negative counsequences in terms of formal evaluation, salary increment, or promotion. In our success-oriented society, it is risky indeed to confess one's shortcomings.

Then again, a supervisor may decide that a worker is not performing one or more tasks acceptably well, either according to some objective standard ("This person's paperwork is consistently late and incomplete") or in the supervisor's subjective judgement ("This staff member takes far too long to develop a working relationship with people"). Often the worker does not agree. In that case, the supervisor ends up attributing needs to the worker, but the worker either does not experience these as felt needs, or, as stated earlier, is reluctant to accept the supervisor's assessment for fear of the potential negative consequences for him or her.

Given these potential difficulties, the individual needs assessment technique to be described is likely to work best in an organization in which staff feel secure in their positions, one that places high value on continuing education for all staff and translates this value into action through a staff development program that involves staff in the planning of that program. If I were introducing a staff development program into an organization, I would be inclined to attempt to install and routinize an assessment of individual–unique needs *last,* after I had assessed commonly felt needs *and* gotten programs based on those needs well under way. I would hope that would create a climate in which the Personal Competency Assessment[5] procedures described next could be optimally productive.

The steps in the Personal Competency Assessment are:

1. An individual staff member and the person who supervises his or her work identify and describe the major tasks that make up the staff member's job. These tasks can be identified by referring to a job description, providing a thorough job description is available, or by having staff members who occupy the same position keep a record of all their activities for a period of time, and then compare notes and develop a comprehensive list of tasks.

A precise way of describing the tasks that make up a job involves the use of Functional Job Analysis (Fine and Wiley, 1971). The primary elements in this system are attention to what workers do in relation to *people* (clients, other staff, staff of other agencies); *things* (equipment, physical facilities, recording forms); and *data* (identifying information about clients, summary reports of service activities). Some tasks require *physical* activity, such as operating a video tape recorder; some are primary *mental*—for example, analyzing data; and some are primarily *interpersonal,* such as consulting with other people. To write a task statement, one answers the following five questions:

1. *Who?* (This is always assumed to be the staff member whose job is being described.)
2. *Performs what action?* (This should always use a concrete, explicit action verb— *asks, listens, writes.*)
3. *To accomplish what immediate results?* (This always refers to an explicit result, thus providing a standard for the staff member's performance.)

[5]The Personal Competency Assessment is dicussed in Lynn Nybell, Tom Morton, Patricia Ruby, Harvey Bertcher, and Roy Gaunt, *Leaders Handbook: Staff Development for Supervisors* (Ann Arbor, Mich.: Continuing Education Program in the Human Services, University of Michigan, School of Social Work, 1977), pp. 38–46, and is based on the work of John D. Ingalls, *A Trainer's Guide to Androgogy,* revised edition (Waltham, Mass.: Data Education, Inc., 1974), pp. 31–34.

4. *With what tools, equipment, or work aids?* (This always identifies the tangible equipment used to perform the task—telephone, tape recorder, interview guide.)
5. *Upon what instructions?* (This always refers to the nature and source of the instructions received by the staff member.)

An example of a task sample offered by Fine and Wiley reads as follows:

> Asks client questions, listens to responses, and writes answers on standard intake form, exercising leeway as to sequence of questions, in order to record basic identifying information. (Fine and Wiley, 1971, p. 12)

Since writing useful task statements takes practice, it would be a good idea for a group of supervisors to write and compare task statements describing their own jobs, so that they can be sufficiently competent to teach this procedure to their staff.

2. The second step in the Personal Competency Assessment is to have the staff member rate his or her own performance in relation to each task, using a form like the following one, in which previously described tasks are assigned a number (for ease of identification). The small boxes are for a few key words that represent the tasks, as

asks
intake
questions

Then the staff member is expected to identify his or her concerns about a particular task (see Figure 3-1).

3. Next, the supervisor completes his or her own assessment of the staff member's performance. The supervisor and the staff member could complete these ratings simultaneously and privately and then compare them, or the supervisor could wait for the staff member's ratings and then check them over to determine areas of agreement and disagreement. I prefer the former procedure, as supervisors are less likely to be biased in their ratings if they do not know what the staff member's ratings are.

Three Examples of Needs Assessment

The first example of needs assessment, a continuation of the DSS project described in the previous chapter, represents a careful use of the questionnaire, followed by a modification of the Delphi technique. Note that the staff developer did not circulate the Delphi for a second round; rather, she pulled the staff together for an open discussion of the results of the first-round Delphi. This is possible in an office where morale is high and mutual trust is strong. In some settings, however, distrust among staff and poor morale could make such a discussion less productive than the one shown here.

FIGURE 3-1 Personal Competency Assessment

Name _____ Date _____ Supervisor _____

Note: 100% mastery means that you are performing the task as it was meant to be performed, and fully meeting the standard for performance.

	1	2	3	4	5	6	7	8	9	10	11	12
TASK DESCRIPTION												
	—	—	—	—	—	—	—	—	—	—	—	—
RELATIVE MASTERY												
100%												
75%												
50%												
25%												
0	—	—	—	—	—	—	—	—	—	—	—	—

Task # _____   Task # _____   Task # _____

Concerns: Concerns: Concerns:

EXAMPLE 5: THE DSS EXAMPLE (Continued) —
NEEDS ASSESSMENT PROCESS AND RESULTS

In deciding on the type of needs assessment process I wanted to use, I first considered the staff I would be working with. Upon viewing the composition of the staff and the working relationships that exist, I felt that an open approach, allowing for discussions and negotiations, would be far superior to any other approach. In the past, the staff have always been allowed the opportunity to openly express their ideas, suggestions, and feelings and have frequently done so. Since this has proved to be a successful approach in the past, it seemed most appropriate to continue with this approach in doing a needs assessment.

Following the decision to conduct a fairly open needs assessment, I then had to devise a tool with which to gather the necessary information. In deciding on a format,

I felt that there were some things that I wanted the staff to do to help them focus in on their potential needs. First, I wanted them to take a few minutes to think about their particular role and function in the department as they perceive it. Second, I wanted them to consider the full range of contacts and resources they utilize as part of their jobs. Next, I wanted them (in the context of how they see their overall role and function) to identify the skills they perceived as necessary to their jobs and also the skills and/or tools they felt they needed or could improve on that would possibly assist them in better fulfilling their responsibilities. Finally, I wanted them to identify areas they perceived as needing to be addressed and acted on. With these thoughts in mind, a needs assessment form was formulated and prepared for distribution.[6]

In order to introduce the form and to provide instructions and clarification, a brief staff meeting was scheduled on Monday. At the time of the meeting, the form was distributed and instructions were given regarding its completion. I further explained the process that would be followed upon completion of the forms and what I hoped to accomplish as a result of this needs assessment. An open discussion followed where staff conversed about their perceived needs, their feelings about the process itself, and so on. Following this discussion, the staff were requested to take the form, complete it after they had had time to think about it, and return it by Friday of that week.

Upon receiving the completed forms from all staff, I reviewed the comments and identified specific need areas. Another form was drafted listing ten identified need areas. One additional area was provided to accommodate input on need areas that might have been overlooked. The form allowed for prioritizing need areas from 1 to 5. The form was distributed and explained to the staff. The requested return date was established as the following day.

Following the return of the second form, a tabulation of the results was completed. Based on the Delphi method, each priority from 1 to 5 was assigned a value—first—5, second—4, and so on. Upon calculating the total value for each need area, a ranking of the priorities was done. The results of the rankings were written up and prepared for presentation to the staff.

Two days later, the staff members were called together for a discussion of the results. All staff were provided with handouts displaying results for their review. A discussion commenced during which the rankings were covered and staff were encouraged to express their feelings on the results.

After reviewing the results, some staff felt that some need areas that were identified, such as foster home recruitment, seemed to be pertinent to only a small number of staff members because of the nature and breakdown of case loads and responsibilities. Others expressed the opinion that a couple of the areas, such as office accommodations, could not be feasibly addressed at this time. Among the top priorities listed, staff centered their interest and discussion on the topics of work organization and planning, and dealing with stress on the job. On the subject of time management, staff discussed their concerns and the frustrations they encounter in trying to meet the paperwork demands and the client demands inherent in their jobs. Each worker related his or her experiences of having to assume a wider range of responsibilities as a result of the loss of one staff position in the unit. One worker summarized the majority of the concerns very well when he stated: "Since the first of the year, we have all been assigned additional duties due to the cut in staffing. We still have our objectives and time frames to meet. How can we do it?" The consensus of the staff was that there might be many benefits to learning some con-

---

[6]She used a one-page questionnaire with five open-ended items, such as "What do you see as your role and function within DSS?"

crete principles about work organization and planning, to aid in this area. They enthusiastically supported the notion of starting to deal with the problem with some assistance in planning the work they have to accomplish. The results, showing time management as the first priority, were felt by staff to be accurate; however, staff did feel that stress management, which had a ranking of 3, should be placed in the second position. They discussed stress on the job and felt that dealing with this factor would also benefit them. The group talked among themselves and came up with the suggestion that first some guidelines should be provided on work organization, followed later on by some training in managing stress.

Having gained a consensus on the area of greatest concern to the group, the focus of the meeting was shifted to asking the group to identify specific problems within this area. Many of the problems identified related to not having enough time, feeling pulled in too many directions, having too much to do, and not knowing how to plan work in order to accomplish all the required tasks. On the basis of the nature of the problems raised by the group, I suggested that what I was hearing the group say was that the basic problem was one of not knowing (1) how to organize, (2) how to prioritize, and (3) how to plan work effectively. The group concurred. Closing comments were made and the group meeting was adjourned. The staff was advised that further information would be forthcoming.

From a management perspective, I was happy to see that the staff chose time management as a top priority. Since the first of the year when we lost a staff member, workers have had to assume added responsibilities. In the past three months, reports and local monitoring devices have shown that the standards of promptness for the various program areas are not being met by a majority of the staff. In addition, redeterminations have been exceeding the acceptable overdue standards, and dictation has been exceeding prescribed time frames. Specific data related to these areas will be provided. At present, the deviation is not serious; however, the noted increases had become a supervisory concern.

The closing comments indicate the staff developer's satisfaction with the staff's decision, since it addressed both the felt needs of staff and the organization's needs.

Doing staff development is rarely as neat as in this example. The examples I have chosen for this book follow my precepts to varying degrees. The next example, written by a nurse in charge of staff development for the nurses in her hospital, shows how a project got started from a discussion between two staff members, which led to an informal needs assessment and then grew into a project that eventually met the organization's need to have a new procedure used correctly by all staff. It also appeared to meet a felt need of staff to deal with a work problem in a uniform and effective way.

EXAMPLE 6: THE HOSPITAL EXAMPLE

One day in late May I was visited in my office by the supervisor of Central Supply. We have enjoyed many previous chats centering around the difficulties of our jobs and the question, "Why in the world aren't we running the show?" Rather than being depressing, these little talks have always perked us up and renewed our spirits. This day she was bemoaning the misconceptions and inconsistencies exhibited by the nursing personnel on the units in returning contaminated equipment in order to protect the health of the nursing personnel and the Central Supply worker. The variations that were showing up either compromised the safety of Central Supply personnel or, more frequently, caused the ruin of valuable equipment when it was sterilized. I certainly agreed with her that a serious problem existed. She informed me that she and the infection control supervisor had almost completed writing up a new procedure on isolation techniques and the correct way to take supplies and equipment out of an isolation room. I replied that this had been needed for some time and that I would investigate the need for an in-service on the new procedure.

Now at this time, my gut reaction was that this procedure was of major importance and a full-blown in-service was warranted. However, my gut reaction does not constitute an in-depth needs assessment, so I took it further. A meeting of the patient care supervisors (head nurses) was taking place the next week, and I judged that group to be the appropriate means to obtain feedback for this cause. I have utilized this group before in needs assessment because they represent all the nursing staff on all the units. However, I had learned that, ideal as this group should be in knowing the needs of the nursing staff, it was by no means foolproof. One of the flaws in using the group for needs assessment is that eight patient care supervisors (PCSs) represent a total of 42 RNs, LPNs and nursing assistants. That might be better representation than our state or national political system, but it isn't perfect. Also, the degree that each PCS knows her staff is difficult to measure. Recognizing these flaws, I approached the group for advice—should the new procedure be "in-serviced" or simply placed in the procedure book. (This is the choice of action when a new procedure is devised. Not every procedure is given the time and effort of an in-service. If a procedure is started *sans* in-service, then the PCS must inform her staff of its existence.)

Overwhelmingly, the PCSs wanted an in-service and this was echoed by my supervisor, returned from a short sick leave absence. I conferred with her about the preceeding events. She was in agreement about the in-service and wanted to be directly involved in planning and carrying it out. The isolation procedure statement was in the process of a final typing to be submitted to the infection control committee the following week, so I was unable to read it at this time. She explained the general contents of the procedure. We also talked about including some other aspects of the isolation technique that were causing the nurses some confusion. We concluded that she would let me know when the procedure was approved and we could begin our preparations. . . .

Example 7: The Domestic Violence Project Example: The New Library. Initially, this mid-level administrator had hoped to initiate some in-service training for line staff. When she recognized that an in-service training program in this area did not meet staff needs and would be strongly resisted, she switched plans, uncovered a much different need, and responded to it. Note that the needs assessment process was quite informal—something that is easier to do when the number of staff involved is comparatively small.

To my knowledge there has been no specific staff development done at the downtown office of the Domestic Violence Project. However, some of the staff have participated in activities which have taken place at SAFE House. There have been many staff development activities at SAFE House, with the majority concerning empathy training and crisis intervention for volunteer and paid staff. The last in-service (which involved a weekend session on empathy) took place in February, and, from the reports of staff, was a "disaster. " Therefore, the sentiment surrounding in-service training is very negative, especially for the workers at SAFE House. . . .

I became a part of the Domestic Violence Project staff in the capacity of assistant to the director. During my initial interview with her, she explained some of the things she would like me to do and reassured me that I could work on any special projects that were of interest to me. We discussed my limited knowledge of the field of domestic violence and suggested I avail myself of the many books and journal articles which the agency had collected. As we talked of the available materials she mentioned the need to organize and catalogue them; a need which she felt the entire staff had mentioned on several occasions. At this point, I offered to work on the library materials because of previous work experience in a library system.

At the next staff meeting the subject of the library was brought up by another staff member. When I explained my desire to catalogue and organize the collections I was met with a very positive response. Each staff member at one time or another mentioned that they would appreciate the opportunity to learn how I planned to catalogue the books and articles so that they could use the library on their own. From that point on they gave me still more materials to include in the library and expressed an interest in learning my system.

Subsequently, the need for the formal needs assessment was taken out of my hands. Without any prompting from me, the entire staff, from the director to the secretary, verbalized the need for an organized library and for the knowledge of how to use it once it was catalogued and arranged.

However, I spoke informally to each of the staff concerning their ideas on how it should be arranged in order to make the materials easily accessible. For the most part, the staff expressed the desire for me to handle it the way I thought would be the best. They did offer suggestions after I mentioned that I would like to catalogue the materials by major subjects. Their suggestions included the subject areas they thought should be set aside and a discussion of how certain materials would fit into some subject areas and not others. Again, they each offered their help in assisting me to decide on which materials pertained to which subject areas.

As I worked on the library they showed interest in my progress, and asked me to plan a small in-service during a weekly staff meeting to show them how to use the library.

Subsequently the cataloguing was completed, the new system was explained to staff, and the library was declared operational, much to everyone's expressed satisfaction.

A Guideline for Assessing Needs

If you plan to use a formal needs assessment procedure, such as the Delphi or a questionnaire sent to staff, you should first negotiate a contract with the appropriate administrator(s) to (1) do the needs assessment, and (2) use the results to create one or more staff development activities. Of course, activities that are designed to improve and/or modify staff performance can get started without any needs assessment being done; for example, for a state agency, a new program, procedure, or policy could be created by the state legislature, and staff would then have to be trained so as to be able to implement it. Budget cuts, for example, might compel the agency to develop more economical ways of getting the job done, necessitating a new set of staff skills. Even then, however, you can assess needs relating to ways to carry out the task. The questions that follow are designed to help you think through the needs assessment process so that you can develop needs-based staff development activities.

1. Describe the contract you have to do a needs assessment:

    a. Who is it with? _____

    b. What does it allow you to do? _____

    _____

    c. What limitations does it place on you? _____

    _____

2. With regard to felt needs:

    a. Whose needs would you assess, and why? _____

    _____

    b. Which of the following techniques related to needs assessment do you plan to use, and why?

    _____ brainstorming—Why? _____

    _____ Delphi—Why? _____

    _____ nominal group technique—Why? _____

    _____ time machine—Why? _____

    _____ questionnaire—Why? _____

    _____ interview—Why? _____

    _____ informal observation—Why? _____

    _____ other (describe) _____

    Why? _____

    c. What will you look for to indicate that you have a consensus on need

    priorities? _____

    _____

    d. What do you plan to do about lower-priority needs? Why? _____

    _____

    _____

    _____

    _____

3. With regard to organizational needs:
    How do you plan to determine organizational needs that could be met with staff development activities? Why would you use this approach?

    _____

    _____

    _____

    _____

4. How do you plan to let others know about the results of the needs assessment process?

    _____

    _____

5. Problems
    a. What problems do you think will be created by this needs assessment?

    _____

    _____

    b. What do you plan to do about these problems? _____

    _____

    Many staff developers omit needs assessment from their staff development projects. Sometimes they do so because they have some special knowledge and want a chance to try out their ability to train staff using that knowledge. Sometimes they claim that others have already done the needs assessment. Sometimes they claim there isn't sufficient time. Almost all of them later note that the weakness in their projects could be traced back directly to their failure to do a proper needs assessment. So be warned: Staff development without needs assessment almost always fails to achieve its objectives.
    Which is one way to introduce our next topic—the selection and specification of objectives.

chapter 4

SPECIFYING OBJECTIVES, EVALUATING OUTCOMES

- How can goals be used in staff development?
- How do you select goals?
- How do you create a behaviorally specific goal statement?
- Examples of goal statements.
- What guidelines can you follow when creating goal statements?
- How do you evaluate staff development?
- When should evaluation be done?
- What methods of evaluation are used in staff development?
- Examples of evaluation.
- What guidelines should you follow when evaluating staff development?

Staff development is always future-oriented—always optimistic. Staff developers should be continually asking themselves: "How can we enhance staff's ability to do their job better?" and "How can we help make staff's jobs more personally rewarding to them?" with the optimistic assumption that improvements are definitely possible—not inevitable, but possible. The problem is, what does "better" look like? If you have no clear idea, how can you chart an effective course to your destination? How can you tell whether or not you need to make midstream changes en route to that destination? And how can you tell when you've arrived? This is no moon shot, with the safe return of the astronauts as a measure of success; no profit and loss statement, with success measured as a profit in dollars and cents. For most human service organizations, success is an intangible, something measured best—but rarely—by an examination of the social functioning of former clients once they have melted back into the community, a formidable task for which an effective technology does not yet fully exist.

To avoid confusion I shall speak of *long-range* goals (for example, staff are better able to do their jobs, so that clients are more successful in resolving their problems); *medium-range* goals (for example, staff are better able to conduct interviews in such a way that clients voluntarily return to the next interview and continue to work on their problems); and *short-range* goals (for example, a new staff member is able to fill in the agency's intake form correctly and completely). (Some people use the terms *short-range goals* and *objectives* interchangeably.)

HOW CAN GOALS BE USED IN STAFF DEVELOPMENT?

Goals as evaluation criteria. Staff development flows from an assessment of need, followed by an attempt to respond to that need, followed by an evaluation of the degree to which the need was met. The more explicit a goal statement is, the better it can be used to measure the degree to which the need has been met through staff development. As we shall see when evaluation is discussed more fully, it is a good idea to begin designing evaluation procedures at the same time one creates goal statements, rather than waiting until later on, as is often done. (That is why I have included *goals* and *evaluations* in one chapter.)

Goals as guides for the staff developer. When you know what you are trying to achieve, you often have at least an initial notion of how to get there. If, for example, your goal is for your daughter to be able to ride a bicycle without anyone holding her up, you had better plan on spending some time with her sitting on a bicycle of proper size, with you—or someone with the necessary stamina—prepared to run alongside, holding the bicycle erect until she gets the feel of it and pedals off on her own. [1] Knowing what you hope staff will achieve guides you into doing something that appears likely to lead to goal achievement.

Goals as pre-measures. It doesn't make sense to work for a goal that staff have already achieved. Just as goals provide criteria for measuring the success of a staff development activity, so too they provide a basis for measuring what staff already know or can do acceptably well. Knowing the staff's level of propaedeutic[2]

[1] At least that's how we did it when I was a boy, and that is how I did it for my kids. Nowadays, training wheels fulfill that function, or so I'm told.

[2] *Propaedeutic:* Having to do with, or of the nature of, preliminary instruction; introductory to some science or art. Propaedeutic knowledge or skill refers to the knowledge or skill an individual brings into a learning situation.

knowledge or skill tells the staff developer where to start, and helps avoid setting the level of activity too far ahead or behind staff's current level of knowledge or ability.

Goals help you to think straight.   As a teacher, I have often found that the exercise of having to define *for myself* just what I hope my *students* will be able to do that they apparently cannot *yet* do forces me to become clearer about what I hope to accomplish. It's much easier (but less productive) to think in *general* terms about the *general* content of a course than to think about what I hope students will be able to *do* as a result of attending *today's* class, that they could *not do* before they came to class. Creating specific goal statements disciplines me, and, as a busy person, I need that discipline. Perhaps that's also true for you.

Goals help to structure correct expectations.   Many studies have been undertaken to determine whether or not people learn better when they are made aware of what they are expected to learn, in specific terms. Much of this research has found that knowledge of goals facilitated learning in some cases but not in others (see for example, Duchastel and Merrill, 1973). A study by Ojemann (1968) suggests that the statement of objectives is useful in those cases in which the learner's motivation is taken into account: Behaviorally specific objectives facilitate learning when learners believe that what they are to learn will be of personal significance or value. To return to my earlier example of teaching a youngster to ride a bicycle: Most youngsters know what "riding a bicycle" looks like and are probably very excited about learning to master the skill. They want to ride solo, and when they do so they feel justifiably pleased with themselves. But suppose you believe that, before your daughter learns to *ride,* she must learn to repair her bike. You tell her that the hours you can set aside for her on Saturday morning will be aimed at helping her learn how to repair the bicycle, not at riding it—that will come later. Knowing your goal, she can at least try to negotiate with you about what she wants to learn first, or whether she even *wants* to learn about repair. In other words, producing a goal statement allows staff to decide whether or not what you are planning for them to achieve is likely to meet their needs. If it doesn't, they are in a position to negotiate for a different set of goals.

Goals for self-monitoring by staff.   In situations where change is sought, the degree to which individuals believe that they, or the problematic situation, or both, are changing in the desired direction is often invisible to the change agent and known only to the "changee." Assuming that staff do accept your goals for them, these goals can provide them with tangible guidelines by which they can assess their own progress and can ask for help with the process of change, if they believe they need it.

I have gone to some lengths to convince you of the importance of developing behaviorally specific goal statements, because I have encountered many people who intensely dislike such specificity. After all, they say, the numerous intangibles with which human service workers work somehow lose their full meaning when reduced to a pseudoscientific scale from 1 to 10. Creating behaviorally specific goals is difficult for persons accustomed to working with goals like "develop a deeper and broader understanding of. . ." or "Conduct an interview effectively. . . ." In short, the objections to specific goal statements are many and varied, but the bottom line— in my opinion—is that they *are* useful and, indeed, essential to effective staff development.

HOW DO YOU SELECT GOALS?

Much of what follows deals with the technology of creating goal statements in explicit, measurable terms. Earlier portions of this book have suggested that goals should be selected on the basis of a needs assessment process that results in a staff consensus on a priority of needs. Identifying high-priority needs implies a selection of high-priority goals. It would be nice if such rationality ruled, but in fact human service organizations, for all their statements of lofty, humanistic purposes, are still organizations—and organizations are run by people who are influenced by political pressures, resource deficits, personal aspirations and beliefs, individual and collective resistance to change, and so forth. So it should come as no surprise that learning to create specific goal statements does not change the fact that the *selection* of organizational goals involves a value judgment—a judgment often made by policymakers or administrators without the involvement of lower-level staff.

Values are simply people's ideas about what should be prized or given primary importance. The recent attention to *values clarification* is based on the recognition that most people are not aware of many of their most deeply held values, even though these values have a profound effect on their day-to-day decisions (Simon, 1972). Staff developers are supposed to value *change*—that is, *improvement,* since doing something better implies change. But do they really value change? People who are assigned staff development responsibilities are often administrators or persons directly responsible to other administrators, and those administrators often value predictability and stability over the uncertainties associated with change. Staff development *can* be used to maintain an effective status quo: "Teach them how to do it right, not some new and untested way." Sooner or later, however, staff development inevitably becomes associated with change, and change implies a challenge to existing values. It is on this fact that much of staff development stumbles, is blocked, or fails. Administrators who are called on to decide how to allocate an organization's resources, including the resources needed to do staff development, are often forced to place a higher value on control—predictability of staff performance—than on change.

When the staff developers are also the administrators who control the allocation of resources within the organization or a subunit of the organization, they would do well to clarify their own values with regard to change. There will be many realistic pressures to discourage change, except where the "change" being referred to means doing what is "supposed" to be done, better. Administrators must ask themselves, however, whether in meeting their own needs as administrators, they are overlooking the felt needs of staff in a way that lowers staff morale, weakens loyalty to the administrator and/or the organization, and is therefore counter-productive in the long run—that is, makes the administrator's job even harder.

On the other hand, the staff developer who is not the administrator has to think carefully about how best to involve the administrator. At what point and in what way should the administrator be brought into the process of goal selection? This question was discussed more fully in Chapter 2 on contracts but is raised here to emphasize that the processes of goal selection and goal specification do not go on in a vacuum.

HOW DO YOU CREATE A BEHAVIORALLY SPECIFIC GOAL STATEMENT?

Use simple words.   It is important to note that a behaviorally specific goal statement must eventually be recorded in the symbols we refer to as *words*—and the study of semantics has clearly demonstrated the many hazards faced when people try to communicate, verbally or in writing, with each other (see, for example, Chase, 1938, or Hayakawa, 1962). To put it another way, any goal statement, no matter how well written, can be open to misunderstanding or misinterpretation. Your aim should be to make this as unlikely as possible, by selecting words that are as un-complicated as possible. To this end, I should like to suggest that a "one-syllable-less" rule be used wherever appropriate. The one-syllable-less rule simply suggests that words of two syllables or more in your goal statement be reduced, wherever possible, to a synonym that has one syllable fewer than the word it is replacing. One of my favorite one-syllable-less examples is to employ the word *way* for the far more popular *mechanism.*

Write goal statements in terms of "doing."   Essentially, staff development deals with changing the knowledge, attitudes, and behaviors of staff—providing more or new knowledge, prompting a review or change of attitudes, enhancing existing skills or fostering new ones. Eventually, whatever is acquired through staff development in terms of knowledge, attitude or skill should become evident in staff members' role performance—in their behavior. Although you may be interested in providing new information (adding knowledge), you hope that eventually the cognitive activity will translate into behavior. In fact, you can't tell whether the knowledge has been "acquired" by staff (or their attitudes or abilities affected) until individual staff members *behave* in some way. With knowledge, this could run the gamut from (a) "Yes, I know that now," to (b) correct responses on a short-answer test, to (c) correct *use* of that knowledge in some problem-solving situation. Each of these is a behavior. In the first instance, (a), the *goal* would be for individuals to assert that they believe that they have indeed learned what was to be learned.

In (b), the *goal* would be to be able to pass a test on the knowledge to be learned. In (c), when faced with a problem requiring correct use of the knowledge, they would be able to do just that. Because people who work in human service organizations are action oriented, however, simply saying, "Yes, I've learned," or passing a short-answer paper–pencil test would not be what most staff developers set out to achieve. The preferred goal would usually be new or improved action-in-particular-situations.

Goals are often stated in terms of "developing an appreciation of. . ." or "deepening and broadening one's understanding of. . ." or "learning about. . .," but none of these phrases refers to an observable behavior. To fulfill any of the six uses of goals discussed earlier in this chapter, goals would have to be stated in terms of the actions in which staff would engage regarding that goal—actions that are visible to others, in a work situation or some simulation of a work situation.

The difficulty in stating goals in action terms is exemplified by this edited quote from a staff developer:

EXAMPLE 8: SETTING GOALS

Our planning committee of three never discussed goals and objectives openly. I know we hoped to generate more enthusiasm for [our] services. The hospital had received a great deal of national publicity in the 1960s because of the. . .research project (being done there), and continued to give lip service to the great need for high-quality. . . service units. In fact, administration had done little to support the existing programs and was gradually reducing them. We hoped to *draw agency support to our programs. At the same time we hoped to inform the resident psychiatrists, all foreign, about the [client population]. . . [and] learn the basic components of milieu therapy. . . . We wanted to teach a few new group work techniques. . . .* [Emphasis added.]

This was an ambitious project, with a number of long-range goals. But there are problems with this goal statement. A review of the staff developer's verb phrases (such as "draw agency support to our programs") may help to clarify what I mean by stating goals in terms of *doing*. Reread the paragraph, pick out the verb phrases, and write down the actions the staff developer hoped *others* would perform. Note my use of *others:* Goal statements should be written in relation to what the staff developer hopes *staff* will be able to do better as a result of participating in the staff development activity. There is nothing wrong with writing goals for yourself, to yourself, but these are not the goal statements you *share* with others; they are strictly for *you*—for example, *"My* goal for *me* is that I hope to *help them* reduce their need by teaching the subject well."

Here is how I assessed the verb phrases:

- "generate enthusiasm for [our] services": *Enthusiasm* is a state of mind associated with very positive feelings, but it suggests no particular behavior.
- "draw agency support": This phrase speaks to actions by others, but what is meant by *support*? Words of encouragement from the director? An increase in the number of appropriate referrals? Doubling the unit's budget? Here, the term is too vague to be measured; as a goal statement, this needs work.

- "inform the resident psychiatrists": This speaks to the committee's goal *for itself;* an action goal would continue by stating what it was hoped the *psychiatrists* would *do* with the information.
- "learn the basic components of milieu therapy": This phase, again, speaks to the committee members' goals for *themselves.*
- "teach a few. . .techniques": Again, this is their goal for themselves. What would they like *trainees* to be able to do with these techniques that would demonstrate that the techniques had been mastered? For example, an appropriate action goal statement here might be something like this:

> During the weekly meeting, staff who manage these meetings will be able to use the technique of *summarizing* in such a way that the group will be able to achieve consensus on the nature of the problems they are trying to solve, and then initiate action that would lead to the next step in the problem's solution, to everyone's verbalized satisfaction.

Nevertheless, the staff developers' statement of their aspirations reflects the hopes, spoken and unspoken, that guided their actions in this project. Their goals were not stated in behaviorally specific terms but did provide orientation for the committee. My guess is that it would have helped them to make these goals explicit within the committee, whether written out in behaviorally specific terms or not. This explicitness might have helped them to unify and clarify their work together. As it turned out (it was later reported), their lack of clarity about goals had a negative effect on the activity's success.

Later we'll return to some of these statements and see what it would take to transfer them into acceptable goal statements. First, however, we need to look at two other attributes of specific goal statements.

Goal statements should specify conditions.   Behavior never occurs in a vacuum. There are always particular conditions, circumstances, or situations in which the action is performed. These conditions are a crucial aspect of performance: An individual who can't recognize the right time to do something may end up doing the *right* thing at the *wrong* time, with the wrong result. Imagine someone blowing out all the candles on a birthday cake at *someone else's* birthday party. Imagine asking someone, in the most considerate tones, "And how did you feel about that?" when you have just been told by the person how he felt about that: You'll soon get an idea of what I mean by the importance of the *conditions* in which behavior occurs.

In the same sense, a *goal* always refers to a particular condition or situation in which it is hoped the desired behavior will occur. For example:

> *When meeting a client for the first time,* the staff member should be able to. . . .
> *During staff meetings,* staff members will be able to. . . .
> *One month after being hired,* every staff member should be able to. . . .

Condition can refer to your physical surroundings, to a length of time, to being in the presence of others versus working alone, to having been provided with certain information, and so forth.

Goal statements should specify criteria for measuring a performance. What's wrong with this goal statement?

> When faced with twenty problems in subtraction (involving whole numbers), the student should be able to do the necessary mathematical computations.

Several things are wrong. First, do you want the student to be able to do the computations *correctly?* Probably—but if so, you must say so. Must they *all* be done correctly, or would you settle for one or two mistakes? If so, you should say so: "At least eighteen out of twenty correct." Would you be satisfied if it took the student all day to get the correct answers? Probably not. You'd want the student to finish in a reasonable time, which would be whatever your experience with similar students suggests—for example, within twenty minutes. And, of course, without cheating and without help.

Now, with the proper criteria, the statement should read:

> When faced with twenty problems in subtraction (involving whole numbers), the student (working alone and without cheating) should be able to compute the correct answers to at least eighteen of the twenty problems, within twenty minutes.

Of course, it's much easier to present a goal statement for learning in math, where there are right and wrong answers. In the human services, the only available and realistic criterion may be the opinion of someone regarded as an expert—for example, "done effectively *in the supervisor's opinion.*"

We can now return to our earlier hospital example and try to create specific goal statements. Let's take them one at a time. As you will recall, the staff developer had written: "We hoped to draw agency support to our programs."

To turn this into a specific goal statement, we would first have to decide on the meaning of hospital support. Although we don't know precisely what this would have been in her situation, we can speculate about the nature of support. Let us assume it meant a return to previous levels of budgetary allotment (including funding for any staff positions that may, over time, have been eliminated) as well as hiring people for positions that had remained vacant because no attempt had been made to fill them. Undoubtedly, there would be other tangible indications of support, but for our present purposes these should suffice. Try writing an action goal statement that improves on the original statement ("We hoped to draw agency support to our programs"). Take a moment to try to rewrite now, and then compare it with mine (no peeking!) in the footnote below.[3]

---

[3]Here's mine: Upon reviewing the agency's budget, the administration of the hospital will, within three months, both restore the unit's funding level to its highest previous level and fill all vacant positions in the unit with qualified personnel.

Such a goal statement could make it clear to the committee that it will have to plan some activity in relation to the hospital's budgetary processes and its personnel unit (or the applicant-seeking procedures of the work unit). Let's review this statement to see if it fits our criteria:

Simple language: It might be clearer to name the individuals rather than speak of "the administration"—a vague term that stands for a number of persons with varying responsibilities, from file clerk to hospital director. The committee would have to ask itself: Who actually makes budget decisions? How are they made? How can we influence them? Similarly, with personnel: Who actually decides which positions are to be filled? Who makes hiring decisions? How can this process be influenced?

Action words: The meaning of "restore the unit's funding level" should be clear: the intention is that a decision will be made and implemented so that the administrator of the unit will be given the power to expend more funds than were originally assigned to the unit.

Conditions: This action will be taken after the agency's budget has been re-examined (reviewed).

Criteria: Finally, are the criteria specified? The goal is that both actions (funds restored, positions filled) should take place within no more than three months, and the amount of money should be set at the highest level it ever was. I'm assuming that that was higher than today's level. If a budget review indicates that cost-of-living factors make that highest figure unrealistically low in today's market, then some language could be added to take that fact into account, such as "to its highest previous level plus a cost-of-living adjustment." Note, too, that "qualified personnel" are to be sought—not just anyone.

Another goal statement was "At the same time, we hoped to inform the resident psychiatrists, all foreign, about the [client population]. . . ." For purposes of this discussion, let's further assume that the committee believed (probably with good cause) that the foreign-born psychiatrists did not know much about what was normal for teenagers in this country.

In thinking about this goal statement, it's important to recognize that the staff developer was really thinking about more than one desirable outcome, since the goal was not the mere presentation of knowledge to the psychiatrists, but their eventual use of this knowledge in their work with clients. First, the committee believed that the psychiatrists needed to acquire some new knowledge (as well as a recognition of their own stereotypical attitudes toward the youngsters based on their own cultural conditioning) that would lead to some change in their attitudes toward the clients in this hospital. In addition, they hoped for some change in the way the psychiatric residents interacted with these youngsters, based on this new knowledge, and a resultant modification of the residents' attitudes. Such changes require more than one action goal statement. Think about writing separate goal statements in relation to changes in the knowledge, attitudes, and skills of the psychiatric residents. Try to do just that, *now,* before you read mine.

Now, here are mine. First, with regard to knowledge:

> If asked, the psychiatric residents could verbally describe the ways in which most American teenagers would be likely to behave when they were with family, friends, or by themselves; when at school or on the job. Members of the Staff Development Committee would assess these descriptions as generally correct.

There is a problem here in lumping together all teenagers when, in fact, factors of socioeconomic class, ethnicity, and the like would be associated with significant differences between groups of teens. Depending on the nature of the patient population at this hospital, it might be essential to qualify the term "most American teenagers" to something like "most lower-class white and black American teenagers, from both urban and rural environments."

Next, attitudes:

> The psychiatric residents (meeting with the committee) would be able to describe (verbally) to the committee how they (the psychiatrists) view and think about American teenagers, and how they believe their own upbringing has affected their views and thoughts. Both the committee members and the psychiatrists should believe that the verbal descriptions of these views and thoughts are sincere and objective.

Now, skill:

> The psychiatric residents will be able to speak to and interact with the teenagers on the adolescent unit in such a way that the teenagers would say, if asked, that they think that the residents understand them, make them (the teens) feel comfortable, and are helpful.

Each of these action goal statements focuses on a different aspect of the same problem, and they differ in many respects. Achievement of the knowledge goal could be measured by the committee, but achievement of the skill goal is best measured by talking to clients. Criteria for the successful achievement of the attitude goals are the combined opinions of the committee psychiatrists and the psychiatric residents. In all three cases, the criteria used are subjective judgments, but judgments by experts who are well qualified to judge. If, for example, an outside instructor was brought in to teach the psychiatric residents about adolescence in the United States, that person's judgment could be solicited to evaluate the effectiveness of learning. More precise measures might be used; for example, the psychiatric residents might be given a short-answer quiz at the end of their training session, in which there are right and wrong answers (although, as we shall see when we discuss evaluation, staff members are generally unwilling to participate in such testing. In addition, the validity of such objective tests is always an issue). Since judgment is often used as a criterion for measuring goal achievement, we will consider it in detail in the section on evaluation.

My goal statements suggest the following observable behaviors: "verbally describe" and "speak to and interact with." Review your goal statement to determine whether or not someone else could observe the performance you specified. If they can, fine; if not, you should consider a rewrite that uses observable action words.

Although I would like to see attitudes change, my goal statement focused only on the exposition of attitudes and a verbalized recognition of the effect of their own upbringing on their perceptions of American adolescents. This reflects my belief, and the findings of relevant social science research, that attitudes are more likely to change when an individual (1) receives information about the object of an attitude that is new or discrepant with old information, (2) then shares his or her own attitudes with others, and (3) finally learns new ways of behaving toward the object of the attitudes, than when a direct effort is made to change an attitude by a frontal assault on that attitude (see, for example, Festinger, Schacter, and Back, 1950, and Feagin, 1965).

The *conditions* portion of one of my goal statements included "If [the psychiatric residents were] asked," an implied situation in which the residents, individually or assembled, would tell the committee members (and each other) about a number of situations in which the residents interact with the clients.

The *criterion* of my goal statements included "Members. . .would assess these descriptions as generally correct" and similar judgment measures for the other statements. Though not as precise as "compute correct answers to at least eighteen of the twenty problems, within twenty minutes," it does specify one of the better measures for learning: expert opinion.

Writing behaviorally specific goal statements takes considerable practice. The best short work I've seen on the subject is Robert Mager's book, *Preparing Instructional Objectives,* 2nd edition (Mager, 1975). You can read it in less than an hour, and since it uses a no-fail (almost) programmed instruction format, you are likely to succeed (in *that* book's exercises) and receive lots of glowing praise (from the book itself!).

EXAMPLES OF GOAL STATEMENTS

Here are some examples of goal statements from a few of the projects presented earlier. The first example is a follow-up of the nurses' project presented in the last chapter. Here the staff developer found that changed circumstances forced her to modify her original objectives.

EXAMPLE 9: THE HOSPITAL EXAMPLE (*continued*)

It is now a few weeks later and I have been informed that the Infection Control Committee has been postponed until the end of June. I am not pleased with this development and more fully realize that some of the aspects of this program are out of my control and at the whim and convenience of others. This, of course, is one of the disadvantages of involving other people. However, I now have in my possession a six-page copy of the isolation procedure. I was surprised at the length of it and knew I would have to reevaluate the goals. I was very pleased at the thoroughness of the explanations and knew that a great deal of time and effort had gone into its completion. I knew this was exactly what the nurses needed to know to do the job correctly and with less effort. Because there was so much content in the procedure, I eliminated some of my earlier objectives, since this information is not contained in the procedure but was going to be additional. I knew we would not have time for it and would have to cover the material at another time. So I was back to square one on the objectives. I held a meeting with J and R to determine our objectives. Our biggest problem was the time factor. We knew we could not have the in-service extended beyond one hour because of the difficulty of the staff being away from their responsibilities. Our second problem was that of measuring the attainment of the objectives. After much discussion and some compromises, we formulated the following objectives:

1. The nursing staff[4] will perform the gown technique (as outlined in Procedure VI. in the handout) correctly as judged by their demonstration of the technique.
2. The nursing staff will demonstrate double bagging of specimens as outlined in Procedures V.E.4 and 5.
3. The nursing staff will perform the transfer of linen by double bagging and cuffing technique as outlined in Procedure V.E.1 as judged by demonstration.
4. Given actual patient care equipment, the nursing staff will separate the equipment in the correct categories for return to Central Supply as outlined in Procedures V.E.6 and 7.

EXAMPLE 10: THE OCCUPATIONAL THERAPY EXAMPLE (*continued*)

The next example was part of the occupational therapy project reported earlier. The staff developer here set a criterion of *one* correct referral to physical therapy. When I suggested that one correct referral might be too limited a sample from which to assume that her objectives had been achieved, she indicated that referral rates in general were not that high.

This suggests a different problem—the degree to which physicians were making *any* referrals to PT [physical therapy] or OT [occupational therapy]—but this was not the issue she had chosen to deal with in her project. Nonetheless, it could be assumed that the physicians who now knew how to make correct referrals might be inclined to increase their rate of referrals.

1. Given information as in the fourth exemplary case study,[5] each physician will be able to make at least one correct referral to the Occupational Therapy Department within one week from the end of the in-service. A referral is considered correct when the occupational therapist agrees she can best fulfill the order. The order is to be written. (By this, it is meant that the correct department will be circled at the end of the case study.)
2. Given information as in the fourth exemplary case study, each physician will be able to make at least one correct referral to the Physical Therapy Depart-

[4]This phrase will refer to RNs, LPNs, and nursing assistants.
[5]Part of the in-service training program she created involved several exemplary case studies.

ment within one week from the end of the in-service. A referral is considered correct when the physical therapist agrees she can best fulfill the order. The order is to be written. (By this, it is meant that the correct department will be circled at the end of the case study.)

EXAMPLE 11: THE DSS EXAMPLE (*continued*)

The final example, from the DSS project, speaks to the hoped-for results of the activity—the payoff, back on the job. While useful, it gives less specific direction to the staff developer than found in the preceding examples. In my view, such objectives could be added, as supplementary to the objectives of the activity itself. In this case, there should also have been objectives stated about the time management training itself.

As a result of the needs assessment and through supervisory review of the unit's performance, a priority need area (time management) was identified. On the basis of the information gathered and the need area identified, the following management objectives were established:

1. By 10/1/80, the seven (7) workers comprising the Services Unit will, on a monthly basis, complete at least 95 percent of the cases due for redetermination of eligibility by the due date indicated on the DSS 5S, Services Case Status Notice.
2. By 10/1/80, the seven (7) workers making up the Services Unit will make a home call on and open, withdraw, or deny at least 95 percent of all new referrals received within the thirty-day standard of promptness.
3. By 10/1/80, the seven (7) workers comprising the Services Unit will, on a monthly basis, dictate or write a quarterly narrative on at least 95 percent of their cases whose due date falls during the month.

In view of the results of the supervisory review, which showed a deteriorating level of performance on the part of the Services Unit in the areas of redeterminations of eligibility, disposition of new referrals, and narrative recording, the foregoing management objectives have been established.

The factors leading to the reduction in performance have been identified as relating to (1) the loss of a staff member through attrition, which led to reassignment of cases to existing staff, and (2) a substantial increase in the number of people looking for help because of the state of the economy. As discussed earlier, staff members have indicated a need to find ways to better plan and prioritize their work in order to better meet prescribed time frames. An increased ability in these areas could, in time, result in improved performance and accomplishment of the objectives in the areas indicated.

In addition to these considerations, the objectives were established because the department's service programs face potential funding reductions if the standards of promptness are not met. The potential ramifications are evident. From a management perspective, this threat of potential reduction provides a great incentive to formulate the foregoing objectives.

GUIDELINES FOR CREATING GOAL STATEMENTS

The following questions are designed to help you create behaviorally specific goal statements.

1. Assuming that you *have* identified high-priority needs (in terms of both organizational needs and felt needs), state the particular need you have decided to address in this project, and your reason for choosing to work on this need at this time.

    _____

    _____

    _____

2. Your goal statement should be written with regard to the staff members who you hope will achieve the goal(s) you are about to describe. This is your *target population.* Be sure to *avoid* writing a goal statement about *yourself* ("I want to be able to teach....").
    THIS GOAL STATEMENT IS WRITTEN IN RELATION TO THE FOLLOWING STAFF MEMBERS (INDIVIDUALS OR WORK UNIT(S)):

    _____

    _____

3. Many goal statements are actually designed to get at some change that can't be measured easily because it is cognitive or attitudinal. For example, you may want a staff member to be able to recognize something when it occurs ("In the videotape we've just seen, where did the helping persons make an empathic statement?"), or be able to analyze something ("What are the factors that have caused this client to behave in this way at this time?"), or develop a new attitude toward something ("Describe their reasons for having avoided doing group work in the past, as well as their feelings that had led them into giving it a try now").

    IF YOU WANT TO ADD TO KNOWLEDGE OR CHANGE ATTITUDES, WHAT SORT OF CHANGED UNDERSTANDING OR FEELING DO YOU HOPE WILL OCCUR FOR YOUR TARGET POPULATION?

    _____

    _____

4. You need some measure of this changed understanding or feeling that is visible and thus measurable. So you have to select one or more action words (verbs) that refer to things that the staff members should be able to do, which are so clearly linked to the understanding or feeling that the behavior is good evidence that the desired understanding or feeling has been achieved. Of course, you may also be trying to teach some motor performance, like riding a bicycle, where it is easier to measure learning by asking the person to perform that skill. "Let's see you get on the bike and ride it by yourself."
    We can't know if someone has understood something just because they say they do, but if they correctly answer, in writing, a series of relevant questions

about that something without any help from anyone or anything, we are pretty safe in believing that they "know" it—or, at least, that they know it at the moment when they write their answers. (How many of the thousands of facts you were forced to learn in school do you still know today?) But if, for example, my objective was to have my staff know the names and properties of psychotropic drugs, I could arrange a staff development activity designed to achieve that objective (knowing names and properties, and so on) and set as my goal (and as evidence of their knowing) the objective that they should be able to write the names and signficant properties of these drugs from memory; or, if it is my intention that staff should be able to use the technique of force field analysis in resolving a policy issue, I would want them to recognize the kind of problem for which this technique is appropriate and then to use it to develop a consensually accepted solution to the program.

WHAT DO YOU WANT YOUR TARGET POPULATION TO BE ABLE TO *DO* THAT WILL CONVINCE YOU THAT THEY HAVE LEARNED WHAT YOU WANT THEM TO LEARN, OR CHANGED WHAT THEY WANTED TO CHANGE, OR SOLVED WHAT THEY WANTED TO SOLVE—AND WHAT THE NEEDS ASSESSMENT INDICATED THEY WANTED TO ACHIEVE?

---

5.   Learning does not occur in a vacuum, and neither does a performance using what has been learned. All sorts of conditions affect performance—for example, time. It's one thing to want an individual to be able to describe the informal relationships among the members of a staff group *one day* after meeting them, and quite something else *six months* after meeting them. Or it's one thing to expect staff members to identify the accurate use of empathy in an interview when they read a typed transcript of the interview, and quite another when they watch and listen to videotapes of that interview. In your goal statement, you need to identify the conditions under which the behavior you described (in item 4) are to occur.

WHAT ARE THE CONDITIONS UNDER WHICH THIS PERFORMANCE IS TO OCCUR?

---

6.   Finally—and this is the hardest part of such a statement—you need to specify how well the staff members have to be able to do this (whatever it is). "Be correct in three out of five cases"; "Written from memory—all twenty items—in ten minutes"; "so that the entire unit agrees on the solution, and puts that solution into motion"; and so on. In some cases there is no easy or "correct" answer,

and expert judgement—for example, "the supervisor's opinion"—is the best criterion you have.

WHAT CRITERION OR CRITERIA WILL YOU USE TO MEASURE THE CORRECTNESS, EFFECTIVENESS, AND SO ON OF THE PERFORMANCE?

_____

_____

Now let's assemble what you've written in an easier-to-read form:

Under what conditions? _____

_____

Will who? _____

_____

Do what? _____

_____

How well? _____

_____

To demonstrate what understanding or feeling? _____

_____

In order to resolve what need? _____

_____

If you have filled this out, you should now have a goal statement. In most cases, sharing this goal statement with staff should make clear to them what the staff development activity is all about, and should enhance the benefits they derive from it. But that can't be accepted at face value. Actual accomplishments have to be tested. This testing, known as *evaluation,* is discussed next.

THE EVALUATION OF STAFF DEVELOPMENT

Given the current pressure for accountability, and the reality of shrinking budgets, we have to be able to demonstrate the value of staff development if it is to receive adequate support. To accomplish this, we must be able to measure the degree to which staff development has enhanced staff members' performance and their satisfaction with their jobs; and we must be able to demonstrate a link between staff development and positive client change. We need measures that will let us know—in the middle of the staff development process—whether or not we are heading in the right direction in relation to the goals we have selected. We also need to know whether or not staff are satisfied with the staff development activities themselves. To do all this, we need methods of evaluation that are valid, reliable, and practical.

MacBride's recent review of research on staff development in the field of education indicates how complex the tasks of evaluation can be (MacBride, 1984).

For example, MacDonald (1981) took the position that it was virtually impossible to use a classical research design to evaluate in-service programs: "The best you can do are field studies and it is absolutely silly to talk about control groups" (MacDonald, 1981, p. 8). In other words, the validity of any measure is limited by the realities of practice confronting any researcher (Joyce and Showers, 1980).

Reviewers generally give poor marks to the reviews of research on staff development that have been done. For example, Nicholson, Joyce, Parker, and Waterman (1977) report that "Of the 2000 items, the only research review which may properly deserve the name was one conducted by Lawrence and others for the Florida Department of Education" (Lawrence, 1974, p. 19).

MacBride found that reviews of research on the effectiveness of staff development in the field of education have found very few studies about the *use* teachers have made of what they were supposed to have acquired from staff development (Loucks and Melle, 1982; Joyce and Showers, 1980). In other words, there is no guarantee that behavior affected by staff development will result in positive staff change. One reason for this difficulty may be that researchers and teachers may not agree on what constitutes effective teaching. A study at Syracuse found that researchers defined effectiveness in terms of teaching behaviors that produced student learning gains as evidenced by achievement scores, whereas teachers looked to such things as students' degree of involvement and affective emphasis (MacDonald, 1981). Brophy noted that researchers have found "virtually no clear results linking teacher behavior and student learning" (Brophy, 1979, p. 3).

Strother's review found that the in-service programs that were most successful in achieving their objectives were those that:

1. Involved teachers actively in initiating, planning, and conducting the program;
2. Were designed as a collective effort of a faculty, with common purposes directed toward general faculty development;
3. Were funded in ways that permitted the teachers and administrators of individual schools to sponsor them, to design activities, and to select inside and outside leadership as appropriate;
4. Were scheduled at times (evenings and summers) that did not compete with but complemented other professional obligations. Programs scheduled during work hours were considerably less successful in achieving objectives;
5. Had diverse program patterns that seemed to emphasize teacher responsibility— self-instruction, peer study groups, college courses, one-to-one consultation;
6. Involved participants in both receptive and active roles;
7. Had sequences in which participants could try out new things in their classrooms

(or in simulations) and then receive considerable feedback from a skilled person. (Programs in which participants were expected to store up new ideas and behavior prescriptions for a future time were distinctly less successful in achieving objectives.);

8. Had leaders who were linked with a university or other center concerned with professional development;

9. Provided opportunities for participants to see demonstrations of exemplary practices and to learn the skills of observing the practices in themselves and others;

10. Did not rely on lecture presentations as the main activity;

11. Were conducted at the school site if the programs emphasized affective or skill performance objectives;

12. Provided participants with relevant printed materials, such as guidelines for learning and applying new skills;

13. Treated their participants as professionals (Strother, 1983, p. 2).

ISSUES OF EVALUATION

Efforts to measure the effectiveness of staff development must deal with the ever-present issues of validity and reliability, practical concerns about the timing of evaluations, and state-of-the-art limitations in our current methods of measuring results (as they pertain to staff development). Let me address these issues in order, starting with validity and reliability.

Validity

A valid measuring instrument has been described as doing what it is intended to do, as measuring what it is supposed to measure, and as yielding scores whose differences reflect true differences of the variable being measured, rather than random or constant errors. (Bostwick and Kyte, 1981, p. 104)

Given this definition, it should be clear that the most valid evaluation is the one that most accurately measures the degree to which the goals of a staff development activity have been achieved. A thorough discussion of validity is beyond the scope of this book, but there are many good research texts that discuss it at length (see, for example, Grinnell, 1981; Labovitz and Hagedorn, 1981; Polansky, 1975). But some of the issues raised for staff developers who give attention to problems of validity include the following:

1. Does my evaluation procedure measure the thing (knowledge, attitude, or skill) I want to measure?

2. Do I have a sufficiently representative sample of the thing I want to measure to have confidence that my results are not just a fluke, but represent a consistent set of outcomes?

3. Are there other ways of measuring the same thing, and, if so, are my initial results consistent with those measurements?

4. Do my results provide an adequate basis for predicting that the thing I've chosen to measure will have some durability over time, everything else being equal?

Let me attempt to make these qustions more concrete by posing them in relation to one of the goal statements I asked you to work on in the earlier discussion of goals. Take the following goal statement:

> The psychiatric residents will be able to speak and interact with the teenagers on the Adolescent Unit in such a way that the teenagers would say, if asked, that they think that the residents understand them, make them (the teens) feel comfortable, and are helpful.

Referring to the foregoing questions:

1. "measure the thing I want to measure": The goal statement makes clear that the thing to be measured here is the statement of teenagers on the Adolescent Unit, giving their opinion about particular actions of the psychiatric residents who were trained through the staff development activity.

2. "sufficient sample": Obviously, getting the opinion of just one teenager would be insufficient. You might find yourself speaking to the newest teen on the unit, who had had little experience with the residents, or with a teen who had had extremely negative *or* extremely positive experiences with the residents that are not characteristic of the experience of most teens. So you would need to speak to several teenagers, perhaps trying to make sure you interviewed some newcomers and some old-timers, some males and some females, and so on.

3. "other ways of measuring": Unit staff, as well as the residents, would have ample opportunity to observe the interactions of the teens and the residents. Their assessments of these interactions could be quite useful, and could confirm or discount what the teens reported.

4. "basis for predicting": One approach here would be to check back at a later date to determine whether or not any observed change had been maintained. The more valid the response, the more likely you could predict correctly the kinds of responses you would be likely to get. Focusing on questions of validity could go a long way in providing an accurate evaluation of staff development.

Reliability

Reliability is defined as the extent to which any way of measuring something will produce consistent results, regardless of who administers it. On a reliable math test, for example, a student should score just about as well whether a particular test is given by teacher A or by teacher B. In the example of the psychiatric residents, the *method* of evaluation is an interview with a number of teenagers: For the interview to be a *reliable* measure of attitudes, two interviewers asking the same questions of the same teenagers should get approximately the same responses. If they get widely differing responses, you can assume that something about the interview procedure itself is influencing the kinds of answers they are getting, and that this interview procedure is unreliable. This might happen if the first interviewer was a member of the staff and the second interviewer was not: The responding teenagers might feel compelled to answer differently depending on who they were talking to. Again, if only *one* interviewer were used (to eliminate such problems) *that* interviewer might have conducted the interview quite differently with one teenager than with another. Perhaps the interviewer was feeling ill the day of the second interview, or was put off because the second interviewee was an old-timer on the unit and was less respectful toward the interviewer. In either case, the poor reliability of this interview (as a way of gathering data) would make the data gathered highly suspect.

In other words, whereas validity questions pertain to *what* is being measured, reliability questions pertain to *how well* it is being measured. Reliability can be enhanced by such procedures as pretesting the measuring procedure on a sample of people who are very much like those you plan to measure, and using this experience to correct unclear questions and other problems and/or by training your data gatherers so that they all eventually perceive behavior and gather information in pretty much the same way.

WHEN SHOULD EVALUATION BE DONE?

The issues of validity and reliability pertain to all four of the points in time when you should plan to carry out evaluation activities:

1. You need a *baseline* measure of each individual staff member's level of knowledge, attitude, or skill, or of the staff's functioning as a unit, in relation to the goals that have been established.
2. The staff development activity itself needs to be evaluated at more than one point in time. I'll call this *on-the-spot evaluation.*
3. Some time after the activity has ended (or as it continues, in an ongoing process such as supervision), the staff developer will want to check—on the job—the effects of the staff development activity on staff performance. I'll call these *on-the-job measures.*
4. Finally, an effort should be made to determine whether or not the activity resulted in any *benefits for clients,* both immediate and long-range.

Baselining Individual Performance

A needs assessment involving a staff group gives us a general picture of what they think they need but usually is not very precise in depicting the performance of specific individuals or particular units with regard to those needs. The process is designed to uncover common concerns, not the degree to which particular people already know about or can do something about these concerns. In this vein, the concept of propaedeutic skill[6] is useful. The term *propaedeutic* (as indicated earlier)

---

[6] *Skill* here refers not simply to an observable behavior itself, but also to the use—in action—of *knowledge,* as affected by the staff member's *attitudes.*

refers to skills already acquired through preliminary instruction that an individual has successfully completed when approaching the study of some art or science. For example, the person who is to learn touch typing must bring several propaedeutic skills to this learning task: the ability to spell correctly, enough manual dexterity to strike the typewriter keys with the fingers; and to strike them selectively—that is, strike the key for *s* when that letter is desired, rather than *a* or *d*, which are immediately adjacent to *s*. In developing an effective baseline measure, you would have to (1) determine the propaedeutic skills that are preliminary to a specific job-related performance and then (2) develop a valid and reliable measure of the individual's possession of these propaedeutic skills.

One could argue that correct spelling is not an ability that is required of a good typist, but it's hard for me to think of a situation in which a person could be a *good* typist without some conception of what *spelling* means, or without the ability to spell well, or at least the ability to use a dictionary correctly. It's also clear, however, that propaedeutic skills are not easy to measure in relation to many aspects of staff development. First, you must be able to describe precisely the components of a particular skill; second, you must be able to devise a valid and reliable measure of the degree to which the individual already possesses the skill itself, or the propaedeutic skills that are essential to mastering the target skill. This can be done using the *task analysis* approach discussed in Chapter 3.

Incidentally, the task analysis process lends itself fairly easily to the writing of behaviorally specific instructional objectives. In addition, Fine and Wiley (1971) note that when a task statement contains all the information called for by the five questions, it becomes operationally useful; that is, it provides clear information such that:

1. Managers can use it to assess the level of complexity of the task and compare its performance requirements with those of other tasks.
2. Supervisors can use it to give clear, accurate instructions to workers and to develop criteria for assessing whether the worker's performance is satisfactory.
3. Selection officers can use it to infer worker qualifications needed to perform the task.
4. Trainers can use it to determine both classroom and on-the-job training needed by the worker to whom the task has been assigned.
5. Finally, and most important to the current discussion, it provides the basis for baseline measures.

Valid measures of beginning skill knowledge or attitude level are not easy to design. I think of how few university courses begin with a pretest. In some areas of curriculum, where objective information ("the capital of Michigan is Lansing") or measurable skill ("$2 \times 9 = 18$") is the core of what is taught, it should be possible to measure what people can already do (or already know) acceptably well and to excuse them from certain portions of instruction that would be redundant for them. However, the design of an objective measure that is both valid—that is, actually measures what it purports to measure—and viewed as fair (no trick questions) is a time-consuming task. Experience has taught me, for example, that it is comparatively easy to create an examination consisting of essay questions, but very hard to grade one (because grading is a function of the instructor's subjective assessment), whereas it is comparatively easy to grade an objective, short-answer test, but very difficult to make one up that is sufficiently comprehensive and challenging without being impossibly hard. For most academics who teach in the human services, the time and effort involved in pretesting students is excessive in relation to all our other assignments at the beginning of a term. We assume that the students enrolled in our courses would not be there if they had already passed a course on our topic exempting them from our course—if we are teaching a *required* course— and that those who register for an *elective* course do so because they believe that they do not possess the knowledge or skills the course will attempt to provide. Their decision to take the course is, in effect, the "pretest."

If a valid written measure of knowledge or attitude is hard to devise (or easy to devise but hard to grade), a skill display assessment—in which the individual, is measured on his or her ability to perform a task skillfully—is even harder to devise *and* to assess. Some tasks involve quantifiable measures of correctness (for example, to be able to fill out the agency's intake form completely during a half-hour interview with no more than a 5 percent error rate). For others, the measures of "correctness" are not quantifiable except on ordinal scales—"more than–less than"— applied by trained judges—for example, "Assess the degree to which a staff member skillfully used verbal empathic responses in conducting an intake interview." For example, in one study of the training of eighteen social work students to make verbal empathic responses, it took several hours to train a group of three qualified judges to a fairly high degree of interrater reliability in assessing the audiotaped performance of the students during a role-played interview, and several more hours for each of them to judge the taped interviews (Kozma and Bertcher, 1974). The kind of time and energy involved in conducting such a skill display pretest is probably not available in most human service agency staff development programs. Yet without it, a baseline assessment of performance is likely to be highly subjective and therefore of limited value in subsequent measures of the effectiveness of a staff development activity.

It should be clear, then, that there are many problems in developing baseline measures that are reliable and valid. In addition, most staff members traditionally view pretests (or any test at any point in time in a staff development activity) as too much like school, and therefore threatening and undesirable. Indeed, any evaluation of work is likely to be unsettling to staff. For example, Jayaratne and Levy, in discussing research on clinical practice, reported as follows:

> One of the authors once accepted a position to conduct research on the mental health workers in a university hospital. During their first meeting, a social worker confessed: you know, we're all pretty glad that you're here to do your research thing. But everyone feels as I do. Please God, just keep it away from me. (Jayaratne and Levy, 1979, p. 1)

The preceding discussion is not designed to discourage attempts to gather baseline data; rather, it is meant to put that effort into perspective. Given all the limitations described, you must do the best you can within those limitations.

Sometimes baseline data is based on self-report: "I don't know how to do it." For example, "I've never led a group meeting that is designed to help clients cope with personal problems." If the staff members were asked to discuss this response further, however, you might discover that they had participated—as members—in a very large number of group meetings, had chaired committee meetings, had read a fair amount about leading treatment groups, had observed an experienced group leader in action, and were highly motivated to experience group leadership—all of which could be important pieces of baseline information that a staff developer would find useful and that reveal far more than the brief statement, "I don't know how to do it."

Baseline information can also be gathered by asking potential participants to describe particular subjects, issues, or techniques they would like to see covered or presented. In a topic area that is comparatively unknown to potential participants, you could list a number of subjects, issues, or techniques and ask people to rank each on the degree to which they would find it "very useful," "somewhat useful," "not too useful," or "not useful at all" to them.

A good clue for determining the kinds of information you need as baseline data can be found by reexamining your goal statement. If it is hoped that the staff member(s) can do X, under Y circumstances, with a certain level of proficiency, Z, then your baseline measure should be an attempt to gather data about the way in which this activity (or one similar to it) now takes place for the potential participant, in relation to the variables X, Y, and Z.

In some cases, baseline data are available from secondary sources—statistics that are available from the organization. Such data might include the error rate in filling out certain forms, the dropout rate for clients of a particular staff member, the number and variety of books that circulate from the agency library, the percentage of clients using the agency who are members of minority groups, and so forth. Such data would be useful if you hoped to achieve the goals of, respectively, cutting the error rate in completing agency forms, determining a way of improving staff members' ability to hold clients in service, improving the services of the agency library, increasing the use of agency service by members of particular minority groups, and so forth.

In my experience, staff developers generally shy away from doing a pretest, or accept the potential participant's self-assessment: "I don't know that" or "I can't do it." And there's the dilemma: Gathering good pretest data is difficult, but lacking it makes the overall evaluation very problematic. Without a baseline to measure from, it is difficult to evaluate the impact of staff development on goal achievement. Given all the difficulties you face, you do the best you can on the assumption that some baseline data are better than none.[7]

---

[7]Some colleagues would protest that some baseline data are *not* better than none because those data may then be treated as more valid than they really are. This is an appropriate caution; nevertheless, I prefer to urge people to go after baseline data, if only because it forces them to think logically about the evaluation process.

On-the-Spot Evaluations

The most common form of evaluation is the short form (filled out as a staff development activity ends) of the did-you-like-it? and how-did-I-do? variety. These forms are more likely to be completed and turned in if you (1) bar the door and let people leave only after they turn in the evaluation form, because once they leave, your chances of getting the forms completed and turned in rapidly approach zero; (2) keep the forms comparatively short (so people will indeed complete them); and (3) allow people to complete the forms anonymously, so that they feel they can openly express their true reactions. These forms may ask participants to place checks on a rating scale—for example, "This activity was (   ) very helpful; (   ) fairly helpful; (   ) not too helpful; (   ) not at all helpful," followed by "Please add any comments that you think might be useful in planning future staff development activities."

Open-ended questions are also used:
"The thing I liked best was. . ." (*Leave adequate space for the reply*, or the respondent will assume you don't really want much of an answer.)
"The think I liked least was. . ."
"I wish you had done more of. . ."
"I wish you had done less of. . ."
Often, specific information is requested, e.g.,

Today's activity was held away from the office so that we would not be interrupted by telephone messages, secretarial crises, etc. How would you rate holding the meeting away from the office?

(   ) very helpful   (   ) fairly helpful   (   ) not too helpful   (   ) not at all helpful

These subjective responses are no doubt useful. They capture people at the moment of highest enthusiasm, greatest frustration, or complete boredom. They *are* subjective, however, and of comparatively little use when they are the *only* means of evaluation, because the data they provide are so limited: They do not measure improved ability—only *satisfaction* with the staff development activity.

Because they *are* easy to make up and easy to score, however, it is quite useful to make up *at least one such evaluation form* to be administered at some point *during* the activity. Such an evaluation can help to tell you how the participants are experiencing the staff development activity up to that point, and can provide valuable clues about continuing with the original plan (when the feedback is positive) or considering a modification (when the feedback is negative). After all, evaluations done at the *end* of an activity have a significant limitation that is often overlooked: They are completed just at the point when the staff developer cannot use the responses to improve *this* activity. Thus, people filling them out see little value *for themselves* in completing the form, except as it informs you, the staff developer, about their impression of how well you did. Midstream evaluations, by contrast, provide participants with an opportunity to improve their own experience by suggesting that you (a) do more of the same, or (b) make a change, or (c) don't forget to include such-and-such. Of course, if you ignore midstream evaluations, you do so at your own peril; on the other hand, it's easy to ignore end-of-session evaluations, because the activity is over.

For a midstream evaluation to be most effective, it has to be short and focused, *and* the staff developer must have time to review it and decide what to do about any suggested changes. In some cases you might want to share a generally negative response with the participants and then say, "OK, what do you want to do instead?" Undoubtedly, this is risky for the staff developer, but it's a lot better than carrying on when everyone is bored to tears. I have also found it useful to circulate all the completed copies of midstream evaluation forms (unsigned) to all participants present (once I have read them) so that they can get a sense of how everyone else has rated the activity, on paper, then mentally compare what *others* have written with their own rating.

The notion of using a simple midstream evaluation in in-service training is fairly easy to envision. Assume a two-hour training session, a ten-minute break halfway through, and a form that looks like this:

I would rate my learning so far (circle one);

5———4———3———2———1

Lots of   Nothing
Learning   Learned

I would rate my satisfaction with this session so far (circle one);

5———4———3———2———1

Highly   Totally
Satisfied   Dissatisfied

Comments?

This "quick-and-dirty" form[8] can provide a trainer with a fast readout of the training group's reaction to the session, besides making it possible to suggest new or modified approaches.

On the other hand, what about midstream evaluation of other staff development activities, such as supervision? For some staff development activities, you should schedule regular evaluation dates, on which all participants in an activity set aside an amount of time to evaluate *the process* itself, not just the result. In graduate school, the semester framework of four months in a field placement sets the schedule for a written evaluation of students by field instructors at the end of the semester. One school I knew of, however, scheduled an additional written evaluation in mid-semester, reasoning that a student in trouble could be put on notice with plenty of time to do something about it.

[8] I am indebted to my colleague Sallie Churchill for this simple but useful form.

It should be evident by now that I think subjective midstream evaluations are much more useful for participants and staff developers alike than are end-of-activity subjective evaluations. Like anything else, however, they can be misused, as witness the following incredible example, recently told to me by a colleague:

> Staff in a large human service organization that sponsored a week long institute were given a mid-stream evaluation at the end of the first day. The feedback was extremely negative, and upsetting to the trainers. Nevertheless, they decided to follow through on their plans for day 2, with no modification. They did make one change, however; they had a new midstream evaluation form printed up for use at end of day 2 that did not allow for the same kind and amount of negative feedback!

If I did not have the highest respect for my colleague's veracity, I would have found this tale hard to believe.

A different form of end-of-activity evaluation attempts to measure in some *objective* way what has been gained from the activity. This focuses less on did-you-like-it? assessment and more on "What do you know (or can you do) *now* that you did not know (or were not able to do) before the activity?" This is closer to an attempt to sample what the individuals have learned or which organizational problem's solution has been developed, whether or not people thought they were learning during the session or liked the way in which the activity was conducted. This kind of assessment should, by definition, be related to the baselining that was done, in order to compare the effects of the activity *at that moment* on the individual staff member, on a before-and-after measure.

EXAMPLE 12: LEARNING DRUG SLANG

In one in-service training session, staff developers clearly avoided the school-like quality of pre- and posttesting by the use of a gamelike activity. Their task was to teach staff in a Veterans Administration hospital to correctly understand slang used by patients that was associated with the use of illegal drugs. Here's what they did: As a pretest, they played a tape-recorded role-played interview between a simulated drug addict and his "social worker," in which the "addict" used as many drug slang terms as he could in a two-minute sample of interaction. Participants were to write down each slang term as they heard it, and briefly define it, then turn in what they had written, signed, to be "graded." The actual in-service training session followed the pattern of a popular television quiz game, which saw all participants divided into two teams, with points awarded for correct recognition of the meaning of particular drug slang. At the end of the session, the same tape recording was played, and participants once again tried to identify and define the drug slang. By comparing each person's before-and-after performances on this test, it was possible to tell (a) whether the group of participants, as a whole, had improved their recognition of drug slang (they had) and (b) the degree of improvement for each person, suggesting who needed more help.

On-the-Job Measures

Staff developers want staff development activities to go well. It enhances their status, makes it easier to get active participation in the future, and contributes to good morale. But a "good" staff development activity—whether it is assessed as "good" in terms of subjective satisfaction or on some objective measure—is only truly good if it translates into on-the-job behaviors. For example, in training staff to work with groups, determining that they enjoyed the training, and assessing the learners as being effective group leaders at the end of the training is of comparatively little value if, once the training is over, no groups are started, or if groups run by these trainees are mismanaged.

Evaluation on the job may simply involve a search for evidence that the staff development activity produced a real and productive change in agency operations, that this change had some enduring quality, and that—over time—this change became part of the fabric of the organization's operation. Take the group work example: Six months after the group work training ended (and assuming there was no group work going on before the training), are there any groups? How many are managed by more than one staff member? If one staff member leaves, will the group work program end? One could also attempt to evaluate the quality of the group work being done, although this is a far more complex undertaking.

To measure the longer-range effects of staff development activities on staff performance, you can draw on a variety of sources. If line staff were the targets of the activity, supervisors can be asked to rate the effects of the activity on their supervisees' job performance. In some cases, the postactivity improvements are routinely recorded in the organization's statistics—for example, a drop in error rates on agency forms, a change in an individual staff member's rate of clients-who-drop-out-after-one-interview, the rate of circulation of books and journals from the agency's library, head counts of the client population, by majority/minority group status, and so forth. In some cases, no such records may have been kept before the staff development activity; it may be necessary, *as part of the activity itself,* to develop a recording procedure. I am not so naive as to think this is easy. Most human service organizations are already overloaded with paperwork. Staff members often must choose between seeing their clients and falling behind on the less interesting, less rewarding paperwork that records what they do with their clients; they often have no choice but to put the paperwork first, if they want to hold onto their jobs. Any new record-keeping form or procedure makes more work for someone, and is understandably resisted. Faced with this problem, staff developers may confront their greatest frustration: Day-to-day operation of the organization may make it all but impossible to gather the very data they need to determine whether or not the investment in staff development is paying off.

There is no easy answer to this dilemma. I can only counsel "patience and fortitude" or, in the words of a contemporary poster, "Plan ahea$_d$." It seems that some, if not most, of this data gathering may become the responsibility of the staff developer: encouraging, checking, counting, trying to exploit—wherever feasible—the already existing record-keeping activities of the organization, seeking prime indicators that "something" happened as a result of the staff development activity.

I can imagine the following conversation during a coffee break:

Staff developer to the "Right Person to Ask": "You remember that in-service we did on group work last fall? As I recall, we had no group work going on at that time. Everyone who came said they were really interested in getting groups started. So how many groups do we have going now?" "Right Person": "None." Staff developer: "Oh, really? How come?" Or, if "Right Person" says: "Well, everyone has at least one group going," staff developer replies (without wanting to appear too eager), "Well, that's fine. What's the average size of the groups?" And so forth. Or, again, "Right Person" might reply: "How many groups? Let's see. Two, no three. No wait, that group didn't ever get enough members. . .let's see. Two—yeah, two." Staff developer: "Two? Well, that's a beginning, isn't it? Of course, sixteen staff participated. I had hoped we'd get more than two groups going. What's been happening with everyone else?"

Drawing on the model of the classical experimental design, it's possible that some staff were involved in an activity and others were not. If so, subsequent checkups (given all the difficulties mentioned earlier) could try to determine whether those who went through the activity are now doing their jobs (with respect to that activity) differently from those who did not.

If the foregoing discussion is not satisfying to the reader, that's understandable: It's not satisfactory to me either. Later in this chapter, I'll suggest, in more specific terms, what the technology of doing evaluations should be. After all, in my imaginary conversation with "Right Person," I neglected to mention that that person may want to know why *you* want to know what happened to group work. Staff members may feel that somehow you are holding *them* to blame for the possible failure of your staff development activity—a "failure" that will somehow put a bad mark on *their* record. Of course, this is less likely to happen if "Right Person" was involved in the activity from the beginning and if you have maintained ongoing contact with participants since the staff development activity to work on the use of what transpired during the activity. If this is their project as much as yours, they are far more likely to *want* to measure outcomes. And because of the nature of their day-to-day work, they may be in a better position to gather data than you are.

Evaluating Benefits to Clients

The goal of staff development in a human services organization is to do something that will eventually benefit clients, directly or indirectly. Measuring the effectiveness of human service organizations is extremely complex: It is difficult to state with certainty that what is being measured as "results" is truly, at least in part, a function of staff development. Recognizing the difficulty, however, shouldn't stop us from trying, but should only serve to make us more realistic about the possibility of succeeding in showing the linkage of staff development to client outcomes.

Studies of client outcomes should start with, but not be limited to, clients themselves. To what do they attribute whatever result they achieved from their contact with the agency—good, bad, or indifferent? If we assume the best of all possible worlds, the clients might say:

> I was getting nowhere until Mr. Jones put me in that group—that's when things began to happen! It wasn't easy, but at least I learned I wasn't alone—that there were others who had gone through what I had—who are still going through it—and, well, the way he ran that group got us all to trust one another, and trust him and—well, I can't really say what it was, but if it hadn't been for that group, I'd still be in the hospital instead of being out here, doing O.K.

Now, if Jones learned his group work approach through a staff development activity, a fair case could be made for the success of that activity. In real life, of course, it isn't that easy. Clients are often hard to find once they've left a program. They may not be satisfied with what happened to them in the program. Even if things did get better for them, they could still easily misperceive the true cause of their improvement. But the studies that have been done suggest that they are willing, indeed eager, to share their opinions about their experiences in the program (see, for example, Overton, 1960; Mayer and Timms, 1970).

Again, the problem lies in choosing relevant indicators of effective outcomes that resulted from staff development, and gathering data with regard to the indicators. Further, one would have to recognize the host of intervening variables that could have an undertermined impact on the former client. In some cases, so many variables combine, over time, that it's impossible to separate out any effects—assuming there are any—of staff development.

A study by Thomas and McLeod (1960) attempted to study the link between a staff development activity—in-service training—and client outcomes, and achieved what the authors describe as "modest results at best." They measured change for both staff and clients, in a public welfare office. In addition to providing in-service training for some staff and none for the others, they systematically varied case load size in order to test the hypothesis that reduced case loads would lead to an improvement in the quality of service. A subsequent discussion of this study helps point up the problems involved in the evaluation of staff development. According to Thomas and McLeod (1967, p. 348):

> A natural query at this point is to wonder just how successful the training was. It is not easy to say. Generalizations must be limited to what has been learned about this program and ones similar to it. Generalizations are limited also by what the positive findings tell us, because the negative ones tell us so very little. This point merits elaboration. It was found, for example, that training did not improve scores on the test of ethical commitment. Failure to find change here could have been due to any of the following possibilities: a lack of emphasis upon this type of content in training, some shortcoming of the test itself, or the difficulty of changing ethical orientations of persons.
>
> One must be similarly cautious about interpreting the rather modest changes in families that were associated with in-service training. Failure to find greater effects of in-service training for families may have been due to the relatively short period of the training program, the relatively brief period of time allowed for families to show changes, or the relatively small number of contacts which were had with the majority of the families.

More is learned about how successful the training program was from the positive results, because there are fewer possibilities for them to be invalid. Two of these findings deserve special emphasis. The remarkable improvement in analytic skill resulting from training needs highlighting because it was just this skill that was found in the assessment phase to be so badly in need of improvement. Workers were aided during training to improve this skill by discussions and exercises aimed toward the development of more precise thinking about the kinds of problems that families have. It appears, in short, that a training program like the one employed in this study can enable public assistance workers to identify more accurately the problems of recipients.

The other finding of note is the high rate of appropriate reassurance given by the workers who had received the training. Past research suggests that appropriate reassurance is important in the casework interview because it facilitates the movement or change of the client in the desired direction. Results from this study not presented here support this supposition. Since reassurance was not taught directly as a technique in the training program, it is probable that the high frequency of reassurance in the training group indicates that the quality of the treatment relationship of these workers improved as a result of training. There was unquestionably an emphasis in the training program upon the significance of the quality of the helping relationship between the worker and the recipient. One interpretation of these findings, therefore, is that a program of in-service training that stresses the quality of the helping relationship is likely to enable the workers to facilitate the movement of families receiving assistance.

METHODS OF EVALUATION

The primary purpose of evaluation in staff development is to measure the degree to which the goals of a staff development activity have been achieved. Since felt needs are assessed subjectively, the degree to which they have been resolved can also be assessed subjectively. However, although it is certainly important to know whether or not staff feel or believe that their need in a particular area has been satisfied, the demands of accountability require more objective proof of goal achievement. The measurement of the degree to which organizational needs have been met can range from the subjective opinion of an administrator, or of professionals in the community who work with the organization, to more objective measures, such as a lowering in the error rate of filling out forms, a noticeable decrease in the dropout rate among clients, statistics on the percentage of minority participation in the organization's program, and the like.

One method of evaluation is to ask for an oral or written response from staff. In addition, staff's actions, either in a skill display exam (judged by experts), or in on-the-job behaviors reported (verbally or in writing) by their supervisor (or some other qualified observer), can also be used to measure goal attainment. Finally, agency statistics can be used to measure the achievement of some goals.

Written Measures of Staff Improvement

Assuming that we want to develop ways of measuring the acquisition of new cognitions, the following are some ways of getting a valid measure of, for example, improvement in "demonstrating an understanding of the treatment sequence in social work practice. "

Knowledge

Define: Write a definition of the term *treatment sequence* from memory.

Identify: Given a list of terms pertaining to treatment, circle those that pertain to the treatment sequence.

Match: Given two lists, one showing terms pertaining to treatment (including all the terms that pertain to phases in the treatment sequence, the other showing correct definitions for all terms) draw a line from each term in the first list to the appropriate definition of that term in the second list.

Name: Write the names of five authors who have written about the treatment sequence, and name the book in which each of their discussions appears.

Comprehension

Rearrange: Given a mixed-up list of terms that describe steps in the treatment sequence, as well as other terms that refer to treatment techniques, write the steps of the treatment sequence in the proper sequence, and omit those terms that are not steps in the treatment sequence.

Explain: Explain, in writing, each phase in the treatment sequence, using no more than three sentences for each explanation.

Examples: Using one of your recently terminated cases, write a brief description of what you did with your client in each phase of the treatment sequence.

Application

Solve: In the case example that follows, the worker made mistakes in the early phases of the treatment sequence that led to the client's decision to drop out. How would you have handled this case in the early phases of treatment so that the client would not have dropped out? (Followed by a brief case example.)

Transfer of learning: Use a role theory framework to discuss the treatment sequence in relation to one of your clients.

Analysis

Compare: Here is a summary of two authors' descriptions of the treatment sequence. Discuss the differences between these two approaches, and indicate what you think are the strengths and weaknesses of each.

Diagram: Draw a flow chart that depicts the treatment sequence.

Synthesis

Design: Using what you know about your agency, and about the treatment sequence, design the most effective and efficient way to use staff at all phases of the treatment sequence.

Develop: Write a brief statement that is designed to orient new staff to the proper procedures for implementing the treatment sequence in our agency.

Assessment

Criticize: Assume that the statement you are about to read was written by a fellow staff member in regard to the "Sequence" question just posed. Write a critical commentary on this answer.

Rate: Using a scale of 1 to 5, in which 5 is "excellent" and 1 is "very poor," rate the staff member's written response to the "Sequence" question in relation to the following criteria: (1) references to professional literature, (2) clarity of expression, and (3) inclusiveness (ample coverage of the topic). Explain each rating. The total possible score is 15, since you can assign up to 5 points on each of the three criteria.

These items are meant to be suggestive rather than inclusive. If you were to use a written test, the discussion of questionnaires in Chapter 3, "Assessing Needs," should prove pertinent.

Skill Display

Using a skill display is time consuming, if you want a valid measure. Typically, you must do the following:

1. Identify and describe the particular skill to be assessed. (The task analysis format discussed in Chapter 3 should be used here.)
2. Identify and recruit one or more experts capable of judging the particular skill to be displayed. If possible, use at least two such judges to avoid the possibility that one judge is biased.
3. Prior to the judging, train the judges so that their interrater reliability is high. This can be done by having them independently judge an earlier sample of this performance (preferably on video- or audiotape), compare their judgments, and then resolve any discrepancies in their judgments until they achieve consensus.
4. Create a situation in which the skill display can take place under conditions that allow for maximum visibility and audibility (for the judges), yet is as natural as possible, so that the staff member's performance will not be unduly influenced by the assessment conditions.
5. If possible, record the performance. Videotape is best if it is feasible, but even audiotape is better than no mechanical recording at all. This recording can then be reviewed for judging purposes.

Other Ways to Measure Goal Attainment

Once the goals have been selected, and the criteria for success have been determined, define the indicators of "success" that are currently available (before the staff development activity begins) or that will need to be gathered but are not currently being accumulated. For example, if the goal of a staff development activity is to change the way in which supervision is done by adding group supervision to the already existing pattern of one-to-one supervision, and if staff members do not know the person who will eventually interview them in order to assess the staff development activity's success, it would be a good idea for the potential interviewer to get to know the staff so that they are not talking to a total stranger when the assessment interviews are conducted. If the goal is to lower the error rate on agency forms, a procedure needs to be developed, if one does not already exist, to measure the error rate easily.

EXAMPLES OF EVALUATION

EXAMPLE 13: THE GROUP HOME EXAMPLE

Staff teams in an agency composed of six group homes for adolescents decided that they needed to improve their performance as a team. Population of youth in each home varied from as few as five to as many as twelve. Here is a statement of the goals of this activity:

The desired outcome behavior will occur when each team returns to its staff meeting; hopefully, they will take the information gained from this exercise and use it to make themselves more effective in their team functioning, so that the team will be able to identify blockages to team functioning. They then use this realization at their staff meetings to work out solutions. These problems will be worked on at subsequent meetings until they are resolved to everyone's satisfaction. The measure of success will be a posttest survey to learn what each team realized as its particular problem in team effectiveness. Also, the survey will seek information on what they plan to do about it and by what date they will work on it. The survey will also ask them to describe the solutions they will be using.

Here is the report of the staff developer who managed this activity. He also describes the staff development activity itself:

My staff development project went better than I had anticipated. Not only did it facilitate communication between team members, but it also resulted in specific actions to improve team effectiveness. One surprising aspect of the rating scale that I did not expect was the intensity with which the members applied themselves. The interpersonal discussion that took place resulted in a deep exploration of working relations and personality conflicts. Also, the project had some areas that were weak and unclear to some of the participants. Before discussing the results and the things that need to be ironed out, I would like to review the goals of my task.

The aim of my project was to increase awareness of blockages to team effectiveness. This was accomplished through the use of a rating scale that was first filled out individually and then with the other team members. The autonomy of each of the six homes was guaranteed in this manner. Since there is a high staff turnover rate, this technique helped accelerate discussion between new team members. I feel that some of the topics presented were never really brought out at house meetings. This rating scale helped the teams to assess their working effectiveness.

The target population of the project was the line staff for each house, along with the supervisor. Some of the topics were unclear to some members, but with a few suggestions, all were able to carry out the task. Team members gave the project more enthusiasm than I had anticipated. Their extra efforts were rewarded by a deeper insight into their working relationship.

The information gained at the staff development project was then to be used at the next team meeting for individual houses. This was the desired outcome of my project. I did a follow-up survey one week after each house's team meeting. From the survey I learned that each house did bring up the staff development scale. The teams had been stimulated to explore and resolve their house's problems. Some of the teams merely congratulated themselves for doing a good job, while other teams arrived at specific resolutions.

The givens for this project were that the front-line staff, along with their house supervisor, would, at their next meeting, discuss and resolve blockages to team effectiveness. After they have learned this technique, it is hoped that it will be generalized to other problem areas (and their resolution) in the future.

The posttest survey revealed some interesting outcomes. House #1 used the rating scale as a measure of how good a job they were doing. This team has been together the longest in the agency, and they rewarded themselves with the good rating they gave to themselves. Thus, in this case, the scale served as a reinforcer, and I was also told that they are planning to use my scale for a six-month follow-up.

At House #2 it was determined that communication during shift change was a problem. They decided that important messages never got relayed through the log book. Their resolution consisted of purchasing a large bulletin board on which messages and important information could be tacked. In this way, letters from doctors concerning the youth or scheduled shift changes could be recognized upon entering the staff office.

At House #3 the supervisor has resolved to open herself up to more feedback on her role as house leader. The supervisor is a student as well as a full-time worker and was told that she tries to do too much. She told me that she now delegates more responsibility and has more free time.

House #4, which deals with the older boys in our program, decided they had a problem at shift change. The members felt that some of the details were not being totally attended to. This meant that newly arrived staff had to finish up the dishes or finish cleaning the living room. To resolve this, the members decided to list all duties not fully finished and to bring out the list at staff meetings.

House #5, the newest addition to the agency, had the most difficulty with this project. The house supervisor was very defensive as his team members opened up and told him some of the problems around the house. It was obvious that he took it personally, but later, at the time of the survey, he seemed relaxed and calm. He informed me that the project resulted in a more democratic procedure in house discussions. I was told that he now seeks a vote on more house matters than he did before. This allows more input for the team and should increase team satisfaction. I explained that this would also serve to motivate the team, because their vote is incorporated into the action that results.

Finally, at House #6 they decided that the division of duties was sometimes a problem. Their resolution was the construction of a staff calendar whereby each staff member was assigned a duty for a week and then rotated to a different task. By using the calendar, they were assured that each member carried out at least one task every week. . . .

The DSS example, quoted earlier, reported a highly successful outcome, according to the measures used by the staff developer:

EXAMPLE 14: THE DSS EXAMPLE (*continued*)

The following objectives for the training session were presented to staff, as part of a handout. They supplement the major goals of the project. . . .

1. Participants will be able to describe, in writing, their normal time use patterns through completion of a Time Management Questionnaire and/or Daily Time log.
2. Participants will be able to write a time management system analysis composed of individualized monthly, weekly, and daily planning and prioritizing of their own work and time.
3. Participants will be able to describe in writing (from memory) five key time wasters and ways to overcome them. They will be able to write a plan for themselves to eliminate one time waster per week.

In reviewing these objectives relative to the actual training session, I feel that the objectives were, in fact, achieved. The first objective was achieved prior to the pre-in-service staff meeting when participants completed the indicated processes. The use of time was discussed at the pre-in-service session as well as at the actual training session. Discussion indicated that the majority of the participants had gained a better understanding and grasp of their individual normal time use patterns.

The second objective was achieved during the session with each worker completing a daily time log. The workers were asked to utilize the monthly and weekly plans after the training session. They were instructed to submit the same to the supervisor beginning the following week. Monitoring of this request was done on a weekly basis by reviewing weekly work plans submitted by the workers for a period of two months. Indications of systems of prioritizing of work was apparent, and workers' plans showed improvement over the two-month monitoring period. Workers also completed monthly plans, which were reviewed for a three-month period. Workers were provided with suggestions for improvement throughout the monitoring period.

The first portion of the third objective was achieved during the training session, with workers listing five key time wasters on the flip chart provided. Although ways to overcome all the time wasters were not totally covered, workers did select one time waster and, as a group, provided suggestions for its elimination. The second part of the objective was achieved following the training session. Workers were assigned the project of selecting a time waster and developing and implementing their own plans for eliminating it. The workers were required to provide a report of their progress two weeks after the training session. At that time, if the time waster had been successfully eliminated, the workers were assigned a second time waster to work on. This was not done on a schedule of one per week as the objective indicated; however, the workers (over a three-month period) worked on eliminating time wasters. The success rate was outstanding even with our resistant worker. . . .

Finally, the evaluation process in the hospital example, referred to before, was not successful. First, the staff developer describes what did not work out as hoped; then she evaluates her own performance and what she learned from the experience. We can all learn from her example: Professionals should always evaluate the effects of their activities in relation to the outcomes for others. In the final analysis, staff developers must continually engage in self-evaluation as well.

EXAMPLE 15: THE HOSPITAL EXAMPLE (*continued*)

On the way out a few people mentioned what a good in-service it was. I understood what they meant because a "good" in-service to most of the staff means one where they do not just sit and get preached at. I smiled, of course, but I was not happy because I had different criteria for this in-service. None of the objectives had been met, and there were not going to be clear-cut methods to evaluate what the staff had learned from the in-service. JR and I agreed that now the evaluation would be largely subjective; in other words, is there a significant change in behavior of the staff in performing isolation techniques? This type of evaluation does not lend itself to precise record keeping and contains a multitude of variables. . . .

What I Would Do Differently

I spent a lot of time thinking about the preparations for the in-service and the actual event itself. To start with, I should have talked to some of the staff to learn how much interest there was, and to better plan what was important to the staff so that I could do better in predicting attendance. If I had done that, I would have planned my objectives to be more realistic about the time element. Or there was a second way to solve the problem: I could have kept the same objectives but asked the supervisors to assign a limited number of staff to any one in-service and then had more in-services to accommodate everyone. I think a combination of the two is the best method. Recently, there was an in-service where it was required of the staff to learn a new procedure. Having learned from my mistakes, we asked each supervisor to send no more than two people to any in-service. We offered the in-service for four consecutive days on all shifts, to allow for days off, illness, staffing emergencies, etc. There was then a very manageable number of people to instruct, and you could evaluate the learning.

Also, my in-service would have gone better if all the resource people had been there. R was off ill, and of course you do not anticipate that, but it brings up the question of what or who is essential to a program. Now, we had covered ourselves for R's absence only by accident, in that I was familiar with her presentation. Next time, when I am planning an in-service involving other presenters, it will be a group decision whether in the case of absence there will be coverage by someone else or the program be rescheduled. Also, we should have had the supervisor of microbiology there in the first place to answer any questions.

At first I was disappointed (if not downright depressed) about how the in-service had turned out. For all good intentions and time invested, it came across as poorly planned and poorly organized. The more I thought about it, though, the more I realized what a valuable experience it was. I learned many things and have since benefited from this knowledge.

On an informal basis the supervisors of the laboratory and Central Supply have reported an improvement in staff behavior concerning isolation technique. JR, infection control supervisor, has observed better techniques and fewer violations. In fact, this month we are having a repeat of the in-service on second shift at their request. Apparently they want to discuss the procedure now that they have lived with it for a while and problem-solve some areas. I will assess the other shifts for their interest in discussing the procedure again and what would be valuable for them. . . .

The guidelines that follow should help you to design evaluation procedures for staff development activities.

GUIDELINES FOR EVALUATION

In order to evaluate the degree to which goals have been achieved, you need to decide who or what you will measure. In some cases, you may want to evaluate directly the knowledge, attitudes, and skills of individual staff members. In some cases, you may want to gather data from relevant others who are in some way affected by the staff who participated in the staff development activity. In still other cases you may want to measure both. Here is your first question:

1. Who or what will you measure? _____

_____

2. Why have you made this choice? _____

_____

3. What plans have you made for each of the following? Include a discussion of why you chose your plan for each.

Baseline measures _____

_____

Midstream measures _____

_____

On-the-spot measures _____

_____

On-the-job measures _____

_____

4. What plans have you made to include independent measures—for example, different people's judgments of the same thing—to confirm the validity of

your measures? _____

_____

5. Why? _____

_____

6. How will you analyze the data you gather? _____

_____

7. To whom (if anyone) will you report your findings? _____

_____

8. Why? _____

_____

9. What form will your report take? _____

_____

10. Why? _____

    _____

11. What do you have to do *now* in order to be ready to gather your data—design a questionnaire, recruit judges for a skill display, and so on? _____

    _____

12. What preparations have you already made to gather your data? _____

    _____

13. What problems, if any, could these data cause? _____

    _____

14. What do you plan to do about these problems? _____

    _____

chapter 5

MAKING USE OF THEORIES OF LEARNING AND CHANGE

- This chapter takes up the following questions:
  How do the following theories of learning pertain to staff development?
    Stimulus–Response
    Cognitive–Discovery
    Andragogy
    Socialization
- How do staff members' attributes, such as race and sex, affect staff development?
- How do the following ways of learning affect staff development?
    Trial and error
    Modeling
    Verbal Instruction
- How do individual learning styles affect staff development?
- What is the significance of the following for staff development?
    Transfer of Training
    Guidance
    Learning Curves
    Failure to Learn

Because most staff development activities involve learning and change of some sort, it seems appropriate to look at what is known about learning and change and consider the implications of this large body of knowledge for the things that staff developers do. This chapter reviews some major theories about and approaches to learning and change and their relationship to various aspects of the teaching–learning process in staff development. In addition, several processes that affect learning and change will be discussed.

A DEFINITION OF LEARNING

"All instances of learning involve the learner in a behavior of some sort: he (or she) learns to do something" (Thyne, 1963, p. 21). In some instances, the results of learning are easily observed—for example, when someone who could not ride a bicycle before rides a bicycle unsupported, from here to there. In other cases the results of learning, although they involve an active response by the learner, do not lead to an immediately observable behavior. For example, when a person learns how to read and understand a blueprint, the observable behavioral result comes only when the person eventually builds something according to that blueprint. Sometimes people learn *not* to do something, such as changing the self-defeating habit of submitting incomplete paperwork after a deadline, but this often implies learning to do something else instead—in this case, turning in the completed paperwork on time.

Learning also implies a new way of behaving in a given situation. Individuals can be said to have learned how to ride a bicycle if, when given the opportunity to do so in the past, they could not ride one unsupported, but can do so now. In every instance of learning, an important factor is the situation itself. In this example that means being in the presence of a bicycle in good repair that is the appropriate size for this learner and is in a space large and safe enough for bicycle riding. The new behavior that has been learned is a response to that situation.

Finally, some learning is transitory. I may "learn" your name well enough to use it when meeting you for the first time, but I cannot be said to have learned it very well unless I can also use it the next time we meet—or, for that matter, ten minutes after I have first met you! We say that a person has learned something when it becomes a relatively regular part of his or her behavior.

Bass and Vaughan (1966, p. 8) define learning as "a relatively permanent change in behavior that occurs as a result of practice or experience." They refer to this as an "operational definition" since it addresses the *observability* of the results of learning. Clearly, people also learn internally—cognitively and attitudinally—and it is not always easy to link particular behaviors to particular "internal learnings." Their definition is operational, they say, because it refers to something that is "readily open to public observation and verification" (Bass and Vaughan, 1966, p. 8).

It would be naive to assume that all on-the-job learning by staff takes place through staff development. As Bass and Vaughan note, staff members are frequently unaware that they are learning:

> In fact, a great deal of learning is acquired below the level of conscious awareness...if questioned about his learning, the trainee in all likelihood would be unable to state what he had learned, or perhaps whether he had learned it at all.

Moreover, learning acquired without the trainee's awareness is typically more lasting and much more difficult to unlearn or change. The learning of basic attitudes and prejudices is the most obvious example of this phenomenon. (Bass and Vaughan, 1966, p. 12)

Although many people could accept Bass and Vaughan's definition of learning, there are several ways of conceptualizing the learning process; each leads its adherents into different approaches to facilitating learning. Biehler (1978) designates two views of learning that I think are relevant to staff development: (1) S–R (stimulus–response) and (2) cognitive–discovery. Also important is the work on andragogy, or adult learning (Ingalls, 1973). After reviewing each briefly, I shall add an equally brief discussion of the sociological concept of socialization as it pertains to learning in staff development.

APPROACHES TO LEARNING

S–R: The Stimulus-Response View of Learning

To understand the S–R view of learning, we can briefly look at four of its basic concepts: (1) drive, (2) stimulus, (3) response, and (4) reinforcer.

Drive (or motivation) refers to an organism's response to some internal or external stimulation or deprivation. There are two types of drives: *primary* (unlearned) and *secondary* (learned). An example of a primary drive is hunger, which is unlearned. An example of a secondary drive might be the desire to satisfy a primary drive, hunger, in a particular way (for example, at a fancy restaurant, in order to assert one's social status). Primary and secondary drives are linked: Secondary drives for such things as recognition, information, and status are viewed as learned ways of satisfying primary drives.

Stimulus (or cue) refers to something that elicits a response from an organism. This book is designed to be a stimulus to its readers, to elicit as a response the desire to learn more about staff development. Staff developers do their job in response to a complex array of drives, including their own need to eat (a primary drive), as well as to be successful in their work and to see their organization run better (both secondary drives). The stimulus for their actions might be a request from their superior to do something—via staff development—about a work problem; their own observation that something isn't working the way it should; or a response to reviewing the results of a needs assessment procedure.

A *response* is a behavioral result of stimulation. Sometimes the staff developer responds to a stimulus by taking action—perhaps by issuing a memo to all staff reporting the results of a needs assessment procedure, or by conferring informally with a colleague about the advisability of issuing such a memo. At other times the staff developer may respond to the stimulus of needs assessment results by going off to a quiet place for some private thinking.

The response B to a response A to a stimulus is called a *reinforcer* if it has the effect of continuing and strengthening response A, or increasing the frequency and/or intensity of response A. If the staff developer does send out a memo describing the results of the needs assessment procedure (A), and is praised by colleagues or by the boss for doing so (and, further, finds such praise (B) to be rewarding), then that praise tends to reinforce the memo-sending response. Chances are that this staff developer will use memos in the future to let staff know about the results of other needs assessment procedures.

This example suggests the introduction of two other important concepts: *punishment*—a response C to the response A that penalizes the individual for having made that response (for example, the boss bawls out the staff developer for having issued the memo before discussing its contents with her, making it less likely that this staff developer will issue uncleared memos in the future); or *extinction*—a lack of response (for example, if the memo is greeted by a deafening silence and is totally ignored by everyone, which again may have the effect of discouraging our staff developer from using memos in the future, since there is no reward (B) for having used a memo).

The S–R approach to learning grew out of laboratory experiments by such people as Pavlov (Yerkes and Morgulis, 1909), and Skinner (1968). Its adherents point to the "scientific" basis for this view. Unfortunately, much of this laboratory work was done with animals such as rats and pigeons, creatures not well known for making a response based on secondary drives. One criticism of the S–R approach is that the principles of learning that are developed from studies of such animals do not always provide a sufficient basis for understanding learning when the learners are human beings. For example, Skinner helped to promulgate programmed instruction, an approach that attempts to translate his research findings into an effective instructional technology. You may have been exposed to written programmed instruction at one time or other. Assuming the learner wants to learn the material taught by the program, the classical program proceeds, frame by frame, to provide stimuli in the form of bits of information or questions to which the learner must write a response. In order to reinforce learning, hints (or *prompts*) are built in to increase the likelihood of making the correct responses, so that the response can be rewarded and thereby reinforced. Unfortunately, Skinner and others sometimes forgot that proceeding frame by frame soon becomes very boring for the learner, and boredom can be a form of punishment. So although the principles of learning were empirically validated through research with animals, translating these principles into instructional activity for people has often proved difficult. (We can't really blame Skinner *et al.,* who probably had not had any experience with a bored pigeon. Satiated pigeons, yes; bored, no. In the final analysis, boredom is a very human affliction.) This frivolous aside is not meant to diminish the importance of the S–R view of learning; rather, it suggests that this approach has not answered all the questions about learning. The approach known as *behavioral modification* arose out of the S–R view of learning and has been shown to facilitate various kinds of learning—for example, the elimination of such bad habits as smoking and overeating—while also providing an extremely effective way for people to rid themselves of phobias, acquire assertiveness skills, and learn to manage test anxieties, to name but a few. And although evaluations of programmed instruction have shown that programs are not always effective, I have found (as both a consumer and an author of programmed instruction) that programs can be very helpful.

The major learning concepts developed from the S–R perspective are very useful to staff developers, as are the laboratory studies that generated them. Human learning, however, is simultaneously affected by so many variables that are not accounted for in the laboratory that an S–R view of learning, by itself, is not an adequate basis for staff development activities. In looking at the other views of learning, you may decide, as I have, that all of them are useful, and that no one of them has all the answers.

Before proceeding to the next approach to learning (cognitive–discovery), there are three more concepts developed by the S–R theorists that I want to call to your attention because they are so important for staff development. These are: (1) scheduling of reinforcement, (2) knowledge of results, and (3) generalization.

Scheduling of reinforcements refers to the time between a learner's performance and the presentation of a reward for that performance—rewarding every correct response to a stimulus, rewarding intermittently, rewarding with no particular pattern, and so on. When someone is learning something that is very new, it is often advisable to reward *every* correct response, since the learner may experience a failure to reward as extinction (no reward, hence no reinforcement). In time, however, it will probably not be feasible to reward every correct response, and occasional rewards will be sufficient to reinforce a response. Eventually, learners reward themselves for a correct performance, and that may be enough reinforcement to maintain or strengthen a response. Studies of scheduling have also examined the length of time between the performance of a new behavior and the time when the learner is rewarded. It has been found that if the reward is too long in coming, the learner may not make the connection between the particular response being rewarded and the reward itself. For example, if someone is learning how to use empathy in conducting an interview, rewarding the learner for effective use of empathy at various points in the interview is likely to interfere with the interview itself. If the interview is videotaped, however, and the learner and an instructor review the tape together, then the instructor can stop the tape (long after the actual interview has ended) each time the learner makes (made) a good empathic response, and praise the learner for it.

The concept of *knowledge of results* (also called *feedback*) is closely linked to reinforcement. It refers to the learner's receipt of information that confirms the correctness of his or her response. A person learning to shoot a rifle at a distant target needs to be informed after each shot whether he or she is aiming too high, too far to the left, and so on, in order to make the necessary adjustments in performance. Our novice bicycle rider knows immediately whether he or she is keeping the bicycle up and moving in the correct direction, but cannot recognize, without feedback from some other source, such as an instructor, that his or her posture is or is not appropriate to the development of riding habits that will lead to eventually doing sixty miles a day with ease. Without knowledge of results, it is very difficult for the learner to know which parts of what is being learned need further correction. Providing useful feedback is a major challenge for staff developers.

Generalization refers to the fact that learners will recognize a particular stimulus in a multitude of diverse situations, and will respond consistently with a correct response to that stimulus. For example, upon seeing a bicycle, our rider will mount it, facing front, and ride it from here to there, using the pedals correctly. He or she will be able to ride with just about as much ease on bicycles made by manufacturers other than the manufacturer of the one on which he or she learned. In one sense, this has to do with memory: I am able to repeat (at a later time, removed from the original learning situation) the things I learned in the instructional situation. As a concept, generalization will become very important when we discuss *transfer of learning* later in this chapter.

The Cognitive–Discovery View of Learning

The S–R view of learning postulates that the organism learns in order to satisfy primary drives (or secondary drives that become associated with primary drives). Piaget developed a view of the individual very different from Skinner's that had direct implications for learning: He believed that children will learn because they have an innate desire to make sense of what they observe and experience, in order to maintain a kind of cognitive equilibrium (Biehler, 1978). In this view, children do not have to be rewarded by a teacher for learning something (or induced to learn by being offered a reward if they learn), for, as children learn more and comprehend more fully, they achieve better coherence in their understanding of this world, which is its own reward. Notice how this shifts the nature of the teacher–learner interaction: In S–R, the teacher provides rewards, thereby reinforcing certain kinds of learning—learning that is controlled by the teacher. But in the cognitive–discovery view, the instructor's responsibility is to set things up and/or pose questions in such a way that the learners seek and discover the answers for themselves. So whereas a teacher who uses S–R principles preselects an instructional objective and may shape desired outcome behaviors through "successive approximations" (rewarding correct attempts to learn that are close to or right on the button of the predetermined steps to learning, while ignoring—that is, extinguishing—or punishing behaviors that are incorrect), the instructor using a cognitive–discovery approach would provide learners with problems to solve, or data to uncover—for example, a blank map on which they have to determine the names of cities, rivers, and so on in the region covered by the map. In a sense, learners in this situation *own* their own learning because they seek out and discover answers for themselves. Obviously, such a teacher must operate somewhere between challenging learners with dilemmas they will be unable to ignore (which would create an uncomfortable imbalance for learners) while providing challenges that are not so far beyond the learners' ability to solve that they end up settling for a simpler and perhaps less complete set of answers.

Those who have been interested in this approach to learning have also investigated it in the laboratory, but have used higher-order animals (such as apes) in loosely structured situations, to observe and learn from the ways in which these animals solve problems. Believing that the way in which individuals perceive situations determines how they will respond to them, they have tended to emphasize the teaching of inquiry and problem-solving skills. For example, Suchman (1965) presents children with a physics demonstration and encourages them to find out "why" by asking questions to which the teacher may only respond with "yes" or "no" (Biehler, 1978, p. 300). The session is tape-recorded and then reviewed, with the teacher helping the students to identify the kinds of questions they asked that identified key information, narrowed the focus, suggested other ways to do the demonstration, and so on. Bruner (1960), in one instructional package, suggests that the instructor emphasize contrasts, stimulate informed guessing, encourage participation in joint problem solving, and help students become more aware of the process they are using to solve problems (Biehler, 1978, p. 299). Bigge (1976) suggests introducing disturbing data that disagree with students' prior assumptions, as well as permitting students to make mistakes and then to review with the teacher why the mistakes occurred (Biehler, 1978, pp. 229 ff.). Perhaps the cognitive-discovery approach is best summed up by Albert Einstein's remark: " 'I never teach my pupils; I only attempt to provide the conditions in which they can learn' " (Walter and Marks, 1981, p. 1).

Bruner (1960) is a leading proponent of the "discovery" approach to teaching. He suggests that students will learn better and retain more when they have an overall view of a subject to be studied and grasp the principles that can be applied to a specific situation. In effect, Bruner would have people learn how to negotiate an enclosed maze by lifting the top off the maze and studying its design, whereas the S–R view would have a teacher instruct students in the particular steps that are most likely to get them through the maze.

Piaget (1970) and Bruner both argue that the understandings children arrive at on their own are usually more meaningful than those proposed by others, and that students need not be motivated or rewarded when they seek to make sense of things that puzzle them. When children are given a substantial amount of practice in finding their own solutions, they not only develop problem-solving skills, but also acquire confidence in their own learning abilities plus a propensity to function later in life as problem solvers (Biehler, 1978, p. 295). As with the S–R view of learning, the cognitive–discovery approach has its limitations. For better or worse, human beings have developed a great deal of knowledge about a great many things, including how to operate in a human service organization, so that it is not always necessary to learn by reinventing the wheel. There are, of course, advantages in giving staff the freedom to struggle with difficult problems, where old ways have not worked and true discoveries are needed. Further, my observation is that simple yet profound truths are often overlooked unless staff are allowed to discover them for themselves through some problem-solving method. For example, in a simulation game I helped to develop, someone in the role of school social worker attempts to influence the outcomes of decisions affecting elementary school students within one school. To do this, the "social worker" must negotiate with other players in the room who take the roles of vice-principal, parent, teacher, education reporter for the local newspaper, and so on. As one player learned while playing the role of school social worker, these negotaitions are most effectively done by going to the other person and talking with him or her privately in a corner of the classroom. This player tried to operate without ever leaving his chair (which, in this game, simulated his office) and steadily lost power in decision after decision. As he told me later, the lesson he learned was strikingly clear, and something he never forgot in later years: If you want to be influential in a complex organization, you have to get out of your office and wheel and deal, both within the organization and in the community—and most of this wheeling and dealing must take place out of public view. Sitting in your office and waiting for others to come to you, he found (during the game) was a sure way to lose power. A powerful discovery, and one that subsequently had considerable influence on the way he conducted his career. Obvious? Perhaps, but all of us overlook the obvious every day.

Nevertheless, to rely solely on discovery is to place the learner at a great disadvantage. Effective learning in staff development must also be efficient, and there are many subjects that can be taught and many problems that can be solved in a prestructured way. There is no reason, for example, that all staff members should create their own theories of personality, when there are so many glorious theories available to be studied.

For staff developers, the implications of the cognitive–discovery approach lie in those areas where the goals of a staff development activity are long-range and not too specific—for example, "better able to manage a particular kind of client population facing a particular kind of crisis"—as opposed to specific skill areas where a behavioral outcome can be observed and measured—for example, "use a word processor so that a letter-perfect copy can be produced." For example, using a simulation game in a problem-solving staff meeting places staff members in the kinds of ambiguous situations that allow for exploration and discovery of new insights, new solutions. To attempt to preprogram such learning according to an S-R approach would deprive learners of the opportunity of learning for themselves in a way that they are likely to remember. In fact, any staff development activity involving problem solving might profit from attention to this view of learning, including supervision, consultation, problem-solving staff meetings, participation in the development of an accountability system, or development of research on practice or organizational issues.

Andragogy

Knowles (discussed in Ingalls, 1973) takes the position that the education of adults (*andragogy*) differs significantly from the education of children (*pedagogy*) in four ways:

1. Adults view themselves as self-directing and do not expect to be treated as children. In a learning situation, they think of themselves as self-directed and see their relationship with the teacher as reciprocal, rather than dependent on the dominant teacher as the child is.

2. Adults bring vast quantities of accumulated experience into a learning situation, and this experience can be used as a vital resource in the learning situation. Knowles's view is that adults are therefore both teachers and learners in the learning situation, whereas children are primarily learners who draw from the teacher's experience.

3. In pedagogy, teachers use the concept of learning readiness to predetermine the sequence and content of what children must learn. Adults, however, having completed their basic education, can participate actively in selecting the content and method of their own learning, based on the multitude of needs they are currently experiencing.

4. Pedagogy is oriented to the child's use—in the future—of what is being taught today. Andragogy is *problem centered* rather than *subject centered* in that is it concerned with learning how to identify and solve problems in the present.

The implication of Knowles's work for staff developers is that they should not treat staff as children in the learning situation, but should make them partners in the learning process. His work is not incompatible with the cognitive–discovery approach described earlier. His work is thought provoking and potentially quite useful, but even adults can benefit at times from some well-organized pedagogy. A prime example has been the introduction of the microcomputer into all aspects of human service agency work. This has created a new type of illiteracy among adults, and it has required my generation of adults to return to "first grade" for a while, until we could learn how to make our computers analyze our data, serve as word processors, print our graphics, and the like.

Socialization: A Role Theory Perspective

A somewhat different approach to learning grows out of the work of sociologists who have attempted to describe and explain human behavior in relation to the expectations people have for one another (Biddle, 1979). According to role theory, individuals occupy social positions—categories of individuals who are similar in some respects, such as the positions *client, social worker,* or *secretary*—and each position has a cluster of expectations that are generally deemed appropriate for the occupant of the position. This cluster of expectations is called a *role*.

The term *socialization* refers to the process by which individuals learn to perform their roles in relation to the expectations of others, as well as internalizing the values that underlie these role performances. Once these values are internalized, individuals will fit comfortably into an existing social system, with their behavior controlled in a way that is acceptable to others in that system. The ultimate goal of socialization is to lead individuals to identify with the values of those who do the socializing in such a way that they control themselves in accordance with the expectations of the socializing agents.

In comparing socialization to the S–R approach, MacCoby writes:

A learning theorist would regard socialization as a learning process in which certain actions of the child are selected out by virtue of reinforcement, others tried and dropped because they are in some way punished or nonreinforced. . . . [However, identification refers] to the child's tendency to copy, to take on as his own, the behavior, attitudes, and values of the significant people in his life, even when the socializing agents have not said, "That's a good boy" or given him a piece of candy for performing these acts or holding these values. (MacCoby, 1961, pp. 29 ff)

How is the study of socialization any different from the study of learning itself? One might reply that in socialization studies, we study not only the child as learner, but also the parent as teacher (MacCoby, 1961, p. 24). In addition, socialization studies are typically carried out with people in real-life situations, not with laboratory animals. As in all social research, such studies involve trade-offs: The researcher may get a better sense of how learning occurs in the real world, but is unable to control for all the intervening variables that could be controlled in the laboratory.

Brim, in writing about socialization into adult roles, suggests that three conditions must be met if successful socialization is to occur (Brim and Wheeler, 1966). The individual, first, must want to perform the role; second, must have sufficient knowledge about the expectations for the role; and third, must have the ability to perform the role. To the degree that any of these conditions are ignored or mishandled, the socialization of the individual will be incomplete. For staff developers, this suggests that any activity that does not either respond to or attempt to build on staff members' motivation to play their job roles is likely to be ineffective in furthering the socialization of those staff members; similarly, if the job description is left vague, socialization probably will not work too well. Or, if the job description is specific but the expectations for the job role come into conflict with values that are important to the staff member, then motivation to play the role will be lowered. Finally, if an individual is hired (or accepted, as a volunteer) who so lacks the abilities required by the position that he or she would be unable to learn to meet the expectations (and/or to unlearn bad habits that could interfere with effective role performance), then the socialization process won't work. This suggests that staff development will be effective to the degree that it attends to *all* aspects of socialization: motivation, knowledge, and ability.

Those who have studied learning from an S–R perspective have tended to study it in a culture-free context, but the study of socialization, by definition, draws attention to the cultural context in which it occurs. The staff developer who wants to make use of knowledge about socialization notes that new staff members are socialized on many levels. In addition to the formal orientation procedure, the degree to which they become socialized to the organization's expectations depends on a complex interaction of several factors, including informal pressure from fellow staff members, previous training and experience, the particular discipline to which the individual belongs, the clarity of and consensus around the new staff member's job description, and various personal attributes of the new staff member—race, sex, ethnicity, socioeconomic background, age, and so forth. Staff development is often used as the organization's formal way of socializing new staff through orientation, in-service training, supervision, and the like. But staff developers would indeed be naive if they thought that theirs was the only set of expectations with which new staff members have to contend. At the same time, it is helpful to know that staff developers can perform a vital socializing function in giving new staff members the knowledge they need to perform their role, training them to hone the skills they have (and to acquire new skills they will need), and enhancing their motivation to do their jobs as staff members of this organization.

A Comment on Staff Attributes and Staff Development

Given developments since the 1960s in civil rights and equal opportunity employment legislation, staff developers would do well to recognize the effects of staff member attributes such as race, sex, and age on staff development activities. For example, Royster (1972) has described the very special set of problems facing the black supervisor. He describes the black movement as emphasizing

> the revitalization of the role and dignity of the black man...to unite the black community in its struggle toward independence and self-determination, and its combat with white racism. (Royster, 1972, p. 78)

This movement has helped to impel many black students to enter the helping professions, such as social work. There they may discover black supervisors experiencing a role conflict:

> Because the supervisor is management, he is caught between fostering agency norms and the black workers' concern for and hopeful championing of the cause of black clients...the black worker can often afford to take the role of client and reflect client moods and desires; the black supervisor does not have this luxury. Reacting only as a black could be disastrous for the agency, its total clientele, the professional, the profession and indeed, for the black community.
>
> The black supervisor is in greater conflict over his commitment to the black movement. The greater the commitment, the greater the dilimma of whether to bring the white workers' racism into focus, and whether to teach and administer from a black perspective. (Royster, 1972, p. 80)

In a different vein, Reed (1981) addresses gender issues in her discussion of the training of female group leaders. She notes that small-group theory and research, until recently, generally ignored sex as a major variable. She then cites this recent research to support her view that there are significant differences in the characteristic behaviors of men and women in groups. One problem these differences create are the expectations women have for themselves when they are training to become group leaders:

> ...a woman trainee is likely to blame herself for not being able to make groups work the way "the books say they should," and the way they do when she co-leads with a man. (Reed, 1981, p. 167)

The two examples just cited represent a very abbreviated discussion of the ways in which staff member attributes can affect the staff development process. It's one thing for the staff developer to be "color blind," by which most of us mean "free from prejudice": It's quite another to pretend that staff attributes have no impact on staff behavior or on staff as learners. It's even worse to *ignore* or be insensitive to the effects of staff member attributes on staff development. One must always ask: What are the significant attributes by which one might describe staff, and how do these attributes affect their views of themselves and their relationships with others? Are there, for example, interracial tensions just below the surface that are affecting team work? Do the women on staff feel that the male director of the agency is insensitive to their felt needs? Do older staff members, faced with a far younger (but professionally trained) supervisor, find that age is a barrier to their learning?

Asking this kind of question (and, in so doing, perhaps uncovering some problematic tension) is no guarantee that solutions can be found. But if we are going to try to base our staff development process on some understanding of human learning, we must include such questions in our planning.

THREE WAYS TO LEARN

There are at least three ways of helping people to learn: (1) trial and error, (2) modeling, and (3) verbal instruction. Each can play a part in producing a relatively permanent change in an individual's response to a situation. These often occur in some combination, but for purposes of clarity, I will discuss each in turn.

Trial and error

This is the most common way in which people learn. From infancy on we reach, we grasp, we crawl—sometimes with encouragement, sometimes without, always moving toward greater mastery of ourselves and our environment. In the human services, trial-and-error learning often occurs because no one has the time to instruct. Many employees, after a short period of orientation to acquaint them with an organization's policies and procedures, are told: "Here are your keys. Now get out there and do your job." Indeed, in an institute on staff development I once conducted, an executive director angrily said to me: "I hire people because they have the experience and ability we need. To instruct them would be to insult them. You seem to think staff development should go on as long as they're here. I don't. Let them figure it out for themselves, is my motto." This sink-or-swim approach is a common philosophy.

The cognitive–discovery approach to learning relies heavily on trial and error, and there is no doubt that it can result in effective—if sometimes painful—learning. By itself, however, trial-and-error learning can lead to the acquisition of inefficient ways of doing things, and the development of bad habits that are difficult to overcome.

So, for example, a staff member can fall into the habit of beginning interviews with a new client in an informal fashion: "Hi, my name is Mary Smith, but you can call me Mary. And I'll call you John, O.K.? Now, John,...", even though the individual addressed as "John" may find this approach offensive and yet feel constrained from saying so. When coupled with modeling and/or verbal instruction, however, trial and error can help individuals learn something extremely well, because it allows them to adapt the response to their own way of doing things.

The S–R approach to learning is often deliberately structured so as to guide an individual into making a correct response, in order to reward—and thus reinforce—that response. Trial and error is therefore less appropriate to this learning approach. As for learning by socialization, unfortunately we are often socialized into certain ways of thinking and acting by the mistakes we make (and the punishment we experience for making these mistakes). Too much punishment, however, may make this kind of learning too painful as well as inefficient. Accordingly, while recognizing the inevitability of trial and error in socialization, it is best not to rely on it alone when socializing a new staff member into a position.

Modeling

Americans who have tried to learn how to eat Asian cooking with chopsticks know that neither trial and error (should I hold one stick in each hand?) nor detailed verbal instruction is anywhere near as valuable as simply watching someone who is already well versed in the use of chopsticks and who says, "Watch me, then do as I do." Learning by imitation is a common and extremely efficient way of acquiring new behaviors.

Research—much of it related to the S–R approach to learning—has taught us a lot about effective modeling. For example, Miller and Dollard (1941) found that imitation was likely to occur when someone who had observed a model in action was rewarded for imitating that model. Subsequently, Bandura and Walters (1963) found that observers would imitate a model even when not rewarded for that imitation, providing they saw the *model* being rewarded during the observation in a way the observers would have liked to be rewarded. For the staff developer who wants to exploit knowledge about modeling, this suggests that learners will learn best if they are given a chance to imitate an effective performer, if they see the performer rewarded (for example, with praise and acclaim) and if they themselves are rewarded for those aspects of their attempt to imitate that are more or less correct. Further, it has been found that people are more likely to imitate a model on the basis of the model's presumed expertise (Divesta, Meyer, and Mills, 1964), higher social status (Harvey and Rutherford, 1960) ability to control rewards that the observer wants (Bandura, Ross, and Ross, 1963), and perceived similarity with the observer (Rosenkrans, 1967). These findings have clear implications for staff developers, whether they offer themselves as models or recruit individuals with particular kinds of expertise to serve as models. For example, using someone to teach computer illiterates like me how to use a microcomputer for data analysis is less likely to work if the demonstrator speaks in computer jargon and goes through complicated steps too quickly. I couldn't possibly imitate that—not for all the M&Ms in the world. But if (1) it's made clear that not too long ago the person designated as a model was also a computer illiterate, like me, and if (2) the model speaks English with only a sprinkling of computer jargon, and if, (3) the model breaks up the demonstration so I can try out what I have observed and be rewarded—both with praise *and* with the computer's continued smooth operation—then I have a good chance of learning from this model.

Flanders (1968), in his review of literature on modeling, found that a combination of model-rewarded-in-the-presence-of-the-observer and observer-rewarded-for-imitative-learning-attempts is probably the best way to learn from a model. My own work in this area has led me to propose the following guidelines for a social group worker's use of modeling: The guidelines seem applicable to staff development.

A. Modeling can be used to teach someone how to say or do something when there is sufficient evidence to indicate that they are unable to do that something acceptably well.
B. A learner will be more likely to imitate a model correctly, in the future, without monitoring, if any of the following conditions are met:
    1. If the learner agrees voluntarily to learn particular behaviors by imitating the actions of a model;
    2. If the model behaves in a consistent fashion when demonstrating the behavior to be learned;
    3. If the learner observes that model being rewarded for the demonstration;
    4. If the learner perceives that the model has expertise with regard to the behavior to be learned;
    5. If the learner perceives that the model controls resources that are valuable to the learner;
    6. If the learner perceives that the model has a somewhat higher status than the learner's status;
    7. If the learner believes that the model and the learner are similar in some respect that is significant to the learner;
    8. If the model's demonstration is highly visible to the learner, and the learner is aware of the cues to which the model is responding[1] during the demonstration; and
    9. If the learner is rewarded for providing a good approximation of the model's demonstration.

[1]In this case, *cue* refers to those things the model perceives that lead to a particular performance; for example, when driving a car and approaching a corner at which the model plans a turn, the model moves the turn indicator, applies foot to brake so as to slow the car, waits for the traffic to clear, and then completes the turn. There are several relevant cues here: recognizing the place to turn, recognizing the appropriate devices to use (turn indicator and foot brake), recognizing the clear road conditions, and finally recognizing the car's appropriate equipment to complete the turn (steering wheel and accelerator pedal). Unless the observer knows about the cues that caused the model to behave in a particular way, the observer may—in trying an imitation—act at the wrong time, with disastrous results.

C.   Learning by imitation is most likely to be effective when it occurs in the following sequence: demonstration by a model, imitation by a learner, feedback to the learner on the attempted imitation, and improvisation—by which is meant that the learner attempts an approximate imitation of the model's demonstration given a different set of circumstances or cues for the learner's performance. (Bertcher, 1978, p. 241)

Given this idealized set of procedures for effective and efficient modeling, it should be recognized that much of what has been learned about modeling has been studied by scholars interested in the S–R approach (see, for example, Flanders, 1968, and Bandura and Walters, 1963). Scholars interested in socialization have also drawn attention to the importance of modeling in learning to perform a role (see, for example, Biddle, 1979). On the other hand, the primary use of modeling in relation to the cognitive–discovery approach would be to encourage observors to emulate a competent individual's approach to the process of discovery. The discovery itself belongs to the individual, and cannot be experienced by watching a model.

Verbal Instruction

I have separated *modeling* from *verbal instruction* because the latter relies so heavily (for instructional effect) on words, spoken and/or written—words that are used to convey information and/or guide action. (Modeling also relies on verbal instruction to call attention to various aspects of a demonstration, but its major impact comes from the visible and/or audible demonstration.) People often learn by some combination of trial and error, modeling, and verbal instruction. For example, the music teacher first lets a student sight-read a new piece (trial and error); then explains some aspect of pianistic technique (verbal instruction); then says, "Now, watch how I hold my hands while I'm playing"; and then plays the new piece in such a way as to demonstrate a particular technique (modeling). But the fact that these three basic ways of teaching can be combined does not rule out the idea that they can be studied separately.

Since verbal instruction relies on words, effective instruction requires that instructor and student use a common langugage and that they continually work on defining and clarifying the meaning of the words they use. Thus, for example, I have started several chapters of this book with definitions. In some cases my definitions may differ from the ones with which you are familiar; you may even disagree with the definition I have chosen to use. But at least you should have a pretty good idea of how I am using key words in this book.

Verbal instruction in staff development can take many forms. (These are discussed in greater detail in the next chapter.) Here are just a few:

The lecture.   This is probably the most common way in which people attempt to impart information and opinion. Lectures provide a good way of condensing and presenting ideas economically, particularly new ideas that are not yet available in written form. The lecture has sometimes been called the professor's "security blanket," because presumably the professor knows the subject well enough to discourse on it for a period of time without an awkward amount of preparation, and, if he or she lectures strenuously enough, disturbing questions and challenges from students can be avoided (McKeachie, 1969).

Although a well-organized, well-presented lecture can inform, delight and even inspire, it has many shortcomings, chief of which is that it does not require or even allow the audience much active responding that would give them a way to test their understanding of the lecture. A study by Natfulin, Donnelly, and Ware (1973) also demonstrated that a well-coached actor who presents an amusing lecture with conviction—a lecture designed to contain nothing of substance—can convince a highly sophisticated audience that they have learned a great deal from the lecture.

Assigned reading.   This is simply a lecture in written form. Unlike parts of a lecture, however, passages in a book or journal that are unclear can be reread if the meaning is at first unclear. In addition, a book is portable, easily available, used at the learner's convenience, comparatively inexpensive, and able to hold much more information than can be delivered in a lecture. In recent years, some books have employed a programmed instruction format, requiring active responding and providing corrective feedback to the reader. Several forms of reading are used in staff development—agency manuals, journal articles, case studies, and the like— although full-length books appear to require more time than many staff members are willing or able to allot.

Group discussion.   Students of small-group theory have demonstrated in some detail the numerous ways in which people's values, perceptions, and beliefs are influenced by group participation (see, for example, Shaw, 1981, or Napier and Gershenfeld, 1981). Discussion seems particularly useful when a teacher wants:

1. to give students opportunities to formulate principles in their own words and to suggest application of these principles.
2. to help students become aware of and to define problems based on information derived from readings or lectures.
3. to gain acceptance for information or theories counter to folklore or previous beliefs of students.
4. to get feedback on how well his instructional objectives are being achieved. (McKeachie, 1969, p. 37)

Combining lecture with small-group discussion is a typical way to deal with the problem that can arise from the absence of active student response to a lecture, referred to earlier. In addition to the foregoing, discussion is used in staff development to develop group solutions to complex problems. In such discussions, participants learn from one another by exposing their ideas to the ebb and flow of group interaction. The value of group discussion for problem solving is often related to the verbal skills of the discussion leader in keeping the group on track, achieving a fair balance of participation, and facilitating movement toward consensus. Ineffective discussion leading can make a sham of "democratic" participation, resulting in diminished benefits for a staff group.

As indicated earlier, each of these ways to learn can be combined with the others. The sequence of verbal instruction, then modeling, and then trial and error appears likely to be effective in helping staff members acquire new or improved learning. In addition, each of these approaches can make use of underlying notions about learning from the perspective of the S–R or cognitive–discovery theories, andragogy, or concepts of socialization.

A NOTE ON INDIVIDUAL LEARNING STYLES

Regardless of the work that has been done on the learning process, experience in the classroom has taught me that no single approach to the teaching–learning process is equally useful for all students: Students learn—as individuals—in different ways. Some students want to experience something first and *then* talk about it, in an attempt to conceptualize their specific experiences; others want to read about it, talk about it, hear about it, and think about it, before they ever try to *do* it. To categorize any one way of learning as better than any other is silly; rather, the motto "Different strokes for different folks" seems to apply. Time after time, students in the same class split fifty-fifty on issues of "You should lecture more, explain the text more, control the classroom more" versus "We should have more in-class discussion, more sharing of experiences, more facilitating (than lecturing) by you."

The important point here is that you, as a staff developer, will very likely find, among the staff you attempt to develop, people who learn best in diverse ways, and you should be prepared to offer more than one method by which they can learn. Additionally, it doesn't hurt to consult with them, before beginning an activity, about their learning style preference. Even there, however, you have to be careful: I have known of agency staff groups that expressed a preference for verbal instruction via a lecture presentation for in-service training, not because they preferred to learn by lecture but because a lecture presented less danger that their failures to learn would be exposed. When that happens (or when you suspect that is the problem) you have to choose between staff's comfort and your wish to engage them in more experiential (modeling and/or trial-and-error) learning experiences, because you are convinced that they cannot learn in any other way. I might be able, for example, to give you an interesting lecture on "how to play the guitar," but until I place a guitar in your hands and show you a few licks, I don't see how I can teach you to play it. Still, I may have to accept your unwillingness to pick up the instrument, here and now, in the hope that you will be more willing to risk failure once you trust *me* better.

When I present the chapter on the management of particular staff development activities, you will want to remember that individual staff members learn best in different ways.

INSTRUCTIONAL ISSUES

A number of issues need to be considered when planning for and using any form of staff development: (1) the transfer of training, (2) practice, (3) guidance or prompting, (4) learning curves, and (5) failure to learn.

Transfer of Training

Anyone who has ever been a student knows that the number one goal in many courses is just to pass the course. All too often, that is not only the number one goal—it is the only goal: Pass the final exam, and then forget it all.

As a teacher, I hope all my students will pass my courses, but I also want something more: I want them to *learn* something from the course that they can take away (that is, *transfer*) and use outside the classroom. In commenting on transfer, Biehler states:

> In order to make learning more than a pointless ritual, teachers need to concentrate on finding ways to help students use what they learn, continue to learn, and feel positive about learning. When such a learning outcome occurs, psychologists say transfer has taken place, because what is learned in school transfers to out-of-school situations. (Biehler, 1978, p. 453)

Bass and Vaughan offer the following definiton of transfer:

> Stated simply, transfer of training deals with whether or not learning in one situation will facilitate learning (and therefore performance) in subsequent similar situations. There are, of course, three possibilities: (1) *positive transfer:* learning in one situation enhances learning or performance in a new situation; (2) *negative transfer:* learning in one situation inhibits learning or performance in a new situation; . . . [and] (3) *no observable effect,* sometimes referred to as "zero transfer". . . . (Bass and Vaughan, 1966, p. 38).

Here's a simple example: Learning to drive one make of car should make it comparatively easy to drive a different make of car, providing they both use an automatic shift. That's *positive transfer.* Learning to drive on the right-hand side of the road can create a situation of *negative transfer* (and, speaking from personal experience, near disastrous results) when you find yourself in a place where it is customary to drive on the left-hand side of the road. *Zero transfer* is what occurred when I found myself trying to learn how to "drive" a totally different transportation device—a small sailboat—where my car-driving ability neither helped nor hindered my learning.

This notion is so straightforward that it seems simplistic. Where we go awry is in thinking that general *knowledge* transfers easily into skillful *performance.* Someone gives a lecture (allowing for questions and discussion) about the best way to conduct an interview with a parent who has abused his or her child. The lecture includes a comprehensive review of research on the factors that appear to cause child abuse, a description of the ways in which child abuse occurs, and a presentation of the best approaches to use with an angry and defensive child-abusing parent. Based on this lecture, the learner is expected to sally forth and manage interviews skillfully with child-abusing parents, or with children who have been abused. Unfortunately, the general knowledge gained from the lecture is probably not sufficient to effect positive transfer of the *skills* the learner is expected to use on the job—skills in conducting an interview focused on a particular kind of problem, with a particular parent. What the lecture and discussion *may* do (in the way of positive transfer) is to make it possible for learners to pass a written test of general knowledge on the subject. For a staff developer, that really should not be a sufficient goal.

There are several things you can do to facilitate positive transfer (I am assuming you want to avoid both negative and zero transfer). First, you can include, in the learning experience, elements that are similar to—if not identical with—elements that are likely to be found in the performance situation. According to Ellis:

> Similarity is a complex variable in that there are several ways in which it can be measured....In general, similarity has been defined in three ways: (1) scales of similarity have been constructed, based upon the judgment of subjects, (2) similarity has been defined in terms of variation along some known physical dimension such as size or intensity, and (3) similarity has been defined in terms of transfer itself, which is most unsatisfactory. (Ellis, 1965, p. 16)

It may not be the *number* of similar elements that affects transfer, however, but the *importance* of any one element to effective performance. In going from the everyday experience of driving on the right to the unaccustomed experience of driving on the left, even though almost all the other elements are similar (steering wheel on the left, lots of cars on the road, good visibility for driving, and so forth), one key element (direction of traffic flow) is so dissimilar, so opposite to all our driving habits, that if we have to make a quick turn into heavy traffic, our driving habits can create a serious accident.

Even in role playing, when rehearsing a common event, if the role-played situation is too dissimilar from the future performance situation, positive transfer may not occur. For example, the learning situation may offer an overly cooperative role player who makes everything too easy; a quiet room, although actual performance will have to take place amid many distractions; or even (for some people) the knowledge that the role play itself is make-believe (with no negative consequences for failure). All these factors can create enough dissimilarity to diminish or negate positive transfer. Therefore, the more similar the learning and performance situations, the more likely it is that positive transfer will occur.

Another factor that affects transfer is one's skill in learning how to learn. The cognitive–discovery approach to learning discussed earlier teaches a process of problem solving, not a number of previously determined answers. Ellis cites studies in which students who were taught list after list of nonsense syllables achieved "mastery" of each successive list with increasing speed; they had learned *how to learn*—for example, how to use some word association device to help implant the nonsense syllables in their memory (Ellis, 1965). Ellis notes that cumulative practice in learning a series of related tasks or problems leads to increased facility in learning how to learn.

For social workers, this could be translated (for example) into learning how to write an assessment of a client's problem by doing a number of practice written assessments—learning how to use words economically, how to recognize and describe key elements in a client's stressful situation, how to describe apparent cause-and-effect relationships, and the like. A good rule of thumb for facilitating positive transfer might be based on the degree to which there is or is not a standardized way to do something. The more standard the event, the harder you should strive for similarity between the learning and the performance situations. There is a fairly standardized way to drive in heavy traffic—a set of skills—but the range of discretion involved in writing an assessment of a client's situation is very wide, so that it is, in many ways, a nonstandard event. In the former situation, you might work for maximum similarity between learning and performance situations (for example, the driving instructor might have you drive your car through the downtown parts of your city so you can learn how to drive in traffic), whereas in situations where the performance is nonstandard (that is, there is no one way to do something correctly), greater attention is given to learning to learn such things as how to quickly recognize the meaning of nonverbal responses during an interview. Bruner describes this as "nonspecific transfer," saying:

> . . . it consists of learning initially not a skill but a general idea which can then be used as a basis for recognizing subsequent problems or special cases of the idea originally mastered. (Bruner, 1960, p. 17)

To facilitate transfer, Ellis also suggests that you provide the learner with adequate exposure to whatever is to be learned, provide for a variety of examples when teaching concepts and principles, label or identify important features of whatever is to be learned, and make sure that general principles are understood before expecting much transfer (Ellis, 1965).

Practice

Almost everyone remembers learning to ride a bicycle. Chances are you would never have mastered it if you hadn't had numerous chances to acquire the sense of balance and control needed to move the bicycle smoothly from here to there. I remember my daughter's frustration when she tried to learn computer math in high school because her time using one of the few microcomputers at her school was so limited (fifteen minutes at a clip) and she was so harassed by the next student in line breathing down her neck that she couldn't devote her full attention to learning. To learn something, we each must have numerous opportunities to try to learn it (with, as mentioned in the discussion of the S–R approach, feedback on the correctness of our performance) so that we can develop the smooth, confident, competent performance of the expert. Bass and Vaughan (1966), summarize a number of studies to show that *distributed practice* (practice spread out over time) often leads to greater mastery than *massed practice* (a large amount of practice at one time). Many people believe this is because distributed practice allows for rest periods and the dissipation of the fatigue and frustration that often accompany learning attempts. In this vein, one of my teachers taught me a maxim that I still find useful: "The head can take in what the seat can endure." Distributed practice recognizes the wisdom in that saying. In a more serious vein, Biehler reports that distributed practice works best when the content to be learned is divided into small parts because of the "serial-position effect":

> The serial position effect is the tendency of people to learn and remember the words at the beginning and end of a long list more easily than those in the middle. When you use short lists, you in effect eliminate the hard-to-memorize middle ground. (Biehler, 1978, p. 438).

For the staff developer, this means that limited exposure—for example, only one or two chances to try to do a new task—is probably insufficient to produce much learning.

Guidance or Prompting

It should be noted that trial-and-error learning, as previously discussed, is a form of practice. Because it often occurs in an unstructured way, however, there is little opportunity for objective feedback, so the seat-of-the-pants learning that can occur may result in the learning of clumsy ways to do things. Guidance during practice can solve this problem. The instructor teaching correct use of a micro-computer at the student's elbow can quickly correct errors, praise correct use of the computer, demonstrate how to program tricky content, and see to it (at least during the lesson) that practice is on target. Programmed instruction is structured to provide guidance (or prompts, or hints) in a way that pretty well assures success as the student learns, step by step. The program asks, "What is the capital of France?" and the reply is written, "The capital of France is PA__IS." You fill in the letter "R," turn the page, and learn that the correct answer *is* "R"! Then, in addition, the program rewards you (assuming you wrote in "R" to begin with) by saying, "Good for you, if you wrote 'R'!" The guidance or prompt you received ("PA__IS") was designed to make your learning attempts successful by allowing you to be rewarded and to have this particular response reinforced. (Not all programs are this simplistic, but the notion of guiding you to a correct response is very common in programmed instruction.) Since an autonomous performance is the eventual goal, however, guidance cannot go on forever, or the learner will learn only *with the guidance as an essential part of the performance to be mastered*—something you do not want to occur. So you run alongside your youngster's bicycle, holding on to the seat in order to maintain her unsteady balance (and, with the aid of this guidance, she experiences the sensation of balancing a bicycle), removing your hand for a bit to see if she can keep going—and then, when you are sure that she can, you let go completely (and, thankfully, stop running). Suddenly the learner has the thrill of knowing that she has learned what she set out to learn and no longer needs your close guidance. In many cases, guidance is what makes learning possible.

Learning Curves

As guidance is removed (sometimes called "fading the prompt") the learner—through practice—becomes a better and better performer. Many attempts have been made to measure the speed of learning so that instruction can be timed in such a way as not to go too slow (and bore the learner) or too fast (and leave the learner, so to speak, in the dust). The concept of a *learning curve* "indicates the extent to which the rate of learning increases or decreases with practice" (Bass and Vaughan, 1966, p. 43.).

Learning curves vary depending on the kind of learning to be mastered, the situation in which the learning occurs, the learner's motivation to learn, and the learner's ability to learn. In some situations, learning may occur very slowly at first, but may speed up after some particularly difficult component has been mastered. In other cases, learning may proceed at a satisfactory rate for a time, followed by a period in which little or no learning is apparent, despite repeated practice. Learning plateaus (in which learning has occurred up to a point but suddenly slows down) are typical parts of learning curves and are often followed by a spurt in learning. According to Bass and Vaughan, several ideas have been advanced to explain plateaus in the course of learning:

1. a series of habits has to be learned, each more complex than the other (e.g., learning a foreign language that uses a different alphabet than ours), the plateau comes at a period in which a new type of more complex learning (e.g., the grammar of the language) is slowly beginning;
2. motivation declines, e.g., the novelty of a new learning method wears off;
3. no new learning is evident but a lot of incorrect learning is being eliminated;
4. when learning complex content composed of several parts, each new part puts new demands on the learner which, in time, are easily managed (Bass and Vaughan, 1966, pp. 46 ff.).

If one can anticipate when plateaus are likely to occur, learning time can be reduced, thereby encouraging both learner and teacher. For example, if motivation lags because novelty has worn off, one could add a different learning approach or a change in pace, spaced in time so as to maintain high motivation.

Failure to Learn

Some people are slower learners than others or are better at one kind of learning than another; some people, as just indicated, experience plateaus in the course of learning. But what about people who don't learn acceptably well?

Some teachers view poor learners as a challenge, but others are very hard on those who apparently can't learn as well as they are expected to learn. It's almost as if teachers experience such learners' failure as a reflection on their ability to teach, so they reject those who fail to learn in order to blot out their own feelings of failure.

In studying the education of counselors, Carkhuff (on the basis of tests he and his associates had devised) found that some applicants lacked even minimal levels of empathy, nonpossessive warmth, and genuineness—three qualities they had found were crucial for effective interpersonal helping (Carkhuff, 1969). These individuals, they found, did not benefit (that is, did not learn) from their instruction, and entry tests were eventually devised to screen out such applicants. Increasingly, they discovered that faculty members (already in place) who fell below minimal levels on these three qualities caused the performance level of acceptable students to deteriorate over time.

Many people have studied students' attitudes toward failure. They analyzed individuals' *level of aspiration* and found that people tend to raise their goals after a success and to lower them after a failure (Hoppe, 1930, and Sears, 1940). Atkinson (1964) developed a more comprehensive explanation of this phenomenon, based on McClelland's (1965) notion that people acquire a need to achieve and a contrasting need to avoid failure. For some people, particularly those who have earlier experienced many failures, the need to avoid failure leads them to set impossibly high goals (if they don't succeed, they can't be blamed for failing to achieve such difficult goals) or very low goals (at which they are likely to succeed, while learning little).

Since learners experience failure as a punishing experience, it seems advisable to create as many opportunities for success as possible. This is where *guidance* is used. In addition, it may be wise to go slower, demand less, and pitch the instruction at a level such that you avoid too many failures. Bass and Vaughan say, "the task should be difficult enough to be challenging, but not so difficult that most trainees cannot successfully complete it" (Bass and Vaughan, 1966, p. 63). Some educators grade on a curve, with the clear intention of eliminating a percentage of students who do not measure up. Most staff development activities do not have this intent; it is unlikely that they could survive if they did. Human service work is difficult enough without designing staff development so as to be sure that some staff will "flunk."

Often, learning attempts produce a mixture of failures and successes. Many studies of the S–R approach note the tendency of the instructor to attend only to the failures, while taking the successes for granted. The result is that *failure* is rewarded (with attention), which can inadvertently serve to reinforce it, particularly when the correct portion of the performance is ignored. The moral is: Always reward the correct portion of the performance to be learned *first,* before trying to correct less-than-adequate learning. If the entire performance is unacceptable but there has apparently been a sincere attempt to learn, reward the attempt.

If we continue to encounter failure, however, we have no choice but to confront it as such. This should follow a conscious, open effort to call the learning problems to the learner's attention, and a stated willingness to work with them on these problems. If staff members receive an annual written evaluation containing the surprise information that they have failed to learn how to do some aspect of their job acceptably well—surprise, because it has never been discussed with them before—then the evaluation system itself has failed, because no prior information was given that the staff member was failing.

Staff development programs that threaten staff members with dire consequences if they fail often produce sufficient motivation to meet learning *requirements,* but they may also make it harder for the individual to learn, or may lessen their motivation to transfer the learning to the performance situation.

Further, staff development activities that create failure (that is, staff members do not believe the goals of the activity have been reached, and their needs remain unmet) will lead to a decrease in willingness to participate in staff development. Blaming staff for failure to learn may be our way of defending against our own sense of failure. We should remember that if the majority of staff fail to learn, staff developers have to ask themselves where *they* have failed, rather than blaming the staff.

As indicated earlier, failure in human service work is not uncommon: we possess imperfect technologies and use them in complex organizations that make success difficult to achieve. Maslach (1982), Cherniss (n.d.), and others have noted that burnout often results from staff members' failure to achieve even modest goals. In a sense, needs in staff development grow out of failures of individual staff, the organization, or both. In that context, it is more important than ever that staff developers capitalize on earlier failures to produce more successful results.

Conclusion

The class was sharing internship experiences. "My field placement," said one student, "is just like sex." I was a bit puzzled: The student was the wife of a local minister and was not noted for making rash or provocative statements. "Could you explain that?" I asked, a little uneasy about the answer she might give. "Sure," she replied. "I'm supposed to be learning how to conduct an interview. So what happens? The client and I go in a room, close the door, and fumble around. It's just like sex." She went on to explain that she had never seen anyone conducting an interview, nor had anyone ever watched *her* conduct an interview and then given her feedback on her performance.

More recently, students have been audio- or videotaped during interviews (with client permission, of course), have engaged in co-workmanship with their field instructor, and have sat in on interviews as nonparticipating observers (again, with client permission) to learn how to conduct one. These procedures represent good use of what we know about learning, in order to enhance the education of a professional helper.

GUIDELINES FOR THE USE OF THEORIES OF LEARNING AND CHANGE

There are several factors to be considered when using theories of learning and change as the basis for designing a learning experience. This is truly a complex issue, and the relevant literature is enormous. What follows, therefore, can only be viewed as "bare bones" suggestions. (Chapter 6 deals with the specific methods that can be used by staff developers in conducting staff development activities. Consequently, you may want to delay using these guidelines until after you have read the chapter.)

1. What are the goals—stated in behaviorally specific terms—of the educational

    experience? _____

    _____

    _____

2. What resources do you have or can you acquire that the participants in the staff development activity would regard as rewarding? Occasionally, staff developers overlook some of the things staff participants find rewarding. One way to find this out is to ask. In one manpower agency, staff who learned how to do group work as part of a demonstration–research project, indicated that a letter to their director from the researchers, that would be placed in their personnel file (a letter thanking each of them for helping, and indicating the kinds and amounts of training they had completed in order to participate in this project) would be the kind of reward they would most appreciate. Those who participate in a staff development activity might prefer praise, given in the presence of their administrator. (For suggestions about locating the best rewards, see Bertcher, Gordon, Hayes, and Mial, 1969, pp. 59–81, and Gambrill,

    1978, pp. 178–191. _____

    _____

3. What circumstances could legitimately exist under which you could distribute these rewards to the participants when they achieve at least a minimal level of the performance specified in the goal statement? (For example, if you use positive feedback as a reward, when and how could you provide this feedback?)

    _____

    _____

4. What can you do to see to it that participants have *a number of opportunities* to practice and then perform at least at a minimally acceptable level?

    _____

    _____

5. Some learning goals are best achieved by studying the things others have learned; others are best learned by discovering the answers for yourself. Given the learning goals you have established (from #1), which appear best achieved (using effectiveness and efficiency of learning as your criteria) by

a. studying what others have learned? _____
b. arranging for participants to discover the answers for themselves?

_____

6. How do you plan to take membership in minority or oppressed groups (of staff participants, of clients, of staff developers, or of others in the organization or the organization's environment) into account in planning for staff development? _____

7. How do you plan to take individual learning styles into account in your staff development activity? _____

_____

8. What will you do to facilitate positive transfer of learning? _____

_____

9. In what ways will you provide guidance (prompts, hints) as part of your plan for the staff development activity? _____

_____

10. What will you do about participants who do not achieve the learning goals of the staff development activity? _____

_____

11. In what ways will you cope with the prior socialization of participants if and when it interferes with the socialization processes you are supporting?

_____

_____

12. What will you do to facilitate the socialization processes attendent to staff development? _____

_____

Staff development activities all involve learning in one form or another, but all too often staff developers appear to ignore what we've learned about learning. This chapter has reviewed several theories and sets of ideas that pertain to learning, in an attempt to show how they pertain to staff development. As in the story of the six blind men who went to study the elephant, each theory adds something different and useful to our understanding of the learning process. The chapter also discussed three major ways that people learn (trial and error, modeling, and verbal instruction). It was noted that each individual has his or her own best way to learn, and that no one approach to the learning process works well for everyone. Finally, a number of issues affecting learning were discussed, including transfer of training, the role of practice, guidance (or prompting), learning curves, and failure to learn.

Keeping this information in mind, we can now turn to the actual "doing" of staff development. Such doing, we hope, will always be informed by what we have learned and are still learning about the process of learning.

chapter 6

THE SKILLFUL "DOING" OF STAFF DEVELOPMENT ACTIVITIES

- How do you manage group discussions when they are used for staff development purposes?
- How do you give an effective lecture?
- When and how can you use role playing and simulation games for staff development purposes?
- What makes for successful one-to-one interviewing in staff development?
- What makes for an effective use of media (such as film or videotapes) in staff development?

"A scout is trustworthy, loyal, helpful, friendly, courteous, kind, obedient, cheerful, thrifty, brave, clean, and reverent." This portion of the scout ritual I memorized as a boy also suggests some of the qualities of a good staff developer. Missing from the list are a few other attributes that seem necessary for survival, to say nothing of success: a sense of humor, political savvy for organizational in-fighting, and patience. In addition, of course, there is *skill*—skill in the use of the multitude of techniques and approaches that are associated with the staff development activities that have been mentioned throughout this book. In some cases, it is the staff developer who needs to be skillful in—for example—conducting problem-solving staff meetings, running a simulation game, or providing individual consultation; in other situations, the key lies in successfully recruiting others who have the appropriate expertise to conduct such activities.

Devoting only one chapter to the skills involved in implementing and managing staff development activities is bound to lead to superficiality: There are entire texts devoted to, for example, the theory and techniques of supervision alone. All I can do here is point to some basic guidelines in the management of staff development activities. For the novice staff developer, this chapter should suggest ways to develop sound and skillful practices. More experienced staff developers will, I hope, find it helpful to review some things they know, including some things they once learned but may have forgotten.

The skills I have chosen to present are not necessarily linked to any one staff development activity. For example, "leading a group discussion" refers to a cluster of skills that could be used in running a discussion of a role play, involving participants in group supervision, drawing out questions and concerns of new staff members during a group orientation, and so forth. In each case, the skill itself is seen as generic; its use will be shaped by the goals of the activity, the nature of the participants, the relationship between the staff developer and the participants, the relationships between the various participants themselves, and the amount and kind of experience they have had with the particular activity.

My selection of skills related to staff development activities is, in itself, somewhat arbitrary—a matter of definition. "Leading a group discussion" is a skill area that pertains to many activities. But within that area are a host of subskills, some having to do with preparing for a discussion, and some relating to the discussion process itself. The skills that will be presented include: leading a group discussion, presenting a lecture, using role playing and simulation games, conducting an individual interview, and using media.

LEADING A GROUP DISCUSSION

Many staff development activities take place in a group context, and many have foundered because the group discussion went awry. Maybe one or two participants dominated the discussion, or the discussion meandered every which way without any apparent direction, or the discussion developed into a gripe session that left problems unresolved, or nonparticipants said nothing because they were bored or offended or felt overwhelmed by the big talkers. Whatever happened, the result was a general wish to avoid staff discussions as much as possible. Accordingly, a good place to begin a discussion of staff development skills appears to be "leading a group discussion."

Pregroup Skills

Let's begin with the skills involved in setting up the physical aspects of a meeting. Rule #1, learned through painful experience, is: Take nothing for granted! Don't assume that the lights work, that there will be enough chairs, that the room temperature will be comfortable, that there will be chalk and an eraser for the chalkboard (or an easel and a large newsprint pad and thick felt-tip markers in working order, plus masking tape to tape up the pages of the pad as you complete them), or that the meeting place is reserved for you and not for some other staff group that has also reserved it. *Check it out!* Preparing a checklist ahead of time will help you avoid overlooking the kinds of details that, unattended to, can destroy an otherwise well-planned meeting.

It's always best to arrive *before* a meeting in time to check things out and take any corrective action that may be needed. I'm a firm believer in the importance of seating arrangements, because they can have a powerful impact on group interaction. Shaw provides a thorough review of research on the physical environment of a group (Shaw, 1981, pp. 118–166). If I arrive and find a room set up theater-style (every chair facing the front) and I want to promote group discussion (which is facilitated by face-to-face interaction), I always try to involve early arrivers in helping me put the chairs in a circle. What about rooms that have seats bolted to the floor? Avoid them, unless the shape they create fits with the kind of session you want to run. Bolted chairs can also make it difficult to subdivide the group into smaller "buzz" groups, should you choose to do so for part of a meeting. I also stay away from long, narrow tables; I prefer a round table, where everyone can see everyone else equally well, or smaller rectangular tables that can be arranged into a square.

Often, you will want to distribute written materials that have been duplicated. Unless these are to be used during the meeting, however, it's better to hold them for distribution at the end of the meeting (tell people they'll get copies). Otherwise, people will be reading them when they should be attending to the discussion. But a written agenda, passed out at the beginning of the meeting, helps people to organize their participation in relation to what is coming; it is also one more way to let people know that you have prepared for this session in a way that will be helpful to them.

If people are coming to a meeting to engage in problem solving, you may want them to have certain information in hand *before* they arrive, so that you don't have to use precious meeting time to present this information. When this is the case, distribute handouts well in advance of the meetings (at least two days ahead of time if at all possible) so that participants have enough time to read and prepare. (Be sure to bring extra copies for those absentminded professors—like me—who sometimes forget to bring their copies to the meeting.)

If you are planning to use audiovisual equipment, make sure you know how to use it *before* the meeting. Using a film or videotape without previewing it is courting disaster. If you want to use a film or tape to initiate discussion, and you only have one hour, a fifty-minute film won't leave much time for what you really want—an exchange of ideas. Previewing allows you to select some portion of the film or tape that is most likely to stimulate the discussion you want, while leaving sufficient time for the discussion to be thorough. If you have *two* hours, and plan to have a break, don't schedule the break to occur right after the film, or you will lose the very intensity of discussion you wanted the film to create.

Decide, too, if you want to serve some refreshments, such as coffee. This can help to set a comfortable tone. Many people add edible refreshments—doughnuts, a large bowl of fruit, or cookies.

These suggestions may sound so commonsensical that even to mention them insults the intelligence. In my experience, however, simple mistakes are very common—and can seriously impede a meeting.

Leading the Discussion

One of my colleagues has likened leading a group discussion to conducting a symphony orchestra—an analogy that doesn't bear close scrutiny. True, an agenda can and often should be used to give direction to a meeting. But an agenda is hardly the same as a musical score. When an orchestra plays together, each musician must play his or her part as written. A conductor will place his or her own stamp on the music by varying the tempo or bringing out certain sections of the orchestra, but a discussion leader and participants must interact according to a much more unpredictable process. If participants believe that their interactions are being "orchestrated" in a supposedly democratic process, they are likely to distrust that process.

In staff development, the role of discussion leader may be complicated by the fact that the staff developer who is trying to conduct a democratic problem-solving discussion may find participants acting in a restrained way because the discussion leader is also their supervisor, Or, if the discussion leader is a high-status person brought in from outside as a trainer, staff may decide there is nothing to be gained from challenging this person and may respond superficially, rather than expressing deeply felt disagreements. Discussion leaders should be particularly sensitive to the ways in which their other roles affect the participants' views of them as discussion leaders. (When this happens to me, I tell participants that I know they may not feel comfortable in challenging me, but that unless they do, the meeting won't be of much use to them. Then, if they take me at my word and *do* challenge me, I have to be sure to *reward* such participation and not react defensively.) One way to facilitate discussion is through small-group exercises, where people become so involved that they forget their inhibitions. The series of handbooks entitled *Structured Experiences for Human Relations Training*, developed by Pfeiffer and Jones, is an excellent source of such small-group exercises (Pfeiffer and Jones, 1965–1975).

Discussion leaders who have strong opinions about a subject are often perceived as biased in the way they manage a discussion. I am tempted to compare a discussion leader to an umpire in an athletic competition—a person who is not *for* one side or the other, but is only there to see that the game is played fairly, according to a predetermined set of rules, with each player enjoying the full protection and support of the umpire. This is a tempting analogy, except that a group discussion is not a game, with a winner and a loser; in fact, a group is often seeking solutions to problems that are acceptable to *all* participants. There are several identifiable techniques that can be used to make a discussion useful. Here is a description of some of these techniques.

Gatekeeping

In most, if not all, discussions, the amounts of participation are uneven; that is, some participants talk more than others.

> Typically, a few group members account for a majority of the total participation in group activities, and this unequal distribution of participation increases with increasing group size. (Shaw, 1981, p. 398)

To this we can add the comment by Napier and Gershenfeld:

> Total group morale will be higher in groups in which there is more access to participation among those involved—the more open the participation, the higher the morale. (Napier and Gershenfeld, 1981, p. 47)

On the basis of these observations (which in turn are based on review of small-group research), the technique of gatekeeping becomes an important one for group discussion leaders:

> Gatekeeping is behavior that helps all members of the group to participate by limiting those members who monopolize the discussion and by encouraging low participators to talk more. (Bertcher, 1979, p. 115.)

Encouraging low participators to speak can be done in a number of ways, including direct appeal ("Mary, what do you think about this?"); subdividing the group ("Each of you pair up with the person sitting next to you, then come up with one question between the two of you that you'd like our speaker to answer. Then we'll go around the room, taking your questions. . ."; and watching for nonverbal cues ("John, you look as if you have some thoughts about this. What's your idea?"). Holding back the talkative members is a bit trickier. Sometimes you can time your move, as they pause to catch a breath, and invite others to comment ("Pete here thinks we shouldn't do anything—just let matters take their course. Do the rest of you agree?"), or you can summarize what the individual has said ("O.K., Beth, let me see if I've got this straight. Your suggestion is to. . .What do some of the rest of you think about that?"), or reward them and then move on ("John—that's really an interesting idea. Sue, what do you think about it?")

Focusing

One major problem for a discussion leader is keeping a group on target. Nothing is more frustrating to all concerned than participating in a discussion that wanders here and there without ever reaching any conclusion. To prevent this from occurring, you can use a technique called *focusing:*

> Focusing is calling the attention of the group to something that has been said or that has happened in order to (a) highlight or clarify it so that the group will be more aware of what has been going on or (b) bring the discussion back to the agreed-upon business of the group. (Bertcher, 1979, p. 95)

Depending on the nature and purpose of the group discussion, you may want to call the group's attention to a contribution that has been overlooked because it was made by a lower-status group member ("I wonder if we shouldn't give a bit more attention to Larry's suggestion. Larry, would you mind repeating your idea for everyone?") or by summarizing an individual's ideas ("So, Larry, what you're suggesting is. . .Well, what do the rest of you think about Larry's idea?"). This is one function of focusing—to highlight. To keep the group on topic, however, you may need to call the group back to its agreed-on topic ("You know, Mary, that's an important suggestion, but maybe we ought to deal first with the original question before we move on to that topic," or "I'm getting confused. I thought we were working on X but we seem to have jumped to Y. Could we stick with one thing at a time, please? Let's settle the X issue, and then, if you like, we can move on to Y."). Sometimes, even with focusing attempts, a group keeps straying from its topic. At that point, it's appropriate to call the group's attention to its own process ("We seem to keep getting off the topic we said we wanted to discuss. Maybe we don't really want to handle it now? If not, let's decide what we do want to work on."). On other occasions, if you know the group well enough, a little confrontation may be in order ("We seem to keep getting off the topic we've agreed to discuss. Why do you think we keep straying?") Of course, you can't use focusing unless you have a pretty clear idea yourself of what the group agreed to discuss.

Summarizing

Groups seem better able to move along in problem solving if they have a sense of what's been accomplished through discussion. This can be achieved through the use of *summarizing.*

> Summarizing is the process of drawing together and briefly restating a number of prior responses into one statement, then seeking agreement or correction from the group members until a summary statement has been produced that everyone considers accurate. (Bertcher, 1979, p. 105)

Summary statements are often best when made by group members ("Corey, I wonder if you'd be willing to take a crack at summing up what we've been saying so far?"). It's a good idea to summarize when you sense that members are essentially repeating what others have said, with no appreciably new inputs ("O.K., we seem to be agreed that X is the way things are. Would you all agree? [pause] O.K.

Now what do we want to do about it?"). Summaries can also be used to start a meeting and give it focus ("Last time, we discussed X and came up with the following agreements...We said we'd start today with Z. Does that check with everyone's memory of what we decided to do?").

Mediating

When conflict occurs in a group, it makes people uncomfortable. They may take the attitude that the conflict is too trivial for them to expend any effort over its resolution, or that it is insoluble and therefore efforts to resolve it can only make things worse, as ways of avoiding communication in the face of conflict. Moos (1974) summarizes several studies of organizations that indicate the devastating effect on clients and on staff morale of unresolved conflicts between staff. On the other hand, Coser (1956) has drawn attention to the constructive potential in conflict situations. From this evidence, it would seem that a discussion leader would do well to deal with (rather than shy away from) conflict. One technique that can help this process to work beneficially is *mediating*.

> Mediating involves putting oneself in a neutral position between opponents to avoid or resolve a disagreement that is keeping the group from reaching its goals. (Bertcher, 1979, p. 153)

Good mediating involves knowing the typical level of conflict that has characterized your group in the past. The trick is to avoid intervening too early (which can stop a potentially useful discussion of a disagreement) or intervening so late that major damage has occurred to the relationships among participants, who may then decide that it is impossible to get anything useful from the group.

To mediate effectively, you have to have a reputation for fairness in the group—to be seen as someone who wants to see the group succeed, rather than as someone who is using the group to further your own particular point of view, or as siding with one party to the disagreement. In the actual process of mediating, you should try to clarify the issue by making sure that the different positions are clearly stated and that relevant information is available to all the participants. You can then ask for a compromise position from anyone in the group and, if none is forthcoming, suggest one yourself. If you can achieve consensus around a compromise, fine. If not, you can do one of several things: Suggest that the group agree to disagree, or set the matter aside until feelings are not quite so strong, or seek a solution by reminding the group of some higher value to which you feel sure they all subscribe ("It's clear we haven't reached agreement on what to put in the report regarding this issue. But I want to remind you that we all agreed to have this report finished by the end of the month, and we're not going to make it unless we can settle this issue now. So something's got to give, or we're stuck, and we won't make our deadline."").

One note of caution: If a conflict is settled in favor of one position over another, rather than by a compromise that all can live with, be sure to pay particular attention to the losers. A loss on an important group decision may drive the losers away, either physically or psychologically. You may need to make an extra effort to retain the involvement of the losers, but if they are important to the success of the group, it will be worth it. In my experience, groups that have dealt openly with conflict and handled the conflict to the general satisfaction of all members are stronger and more cohesive for the experience.

A few more remarks about discussion leading. I am assuming that the earlier chapter on contracting (Chapter 2) provides the guidelines for a basic aspect of the successful group. I am also assuming that the contract for a group meeting results from a needs assessment, and that participants are aware of that needs assessment and will support the contract to the degree that they helped shape it and believe there will be a payoff to them from honoring the contract. The actual negotiation of the contract (and ongoing renegotiation and redefinition, as needed) will come about through the use of discussion leading techniques such as gatekeeping, focusing, summarizing, and mediating.

Responding to Feeling

Empathy is the ability to *sense* how people feel about something. Responding to Feeling refers to the action—verbal or nonverbal—by which we communicate empathic understanding to people about their feelings. (Bertcher, 1979, p. 83)

Responding to the feelings of participants is an important way to facilitate full and open communication in a group ("Jane, I get the impression that you're uncomfortable with the group's decision."). Then again, when a participant has presented some information to the group, you can acknowledge the content of what he or she has said, perhaps even summarizing it to make sure that it's understood in the group and that you've heard the speaker accurately; but you may also want to let speakers know that you understand how they feel about the information they have shared, and to alert the group to the participant's feelings ("So I gather that I've summarized what you said correctly. But I'm also wondering if you weren't feeling pretty scared when it happened?"). I am not proposing here that you do therapy in a group meeting that has a problem-solving focus and a group task to be managed, only that the group will work best when full communication takes place. If a participant makes a contribution that includes a strong feeling component, ignoring that feeling means ignoring an important part of the message, which makes for incomplete communication.

In summary, a good discussion leader continually scans the group, looking for nonverbal cues that indicate interest or boredom, such as facial expression; leaning forward with interest, eyes on the speaker versus out the window; doodling versus listening actively, and so on. A good discussion leader tries to keep track of who has and has not participated, and is particularly aware of low participators who look as though they want to say something. Discussion leaders should try to keep their own participation level down so as not to dominate and cut off other speakers; they should avoid taking strong stances themselves early in a discussion that might serve to cut off disagreement; they should keep an eye on the clock and the agenda; and occasionally, as needed, they should gently but firmly move the discussion along. Group meetings have a life of their own. They can go through several phases, and it's important that the discussion not be allowed to fritter away as people gather up their things preparatory to making a hurried departure. In order to avoid a crumbling ending, a concise, accurate summary of what has transpired, plus clear statements about the next meeting, if there is to be one, are in order.

Ultimately, if you are managing a group discussion, it is *your* responsibility to see to it that the contract is fully negotiated, that the distribution of participation is fairly even, that members' feelings are recognized, that the group handles its conflicts effectively, without sweeping them under the rug, and so forth. Always remember, however, that *any* group member can gatekeep (by asking another member what he or she thinks about something) or mediate (one member can say to two others, "You know, unless you two settle your disagreement, we're never going to get anywhere."), or perform any of the leadership acts I have described as *techniques.* Cartwright and Zander define leadership as "the performance of those acts which help the group achieve its preferred outcomes" (Cartwright and Zander, 1968, p. 304). There is no rule that says that only a designated leader can perform leadership acts; sometimes members respond better to leadership acts that are performed by fellow members. For the staff developer, this means that when group members perform leadership acts effectively, you should support their efforts and even reward them for what they have done ("Sue, I think your idea about settling this argument is really excellent because it is such a good way for both sides to see their ideas incorporated in the group's solution.").

Cartwright and Zander define leadership in terms of achieving "preferred outcomes":

> ...most objectives can be subsumed under one of two headings: (a) the achievement of some specific group goal and (b) the maintenance or strengthening of the group itself. (Cartwright and Zander, 1968, p. 306)

The latter refers to such things as keeping interpersonal relationships pleasant, helping members to feel satisfied with their membership in the group, and—in the case of staff units—developing good morale within the unit. Clearly, the techniques described here could be used to carry out either the function of task achievement or that of group maintenance (for example, mediating a conflict can be used to resolve an issue, and thus move the group along in relation to its task goal, but it can also make the group a more satisfying place to be because the parties to the conflict believe that they got a fair hearing for their point of view). Studies by Bales and Strodtbeck (1968) found that in problem-solving groups with no designated leader, the people who pressed for task accomplishment were usually not the ones who tried to achieve member satisfaction. An effective staff development group leader can consciously attend to both functions—at times helping to move the group along, and at other times encouraging members in such a way as to help them feel good about the group. If you pay attention to the group interaction, however, you will soon see that some people devote more energy to task issues, whereas others gravitate toward group maintenance behaviors. Good discussiuon leaders encourage both kinds of behaviors, because both are essential to good group functioning. Ultimately, however, it is the discussion leader's responsibility to see to it that both functions are performed. If the group lacks people who can be effective in one of these areas, the discussion leader will have to take on that function. If a group has a lot of task-focused idea people who tend to ride roughshod over less influential members, thus alienating them from the group, it is ultimately the responsibility of the discussion leader to act to keep those members involved. On the other hand, if the group is a cozy, friendly place where no goal achievement ever occurs, it is the discussion leader who will have to draw the group on to task–goal achievement. In time, group members should take their cue from the discussion leader and assume their share of leadership acts.

PRESENTING A LECTURE

Novice teachers frequently report that they entered their first classroom sessions with a terrible fear that they would run out of things to say. Once launched on their subject, however, they found they had quite a lot to say. The inherent problem with the lecture is that it can be used to fill the entire teaching time, thus making it unnecessary for the student–trainee–participant to participate at all. In addition, the lecture does not require learners to use the knowledge they are supposedly acquiring in order to determine whether or not they have indeed acquired it correctly. I recall serving as a teaching assistant for a professor who relied almost exclusively on the lecture method in conducting a history class. "What I want," she told me, "is for the students to be able to give back to me, in writing, what I tell them during the term." Information in, information out. At the end of the term, that's precisely what happened: The students poured out all the minutiae they had memorized, some of which they had clearly not understood. It was my job to read their final exams—a number of short essay questions. They had almost all the facts, but in several cases they presented these facts in a way that suggested they had memorized words without understanding them.

I suspect you have endured such courses and taken little of value away from them. On the other hand, you may also have been fortunate enough to have studied with a spellbinding lecturer whose words made eminently good sense to you, so that you filled your notebooks with stimulating ideas—ideas and information that inspired you into new channels of thought, words that helped you put your thoughts together. This was a lecturer you looked forward to hearing, a lecturer who made the subject come alive and inspired you to want to know more about that subject.

What, then, are the secrets of a good lecture? When is it a good idea to use a lecture, and when do you want to avoid it? How can you present a lecture that will hold participants' attention without boring them?

To answer these questions one should first think about the lecture in terms of the human processes involved—the communication of a body of information. Essentially, a lecture provides the occasion for giving information—some of it objective information about a subject, some of it the lecturer's opinions about that information. Studies of information giving suggest that the lecturer should consider the following when delivering information of either variety: (1) when the information should be given, (2) in what order it should be given, (3) how much should be given before the listener experiences information "overload"—receives more information than can be absorbed, (4) the listener's expectations about the information to be received, and (5) the ways in which the source of the information affects its reception.

Studies of Information Giving

When to give information. When to give information depends in part on the nature of the information and how it is to be used. Experimental studies (Freedman, 1965; Zimmerman and Bauer, 1956) indicate that the retention of information is highly dependent on the receiver's need for it. This suggests that information given in response to a needs assessment is likely to be well received. In addition, it helps if the information is situationally relevant—that is, likely to provide the basis for action in the very near future. Studies of retention curves show that the bulk of material a person forgets is forgotten in the time period immediately following the presentation of that information (Murdock, 1961; Peterson, 1963). In other words, the quicker the information is put to use, the less chance there is that it will be forgotten before it is needed. There is at least one exception to this rule. Since retention is influenced by a person's beliefs, values, and attitudes (Jones and Aneshansel, 1956; Jones and Kohler, 1958; Taft, 1954), information that challenges an individual's personal convictions will probably need more time to be incorporated between the presentation of the information and the person's need for using it. Indeed, when lecturers suspect that the information being provided is likely to create such a challenge, they would do well to rely on more than a lecture if they hope to effect a change in values and attitudes—for a lecture, by itself, does not appear to be an effective way to present challenging information. For example, announcing a major shift in policy just before it is to be put into operation may be situationally relevant, but it is unlikely to induce acceptance of the policy, should that policy challenge existing staff values and attitudes.

The order in which information is given. Research on the order in which information is given suggests a *primacy* effect: The information that occurs first in a sequence makes a greater impression on the listener and will be remembered more easily and more often. Asch (1946) presented subjects with a list of character traits of fictitious people. Some of the lists were arranged so that the traits read from good characteristics to bad characteristics; other lists, using the same traits, reversed the order of presentation, going from bad to good. When Asch asked his subjects to describe the fictional person, those traits that were listed first (regardless of whether they were the good or the bad) were recalled more accurately.

Anderson and his colleagues (Anderson, 1965; Anderson and Barrios, 1961) studied the degree to which a person's recall of information at the beginning of a list, story, or any other form of presentation could be explained by the idea that the "weights" of initial information are greater than those of later information. The result of their work was a mathematical formula that suggested how to counter-weight information that comes later in the presentation so as to balance the primacy effect. Anderson and Hubert (1963) found that the primacy effect could be reduced if the subjects were asked to restate verbally all the information in a particular message before they formed an impression or filed it away in their memory.

Problems of information overload.   The amount of information a person can comfortably take in and retain is another concern for the lecturer. Miller (1956) argues that a person's memory span has a fixed capacity, regardless of whether the individual is asked to memorize numbers, words, rhyming lines, or nonsense syllables. He indicates that raw information is coded into chunks or cognitive units, which are created by the individual. Immediate memory is said to hold between five and nine such chunks, which can be recalled at any time. Pollack and Johnson (1965) have shown that by teaching a person new coding methods, the amount of information in a chunk can be increased, although the number of chunks that can be retained remains the same.

The foregoing suggests that it is not merely the *amount* of information that affects retention, but also the ways in which chunks of information are presented. For example, Ausubel (1960) found that students remembered better when they were given a preview of what was to be presented, referred to as "advanced organizers." So, for example, in this section of this chapter, I wrote a brief listing of the five areas I would be covering, each of which became a chunk of information.

Memory can also be helped by linking new information to information already known to the learner. According to Johnson, what a lecturer should try to achieve is "meaningfulness":

> Learning may be said to be meaningful to the extent that the new learning task can be related to the existing cognitive structure of the learner, i.e., the residual of his earlier learnings. (Johnson, 1975, p. 427)

Lecturers who provide their listeners with mnemonic devices (jingles like "Thirty days hath September, April, June, and November," or phrases or acronyms) can help them build retainable memory chunks. For example, Biehler (1978, p. 426) presented pairs of words to three groups of twelve-year-olds. The first group was simply asked to memorize the pairs, the second was asked to make up what Biehler called "mediators" to link the two words in the pair, and the third was asked to use mediators that had been composed by the second group. The second group, who supplied their own mediators, were able to remember up to 95 percent of a list of thirty pairs when tested shortly after they had studied them. Those who had been asked simply to memorize the pairs recalled about 50 percent, and those who used mediators proposed by others were about halfway between the other two groups. This suggests that lecturers who propose mnemonic devices will achieve better results than those who do not, and lecturers who encourage their audiences to create their own mnemonic device may have the best results, providing the listeners are willing to make the attempt.

Expectations about information.   Here I want to call your attention to the relationship between information giving and the listeners' cognitive set—the extent to which the information is congruent or incongruent with what the listeners expected to hear. Research on person perception and impression formation summarized by Jones and Gerard (1967) strongly suggests that when persons are given information congruent with their expectations about a person or event (and the information is consistent with the situation in which it appears), listeners are likely to gloss over the information or take it for granted. If the information is discrepant or incongruent with what the listeners were expecting, however, then the discrepant fact would be most noticeable. For the lecturer, this suggests that there may be some value in presenting information that includes some surprises or unexpected bits of information.

Studies by Asch (1946) and Luchins (1957) in which the subjects were given a description of a person and later asked, "What is this person like?" found that it was usually the discrepant information that received the greatest attention. On the basis of these observations, a lecturer might experiment not only with surprises but also with novel ways of saying the same thing—a mnemonic device, colorful examples with unexpected outcomes, reports of data that challenge accepted "facts," and the like.

Sources of information.   The perception of the source of a piece of information has been shown to be associated with the degree to which individuals are influenced by that information. Kelley and Woodruff (1956), in an investigation of influence groups, found that peer group influence was much greater than non-peer group influence. Using student subjects from a teachers' college known for its progressive philosophy, the experimenters asked their subjects to listen to a tape-recorded lecture that took a very traditional view of education. The subjects were asked to evaluate the speaker's diction and delivery. At seven points during the presentation, the subjects heard an audience applaud the speaker. There were two experimental conditions in the study: In the first, students were told that the audience was composed of former graduates of the college; in the other condition, the subjects were told that the audience was a group of educational experts. Attitudes toward education were assessed both before and after the speech. The subjects in the former condition (the peer orientation) changed their attitudes toward the position advocated by the speaker significantly more than did the subjects in the non–peer (educational experts) oriented condition.

The degree to which listeners' perceptions of a lecturer affected their response to what was said was demonstrated in a study by Natfulin, Donnelly, and Ware (1973). They hired a professional actor, provided him with a fictitious name and background (Dr. Myron L. Fox, an authority on the application of mathematics to an understanding of human behavior) and coached him to present his topic and conduct his question-and-answer period with an excessive amount of doubletalk, neologisms, *non sequiturs* and contradictory statements. All this was to be interspersed with parenthetical humor and meaningless references to unrelated topics. Source material for his lecture came from an article in *Scientific American.*

"Dr. Fox" presented his one-hour lecture and half-hour discussion period to a group of eleven psychiatrists, psychologists, and social work educators. The entire session was videotaped and shown later to two other groups of professionals (forty-four in all) with similar backgrounds. The audience were then asked to fill out, anonymously, a questionnaire evaluating the lecture. Fox was a smashing success, particularly with the first group, who saw him "live." In Group 1, 100 percent thought he was interested in his subject, 90 percent thought he used enough examples to clarify his presentation, 90 percent thought he presented his material in a well-organized way, 100 percent said he stimulated their thinking, and 90 percent thought he put his material across in an interesting way. In general, the other two groups had similar evaluations, albeit with a bit less enthusiasm; for example, 91 percent of Group 2 thought he was interested in his subject, and 97 percent of Group 3 thought so. The only major difference between the groups had to do with the question: "Did he dwell upon the obvious?" Group 1, 5 percent, Group 2, 0 percent, Group 3, 28 percent. The answers to "Have you read any of this speaker's publications?"—Group 1 and Group 3, 0 percent, Group 2, 9 percent.

The experiment was not done as a joke or a put-down, but as a test of earlier findings that student ratings of teachers depend more on the personality of the teacher than on educational content. The researchers admit the cards were stacked against the audience. If the topic had been more concrete or the audience more knowledgeable about the subject, the deception would have been harder to pull off. Despite this reservation, the fact is that a group of professionals were effectively seduced into believing they had learned something when they had not.

When the audience was told how they'd been had, and why, many of them asked for copies of the article in *Scientific American* on which the lecture had been based, saying the lecture had stimulated their interest. This raises an intriguing possibility

> of training actors to give legitimate lectures as an innovative educational approach toward student-perceived satisfaction with the learning process....The corollary would be to provide the scholar–educator with a more dramatic presence to enhance student satisfaction. (Natfulin, Donnelly, and Ware, 1973, p. 635)

In concluding their article, the authors note:

The extent to which . . . students are satisfied with . . . teaching, and even the degree to which they feel they have learned reflects little more than their illusions of having learned. (Natfulin, Donnelly, and Ware, 1973, p. 635)

How to Lecture Skillfully

Based on this discussion of information giving, we can now address the issue of how one gives a skillful lecture. Clearly, it is important to view any lecture as a dramatic event, in which listeners are impressed by the lecturer's dramatic virtuosity. For example, anyone can give a lecture on the works of Charles Dickens, but chances are the impact of that lecture will be considerably enhanced if the presenter dresses up with beard and clothes to look like Dickens, and affects Dickens's English pronunciation when delivering such a talk. This is not to say that staff development lecturers should don costumes or affect accents when giving a lecture; rather, they should view the lecture as a dramatic event, and pay attention to its dramatic aspects—setting, lighting, audibility, general deportment of the lecturer, and so forth.

The well-worn advice "Tell them what you're going to tell them, tell them, then tell them what you've told them" bears repeating, particularly since the first part of that advice refers to the provision of "advanced organizers" referred to earlier. There are other ways to alert listeners to what is coming in a lecture—advance publicity, for example. If a lecture is based on a needs assessment of staff, one can call attention to this fact when announcing the upcoming lecture. Should the lecture not grow out of a needs assessment, however, it is crucially important that the advance publicity make as clear as possible what the focus of the lecture will be. I recently attended a presentation on the uses of the computer for research purposes. I hoped for some content I could pass on to my research class. I expected a mix of short lecture and hands-on experience, with a comparatively small group in attendance, as I had encountered in the sponsoring organization a few years earlier. Instead, the audience was large (about forty-five, too many for any hands-on experience), the lecture long and for the most part over my head, and the content a presentation describing two pieces of software. In subsequent contact with the organization that presented the speakers, I learned that about half the audience were quite satisfied with the high degree of sophisitication of the lecture, whereas the other half, like me, were displeased. Some were displeased because there was no opportunity for a hands-on experience; others had come in hopes of learning more about a much larger number of software packages than the two that were presented. Incidentally, the presenters had fine credentials and were enthusiastic and knowledgeable in their manner of presentation. Their lectures, however, each of which took an hour, were supposedly thoroughgoing, objective critiques of these two packages. Although they were particularly well suited to discuss the first package (since they were its co-authors), the credibility of their critique was somewhat marred for me by the fact that they made no bones about telling the audience that the package could be purchased for such and such a price. What turned into a disappointing afternoon for me and some others could easily have been avoided if the brief announcement of this session had provided a more accurate description of what was to transpire.

Given the possibility of a primacy effect—what is presented first will be retained best—you should plan to cover your most important content first. On the other hand, if you have several important points to present, you can reduce the primacy effect by building in opportunities for listeners to participate in the lecture. I do this by writing in my notes "ask class for summary" at various points in my lectures as a way of reminding myself to involve them and to give me a check on whether or not they have been listening. If I receive an incorrect response, I'm unlikely to say, "That's wrong," since that discourages widespread participation. I'm more likely to say something like, "Well, that's one way to put it. Anyone else want to add to or change that?"

If you would prefer to leave the questions until the end of your lecture, tell this to your audience. Personally, I prefer questions during the lecture, since the response comes at the point of the learner's expressed need and is therefore most likely to be retained. But when you allow questions during a lecture, you run the risk of being drawn off your topic in a way that is of little interest to most of your audience.

The earlier discussion of information overload and the limits on retention of too many chunks of information suggest that you should select a limited number of issues or topics to cover—and stick to them. Make clear how any new content relates to things the listeners could reasonably be expected to know. Sometimes you want to give your listeners a set of data that, if presented in a lecture, would be so complicated as to boggle the listeners' mind. If you want the listeners to follow along and make use of these data, you can use an overhead projector or have copies duplicated before the lecture so that they can be handed out and read along with you as the lecture proceeds. Never hand out at the *beginning* of a lecture duplicated copies of information you want your listeners to have for *subsequent* study. Tell them you will distribute this material at the end of the lecture so they need not try to take notes on all the data.

I have not yet mentioned the length of a lecture. Long lectures tend to create listener fatigue, not to mention lecturer fatigue. In recent years, the minilecture—a brief five- to fifteen-minute talk—has been employed to introduce a simulation game or small-group exercise. Such lectures are tightly focused and are designed to set the stage for a longer activity to follow. Where you need to present a lecture that requires more than one hour, you should plan a break at least every fifty minutes. In addition, you may want to leave time for questions, invite them as the lecture unwinds, use part of the time to divide the audience into small groups to discuss the content (such groups can be given an assignment to report their major conclusions back to the larger group when it reconvenes), introduce audiovisual materials that amplify the lecture, and so forth.

Incidentally, there are several ways that a lecturer can elicit questions. Listeners can be encouraged to ask questions verbally, or asked to write their questions on a slip of paper and then turn them in, thus allowing the questioner to remain anonymous. Or listeners can be paired up where they sit, and each pair asked to produce at least one relevant question or comment within a couple of minutes.

USING ROLE PLAYING AND SIMULATION GAMES

> Experiential learning is defined as a sequence of events with one or more identified learning objectives, requiring active involvement by participants at one or more points in the sequence. That is, lessons are presented, illustrated, highlighted and supported through the involvement of the participants. The central tenet of experiential learning is that one learns best by doing. (Walter and Marks, 1981, p. 1)

In role playing, individuals act as if they were someone else in a situation, or act as themselves in some imaginary past or future situation. In simulation games, participants may play a role other than their own, or may react spontaneously as themselves in a gamelike situation (that is, competitively, according to a set of rules that includes guidelines for winning) that attempts to simulate some social situation.

I want to concentrate my remarks on the role of the staff developer in managing the use of both these methods. I shall try to answer the following questions: When do you use them? What are the advantages and disadvantages of using them? What are the guidelines to follow when using them?

When to Use Role Playing

There are several uses of role playing in staff development, and the specific use in part determines when to use it. These include:

1. To help an individual prepare for a coming event, sometimes referred to as *behavioral rehearsal*
2. To help an individual develop empathy for, or a change of attitude toward, another person, by acting out the role of that person
3. To help an individual review a past event by acting as if he or she is in that previous situation
4. To learn new behavioral skills by observing a model in action and then attempting to imitate the model's performance through role playing
5. To present a problem for group discussion, using a role play to highlight different aspects of the problem dramatically.

Part of the answer to "When?" is: Whenever you face any of the five situations just described. For example, if you are trying to help prepare a new worker for a first contact with a client, you yourself (as the staff developer) could play the role of the client (with whom, it can be assumed, you have some familiarity), and the new worker could play himself or herself during his or her first encounter with the "client." In this example, I have focused on the use of role playing to enhance service delivery skills, but behavioral rehearsal role playing can also be used (for example) to help a staff member prepare for a presentation to a community group, in order to interest this group in giving money to the agency.

Placing a staff person in the role of another individual can increase empathy for or modify a negative attitude toward that individual. There is considerable evidence that this kind of role reversal is an effective way to produce behavioral and attitudinal change. For example, Z. Moreno (1951) describes its use with mothers in a well-baby clinic to give them insight into the feelings of their infants; Ablesser (1962) describes its use with four boys who had stolen cars as a way of alerting them to the rights of others. J. L. Moreno (1952) also describes the use of this approach to reduce prejudice toward minority group members.

The third use—to review a past event—might occur in supervision, where the supervisor asks a staff member to show him or her what happened. The request here would be, "Show me, don't tell me," perhaps because in the telling, the supervisor thinks something is being overlooked, or the staff member is not aware of how the behavior affected others.

The use of role playing as a way of teaching a new behavior to staff members by having them attempt to imitate the performance of a model has received considerable attention in the literature (see, for example, Bertcher, 1978). For one thing, modeling provides an efficient way to teach behavior:

> Teaching a child to use a spoon by modeling permits him to see the entire process—how to grasp the spoon, dip it into his food, bring it to his mouth, insert and withdraw it, and repeat this procedure. To teach this to a child without modeling would involve a lengthy and complex explanation, plus a cumbersome step-by-step introduction to the correct way of using a spoon. (Bertcher, 1978, pp. 235 ff.)

For another, it allows the model to witness this attempt at imitation and to provide positive as well as corrective feedback in shaping the new performance.

The fifth use of role playing is to present a situation, perhaps in a problem-solving portion of a staff meeting, in which the role play dramatizes a serious issue with which a staff member is grappling. Perhaps, simply because it *is* dramatic, a role play can be used to kick off a staff discussion. I knew of a supervisor who had to teach her staff the use of a new federally mandated form. "Ugh," said a disgruntled staff member. "Another complicated piece of paperwork!" But the supervisor was ready for this response: She role-played an interview with a "client" during which the form was filled out. Seeing her use of the form *in action,* so to speak, was intriguing for staff (who were accustomed to and bored with the standard lecture-style presentation of new forms) and provided an opportunity for an animated discussion of problems in using the new form, as well as the many problems staff faced when confronting the enormous amount of paperwork required by the agency.

This last example suggests that there may be times when role playing is preferable to a lecture simply because it is more interesting. But there is nothing to prevent a combination of the two—an introductory lecture followed by a role play. Indeed, to make the picture complete, a role play should *always* be followed by a review of the role-play experience; when the role play takes place in a group context, this requires the use of group discussion (see the presentation of that method earlier in this chapter).

Guidelines for the Use of Role Playing

1. In Chapter 2, I discussed the use of contracting as a way of making clear to all involved what the roles and goals of a particular staff development activity are. The first step in the use of role playing is to establish a contract for its use. Participants should know why the role play is being used and what their role in it will be. Just as it is unwise to force people into a contract, so it is unwise to force people into role playing. There is nothing more embarrassing than asking for volunteers to play particular roles in a group setting and getting none. I often approach potential "players" before the session starts and ask them if they would be willing to play a particular part, for a particular purpose. If anyone I approach seems reluctant, I drop the subject and go in search of another volunteer.

2. Assuming the satisfactory negotiation of a contract, the staff developer using role playing should then set the scene. Parts should be distributed and the situation described, including what has led up to the particular situation being enacted. Simple props can be used—a chair, a telephone, and the like—or costumes, such as a hat and coat. An effective way to help someone get into role is to interview the person *in the role* before the role play actually begins. In addition, a role description can be written out and handed to all players to help them understand their roles.

3. Before you start, introduce a time-out norm, whereby any role player who thinks the role play has strayed from believability, or is feeling lost or uncertain about his or her role, can simply say, "Time out," to stop the dramatic action. I recall a role play in which students were enacting a mother–teenage daughter interchange. The other students watching the role play thought that the "mother" was not acting like any credible mother they had ever seen, so one called, "Time out." The class then discussed the question, and the student playing the role of mother (who was only twenty six years old and had never been a mother) admitted that she was not sure where to go with the role. The class then gave her some simple, straightforward suggestions, and asked her if she thought she could now handle the role. When she said she could, they began the scene again. This time, it played in a convincing fashion, providing the focus for a lively discussion. A good way to start a role play (assuming you have planned to use one, as opposed to a situation in which—with no preplanning—you spontaneously decide to use a role play) is to prepare a script that tells the players what to say the first few times they speak. The script ends (in midstream, as it were), but the players, launched by the script into the action of the scene, continue.

4. Once a role play starts, you have to watch to see that it does not run on

so long that there is too much to be reviewed when it is over, and that no one is suffering in his or her role. Occasionally, role players get so caught up in their roles that they reveal more of themselves than they had intended to reveal, with devastating results. It takes good judgment on your part to know this is happening, but it is always something to watch for. When using a role play to set up the imitation of a model, it is important not to let the modeling go on for too long, because the potential imitator may find there is simply too much content to reproduce. Better to break up the model's performance and let the learner attempt the new behavior one piece at a time. Later there will be a chance to put it all together in a longer role play.

5. Should you, as the staff developer, play a role yourself? Sometimes this is necessary to overcome the reluctance of others to get into a role play. Sometimes, of course, as in one-to-one supervision, *you* play the role of model to demonstrate a particular approach to your supervisee. By and large, however, it is better not to play a role yourself if you do not have to, so you can keep an eye on the clock, watch out for persons who may be upset by the demands of their roles, and in general be free of personal involvement with any of the roles so that you can manage the discussion that follows in a fair and impartial way.

6. When do you stop a role play? Assuming that all is going well—that is, no one is being made too uncomfortable by the performance—you should consider negotiating a general agreement about a stopping point when you work out your contract. (For example, "Let me show you how I would handle that referral on the phone, then you can pretend you're making a similar referral on the phone and I'll play the person on the other end, then we'll talk about your handling of the call.") As a general rule, do not let role plays go on too long. It helps to know what *too long* is by defining what you are trying to achieve with the role play, so that you can tell when you have done enough.

7. I said earlier that you should never stage a role play without allowing time to discuss it. In some cases, the discussion will focus on feedback to the players; in other cases, the role play will serve to stimulate a discussion, and there must be time for participants to have their say. You should see a role play as a means to an end, not an end in itself. In discussing it, observers may give their own views of what went on, but it is usually a good idea to let the role players themselves talk about the experiences they had while playing the roles—their feelings, their insights, and the ways in which they saw the others in the role play. Considerable learning occurs in an exchange like this: "The further we went with this, the harder it was for me to reach you, and the angrier I felt toward you." "Yeah, I could tell you were getting annoyed with me, but honestly, I began withdrawing because I didn't know how to respond to your earlier questions. And the more inadequate I felt, the more I withdrew. Then, when I sensed your anger, it only made it worse. I wanted so desperately to respond, but I just didn't know how. " Such an exchange shows participants how observable behavior can be misinterpreted, and sets the stage for ways to handle feelings of inadequacy. It may even lead an observer to

say, "Can we replay this scene? I'd like to try what I think might be a better response for the worker to make, when feeling inadequate."

To summarize, when you are role playing, you should:

1. Negotiate a contract for the role play. If you need volunteers, recruit them before the session begins.
2. Set the scene, and help players get into their roles.
3. Introduce a time-out norm.
4. Begin the action, but do not let it run on too long. You may want to use an incomplete script to help the players get started.
5. Decide whether you want to play a role yourself. Unless you have to do so (either to serve as the model, or as a way of encouraging others to participate), it is better to be the stage manager than to be an active player.
6. Stop the role play, either when you have done what you set out to do or when you have covered a sufficiently large piece of it that it would be unwise to proceed without first reviewing that portion.
7. Never role play unless you are prepared to review the role play, once it ends. In reviewing the role play, make sure to ask the players themselves to share how they felt in the role. When the role play occurs in an audience situation, ask the audience first what it saw, and then ask the players to respond to the audience's perception.

Simulation Games

In writing about simulation games, Lauffer says:

> Participants in [a simulation game] do role play. Because they participate in the gamed simulation, however, they may be only minimally concerned with expressing the way they feel or think. Their behavior tends to be instrumental. Like players in any game, their decisions and actions are oriented toward the accomplishment of defined objectives. The play of any game, in fact, reveals a real world of structure or process that the designers wish to teach about or to investigate. As analogs of the real world, gamed simulations include selected variables in a patterned or organized arrangement. Like real social situations [games] include imbalances in power or in access to scarce resources. (Lauffer, 1978a, pp. 237 ff; see also Lauffer, 1973)

Lauffer's mention of "objectives" refers to the objectives of the game, not to instructional objectives. Unlike the objectives of a method like the lecture, the specification of learning outcomes in measurable terms is not in the province of simulation gaming. As in the earlier discussion of the cognitive–discovery approach, the emphasis is on discovery through experience rather than the attainment of specified objectives. In my first exposure to simulation gaming, I found myself assigned the role of a school board member who was expected to vote on a number of complex issues, as one of the "moves" in the game. An issue was discussed, pro and con, that I did not fully understand. Suddenly I found I had thirty seconds to make up my mind—yes, no, abstain. "But," I protested, "how can I vote intelligently when I don't understand the issue?" Notwithstanding my plea, the vote was held, I abstained, and I suddenly understood what it must feel like to become a new member of an ongoing board of education, faced with the obligations for which one was elected, and feeling totally unprepared. I suppose I knew, intellectually, what pressures faced a new board member, but experiencing them within the game was an "Aha!" experience I have never forgotten.

Every game has its coordinator (known as a referee or umpire), and simulation games have a director (and sometimes ancillary staff as well). The role of director varies with the game but involves three main activities: warm-up, play, and debriefing. Because games are often complex, warm-up may take longer than role play. On the other hand, since the emphasis is often on discovery, you are more likely to be explaining rules of the game than helping players understand their own roles in any detail. During this phase it is quite appropriate to allow participants to ask as many questions as they wish about rules, limits, and the like. If the game has any equipment, as many do, it is your responsibility to see that it is all in place and ready to go. In my own experience, I have found it essential to have played the game myself, as a participant, before trying to run it for others. When you participate, you become aware of the ways in which incomplete or unclear explanations of game rules have a negative effect on play. In addition, you get a feel for the game that helps you to determine whether or not it fits your needs as a staff developer.

Typically, the role of game director precludes playing, as you are keeping track of time and monitoring observation of rules. As director, however, I have frequently found players involving me by asking for rule clarification, ways of getting hold of additional rules, and the like. Since the emphasis is on learning by discovery, I avoid giving advice. However, I will clarify rules when it is clear that players have honestly not understood or I have inadvertently left something out. On the other hand, if I am satisfied that players understand the rule and are actually seeking advice on *how* to play, I shrug my shoulders and move off, leaving them to figure it out for themselves—which is precisely what the game is all about.

The debriefing session involves a group discussion among the players. All the comments about group discussions apply here, but let me add a few points. It is particularly important to help game players recognize that *whatever happened* during the simulation is significant if the review process is to be meaningful. Players who report becoming very anxious during play may pass this off by saying, "But it's just a game." At that point I would ask the group whether or not the simulation was true to life. Once it becomes clear that it was, feelings of anxiety (or any other feelings) become real and need to be addressed. Debriefings often involve a great deal of tension release, often expressed in the form of humor, some of it barbed. It is important to encourage these expressions, lest people leave a simulation with unexpressed resentments. I have seen situations in which people were still angry six months later about something that happened to them in a game.

This brings me to a discussion of when to use a game. Games are powerful.

They can make an indelible impression on people, leading to insights (such as my "Aha!" as the school board member) that have an intensity rarely if ever experienced during a lecture or group discussion, or even a role play, where the manager of the role play or anyone else can call "Time out." There is usually no time out in a game, just as there is no time out in the real world that the game is simulating. Sometimes the lessons learned are fascinating and worthwhile, but they can also be frustrating or embarrassing. So you need to use a simulation game with some care. The players should have some idea of what they are getting into. And some games should not be used with some populations; for example, a game about aging, in which people "die" ("End of the Line" by Fred Goodman) is not a game to play with a group of senior citizens; a game in which the deck is secretly stacked against two-thirds of the players so that the game typically ends in a revolt of this two-thirds, who refuse to play any further, should not be used (in my opinion) with people who must play the game because it is part of a required college course.

Given these cautions, games are a marvelous and delightful way to take a fresh look at old problems. They are potentially full of surprises, "Aha!" insights, and a deepened understanding of complex issues. On balance, it takes a pretty good lecturer to generate the enthusiasm for learning that a game can. Staff developers who are looking for a novel approach will find that a simulation game can fill the bill very nicely. To learn more about particular games for particular situations, you could start with Robert Horn, ed., *The Guide to Simulation/Games and Training,* 3rd edition (Cranford, N.J.: Didactic Systems, Inc., 1977).

CONDUCTING AN INDIVIDUAL INTERVIEW

Individual interviews are used in staff development for a variety of reasons, ranging from contract negotiation with an administrator to an evaluation interview with a supervisee. Some interviews, such as the two just mentioned, are formal (scheduled), with a clear purpose in the minds of both participants; others are completely happenstance, as when two staff meet accidentally at the office coffee pot, or one staff member grabs another for a quick thirty-second consultation on a problem that has just come up. A great deal has been written about the interview. Here I will limit myself to some basic considerations and some fundamental guidelines.

First, purpose. Most interviews are meant, in part, to be persuasive. When you interview someone to gather information (as in a needs assessment interview) you are trying to persuade the other person to trust you enough to honestly share the person's view of his or her needs. When you meet with an administrator to negotiate a contract for a staff development activity, you are trying to persuade the administrator to go along with your contract proposals as far as possible. When you meet with supervisees for an evaluation interview, you are trying to persuade the interviewees that the evaluation is being conducted in their best interests as well as those of the organization and, if anything they are doing needs to be changed, that they should change it with a minimum of resistance. To be a successful interviewer, then, you have to understand something about persuasiveness.

Persuasion is but one form of what French and Raven (1968) call "social power." Simply stated, *social power* refers here to the ability of an individual to change the thoughts, attitudes, or behavior of another person in a particular direction. Power is based, they say, on any one or a combination of five distinct factors, the potential influencer's perception of the person(s) to be influenced: (1) the ability to reward them, (2) the ability to coerce them, (3) a legitimate right to have power over them, (4) the ability to attract the desire of others to identify with the individual, and to do as that individual does (called *referent power*), and/or (5) expertise. Translating these notions to the interview in staff development, I would suggest that you will be a persuasive staff developer to the degree that you can make use of one or more of these bases of power. For example, staff developers have reward power to the degree that they can convince others that they (the staff developers) can respond to the others' felt needs (through staff development activities) so as to reduce these needs. The use of coercive power may produce so much resistance as to be counterproductive, but there is a question of degree here; sometimes the person in charge has to crack the whip a bit, in an interview, in order to motivate staff to undertake an unpleasant task. Staff developers often have the legitimate right (and obligation) to initiate any and all of the staff development activities that are discussed in this book; their failure to do so probably weakens their power overall. Although not all staff developers can themselves generate much referent power (we cannot all be charismatic, for example), they can recruit charismatic others to put across the staff development message (in an interview), both from within the organization and from outside. Finally, the degree to which staff developers are viewed as experts, at least in managing the staff development process itself, will affect the response of others (in an interview) toward the staff developers. In sum, the response of others toward staff developers, in an interview, will be influenced by their view of the staff developers' social power.

Sometimes this view precedes an interviewer as part of his or her reputation within the organization. But much can be done within the interview itself to enhance or maintain that reputation. Herewith, then, some necessarily brief ideas about the management of the interview itself.

1. Ask yourself, "What am I doing here?" It helps to go into an interview with a sense of purpose, some idea of what you hope to achieve as a result of this interview. Often you will discover, during the interview, that you have to modify your purpose—make it more modest, or move in a new direction. But if you do not know where you want to go, your chances of getting anywhere are quite limited. Besides, if you have some sense of purpose, you will prepare for the interview in a particular way. With no sense of direction, you may fail to prepare, enter the interview unprepared, and end up looking foolish (which does not do your image of "expertise" any good).

2. Identify the reason for meeting at the very beginning of the interview. In some cases, this may require problem description; in others it may mean developing an agenda for the session, to which both parties many want to contribute, as in a supervisory or consultative conference. Even if the other party does not choose to contribute, make sure he or she understands and agrees to your agenda.

3. Throughout the interview, attend to what the other person says. It is also important to pay attention to what he or she does not say out loud by "listening" to their body language as expressed in facial expression, nervous tapping, body posture, direction of gaze, head nodding, and so forth. There is nothing wrong with checking these out when their meaning is ambiguous ("You smiled. Does that mean you agree with me?").

4. The term *active listening* has been coined to describe a way of listening that is not merely a passive process, but encourages the other person to continue participating actively, firm in the belief that he or she has your attention and your comprehension. Active listening includes the following:

a. *Attending:* Allen Ivey describes attending behavior as basic to effective interviewing (Ivey, 1983). It involves looking at the interviewee, looking relaxed (as opposed to appearing to be in a hurry to end the contact) and interested, and making verbal comments to show that you are paying careful attention to what the other person is saying. Tone of voice should also communicate interest in the interviewee. Incidentally, for some cultural groups, eye contact during a conversation is considered rude; depending on who you are interviewing, you should be sensitive to this issue.

b. *Responding to feelings:* I have already referred to the use of this technique in the earlier section on group discussion. Those remarks are relevant here as well, and it may be easier to use this technique in an interview, where you need to respond to the feelings of only one other person. Here is one formula: a conditional statement ("You seem to be saying. . .") that attempts to reflect an expressed feeling accurately (". . .that it worries you. . .") in relation to a particular situation (". . .to think about spending any money on staff development, at this time. ") Making the statement conditional invites the interviewee to confirm the statement's accuracy, or to correct the interviewer's perception of the feeling, if it is inaccurate (see Milnes and Bertcher, 1980).

c. *Information seeking:* In the section on lecturing, I discussed some things to think about when *giving* information. Here I am concerned with ways of *gathering* information. A few simple rules should prove helpful: In asking a question, decide whether or not you want a yes-or-no answer ("Would you agree that she is the person I should talk to about this?") or a fuller response ("Could you tell me a little more about her?"). Inform the interviewee of your reasons for needing the information, what you plan to do with it, and— when appropriate—how you plan to guarantee confidentiality. Keep the question as brief as possible, and try not to ask two questions with the second following right after the first, supposedly for clarification ("Could you tell me a little more about her? I mean, is she likely to want to help me?").

d. *Focusing and summarizing:* Both these topics were dealt with in the section on group discussion. During the interview, it is your responsibility to keep the discussion on topic (via focusing); from time to time, you should use summarizing to make sure that you and the interviewee agree on what has been said up to that point. Check it out: Is this what we have agreed to? Are these the issues that remain?

e. *Confrontation:* This is a form of information giving whereby you inform the interviewee of a contradiction between two things he or she has said or done, or of a discrepancy between what the person is saying and what you know to be fact. Some people are afraid to use confrontation because they perceive it as an aggressive act, in which you *force* someone to deal with something that—to the other person—is unpleasant. Indeed, if you are out to nail someone with the contradiction or discrepancy, chances are he or she will sense this as an attack and will resist it. On the other hand, if you simply point out the contradiction in a calm, objective way, insisting gently but firmly that the interviewee pay attention to the contradiction, the person is less likely to experience this as a personal attack by you. This compels the interviewee to deal with and consider reducing the discomfort created by the contradiction or discrepancy.

5. Consider the mix of interview–interviewee attributes. Everyone can be described in terms of a multitude of attributes—age, sex, race, socioeconomic status, and so forth. Members of minority groups, particularly those that have experienced negative stereotyping and discrimination, are often particularly sensitive to others' reactions to the attribute that links them to that group. Thus, women in an organization dominated by men are likely to be keenly aware of their sex in their dealings with male fellow workers; black staff members in an agency whose staff is largely white are likely to be particularly aware of their racial attribute. Interviewers need to take into account the way in which their own key attributes affect the interviewee's attitude toward them and toward the interview process itself. One of our graduates told me of an incident in which he was involved that exemplifies this point about sex differences between interviewer and interviewee:

> The social worker was employed by a hospital that had run out of space for its out-patient mental health clinic. The need for space was resolved by purchasing a nearby motel and remodeling the rooms into offices, so that clients could be interviewed there. During one interview, the worker sensed that his client, a woman about his own age, seemed hesitant to get involved in the interview. He stopped the interview, and asked her if something about the interview was bothering her. With some hesitancy and embarrassment she told him that yes, it was a little difficult for her to proceed because this was the first time in her life that she had been alone, in a motel room, with a man who was not her husband! It was the worker's opinion that if he had not asked his question, the issue would have remained unresolved between them. As it was, they both laughed, discussed the issue briefly, then moved back to the more serious issues that had brought her to the clinic.

Moral: Interviewers with significant attributes that are markedly different from those of the interviewees should spend some time thinking about and perhaps discussing (with the interviewee) how their personal attributes are affecting the quality of the transaction. Interviewers may find, however, that too many questions about this can prove embarrassing to the interviewee. In that case, the interviewer needs to do some homework about the cultural expectations of members of particular subgroups.

USING MEDIA

Instructional aspects of staff development can use a number of media approaches, including audio- and videotape recordings, films, slides, photographs, charts, overhead projection of transparencies, chalkboard (or large newsprint pad with heavy felt-tip pen), books and journals, and—most recently—computers. Using media has several values and drawbacks. Media are certainly no panacea for the staff developer—they can, if used incorrectly, be a real pain in the neck. Used correctly, however, they can certainly enhance the attractiveness of any staff development activity.

A lot of attention has been paid to the comparative educational effectiveness of the different media just listed. Although the findings are mixed, one fairly consistent finding is that media used in instructional institutions, such as colleges and universities, do not produce significantly better learning than, say, lecture and discussion, when this learning is measured by performance on a final examination. For example, McKeachie, reviewing studies on the effectiveness of the use of television in the classroom as a major medium of instruction for an entire course, found that:

> (1) television instruction is inferior to classroom lectures in communicating information, developing critical thinking, changing attitudes and arousing interest in a subject, but that (2) this inferiority is probably not great. (McKeachie, 1969, p. 108.)

The staff developer who is hoping to plan an interesting session in response to assessed needs may hear about a "really good" movie that sounds as though it could fill the bill, only to find that the movie runs for forty-five minutes, and the staff development session is scheduled to last only fifty minutes, allowing almost no time for an exchange of ideas about the film among the staff viewers. In fact, a great many things can go wrong when you try to use media. I list them here not to discourage the use of media, but to discourage misuse that can defeat the purpose the particular medium is designed to achieve. I will follow up this gloomy listing with some suggestions of how to avoid the pitfalls listed here.

Equipment Problems

Sometimes equipment breaks down (for example, the projection bulb in the 16 mm movie projector burns out). More often, however, the problem is that the operator does not know how to use the equipment. I recall a cry for help from a colleague who had planned an entire two-hour class around the display and discussion of a particular videotape, and then could not produce either sound or picture.

Fortunately, on this occasion, I was able to walk into the classroom and play the role of hero successfully by turning the switch that brought the machine to life. (I have not always been that successful, of course.) Films that break in the middle, rooms that have only two-pronged outlets when your equipment has three-pronged plugs (and you do not have an adapter), the absence of an extension cord—at one time or another I have faced all of these situations, and it has not helped the activity one bit. I still remember the day I invited a hundred students to see a particular film that "starred" several faculty members they all knew. When I tried to thread the film, I discovered that it had been rewound upside down and backwards, and I was simply not sufficiently adroit to correct this problem.

Distraction

The use of films and videotapes can suffer when the dress or hairstyles of the performers are so out of date as to invite catcalls and laughter. Poor acting, bad lighting, and inaudible sound are all distracting aspects of films and videotapes made by nonprofessionals. My particular dislike is the novice videotape camera person who uses the zoom lens with such reckless abandon that sensitive stomachs begin to turn over and heads begin to reel. In short, anything about the medium that calls unnecessary attention to the medium itself, rather than allowing the viewer to focus on the content of the message being delivered, is distracting. I recently previewed an instructional program designed to be used on a microcomputer, and found that the program did not clearly guide users (many of whom could be expected to be computer illiterates) into appropriate use of the computer itself, so that the program did not work as it was supposed to work. When media are used effectively, viewers can quickly forget the medium itself, and focus on the message being conveyed.

Relevance

Often you find yourself using a media product that was not developed specifically for your use but seems sufficiently relevant to be adapted to your purpose. But locating just the right item may involve time-consuming effort. Catalogue descriptions are brief, and what another staff developer loved may strike you as mediocre for your purposes. Those of us who sometimes teach from films or prepared tapes generally believe that we can teach from either good or bad examples, but staff generally prefer to see the correct way to do something. Creating a good fit between staff needs and available media is often problematic. Not only is it difficult to locate the most relevant material, but that material is often too costly or is not available when needed.

Given these drawbacks, staff developers might be inclined to forgo all but the simplest of media (such as a chalkboard). But because media *can* pack a dramatic punch, and that is what you believe you need, or because they can provide a close-up view of something that might otherwise be hard to see and/or learn about, you certainly should not rule out their use. Rather, you should plan for their use in the way that is likely to provide optimum payoff. Here are a few suggestions:

1. *Develop a resource file.* You need to know where you can secure media quickly and inexpensively, as well as gaining any expert assistance you may need to facilitate efficient use of the media. Some resources to investigate include:

a. *Your local library:* Indeed, the very word *library* has been replaced by *media center* in many places. Media centers are repositories of materials and the equipment with which to display them. They can also provide catalogues, and offer the librarian's assistance in locating relevant materials.

b. *Colleges and universities:* These institutions, in addition to having their own centralized media centers, also allow specific departments to develop their own media centers, with resources that are particularly relevant to their program (and thus to yours).

c. *The local public school system:* In addition to having their own media centers, schools may have available used equipment that you can borrow or purchase. As with libraries, colleges, and universities, it is a good idea to get to know the key person(s) in the organization who can help you with media acquisition.

2. *Never buy if you can borrow.* This principle of frugality is a result of several years of working for human service organizations with limited budgets. Shakespeare may have said, "Neither a borrower nor a lender be," but he never had to deal with the kinds of budgets with which staff developers are all too familiar. Notes on *where* you can borrow *what* should be an integral part of your resource file.

3. *Always preview.* You need to preview to make appropriate selections in relation to the concepts of *relevance* and *distraction* already discussed. In addition, you might find, for example, a portion of a film that is highly relevant. Say your session is fifty minutes long; a fifteen-minute portion of a film might be precisely what you need to get the staff discussion started where you want it to start. Previewing might also help you to think of other uses for the medium than were originally intended; for example, turning off the sound when showing a movie allows the viewers to concentrate on nonverbal behavior.

Previewing takes time, but it is essential! Never use media material that you have not tried yourself. If it does not work for you, it probably will not work for others. I will go even further: If you cannot preview the item, do not use it.

Further, in connection with previewing, make sure you know how to operate the equipment you will need to use. In some cases, you will need special training. If that is impossible, be sure to arrange for the services of someone who can operate the equipment for you.

4. *Get a budget.* The use of media often involves spending some money, and it will help you to know just how much money you have or how much you want to have in order to accomplish staff development goals. But do not let the lack of money stop you. That is when your creative borrowing or bartering skills need to be brought into play.

CONCLUSION

I have tried to present some basic ideas about the hands-on doing of staff development. Much more can be said—and has been said—about each of the areas I've addressed here. Library shelves and bookstores bulge with how-to books in every one of these areas. I hope my distillation of some key principles can lead you in the right directions.

chapter 7

MANAGING STAFF DEVELOPMENT

- This chapter takes up two major questions:
  How do you locate and use resources for staff development, including information, money, services, equipment, and volunteers?
- How do you plan staff development in order to achieve maximum efficiency, including use of flow charts, Gantt charting, PERT charting, and payoff/loss analysis?

LOCATING AND USING RESOURCES FOR STAFF DEVELOPMENT

Resources are all those things—material, informational, or human—that you need to accomplish a task. Too often, new ideas die a-borning because people *assume* they lack the resources to bring them to life. There is a tremendous range of resources available for all kinds of staff development activities, but people don't know about them or don't know how to find or get what they want when they want it. In this section I will identify the kinds of resources needed for staff development activities that are not immediately or obviously available, and suggest ways of locating and acquiring them. My not-too-hidden agenda is to get you started on developing your own file of local resources, so that when individual staff who know about particular resources leave your organization, their knowledge of resources does not depart with them.

I will deal with five different kinds of resources: (1) information, (2) money, (3) services, (4) equipment, and (5) volunteers.

Information Resources: The Computer

Some people say we have left the Industrial Age behind and moved into the Information Age, thanks to the development of computers and, especially, personal computers (PCs) for office use. Libraries have always been wonderful places to find information, but the time required to find it was often disproportionate to the amount of information found. Now, with the aid of computers, we can scan vast collections of information, locating particular kinds of data with tremendous speed. Most libraries now have computers, and librarians are trained to conduct searches of information systems.

Nowadays, many human service organizations are purchasing their own PCs. Through the use of a device known as a *modem,* it is possible to hook up a PC, through the telephone lines, to any one of a variety of information referral services (or vendors) who market information. With most vendors, you can open an account with an initial fee and then pay for information you get from the computer, based on the quantity of information you collect. Vendors who sell information link you— through their system—to an enormous variety of data bases, which are simply large collections of information. For example, all of *Psychological Abstracts* makes up one data base, all of *Dissertation Abstracts,* another. Each vendor continues to add data bases, as well as providing training for persons using their system. In addition, people who use the same model of PC often form informal user clubs that meet regularly, as well as calling one another up for consultation and support.

Once you have decided what kinds of information you want, local university librarians can tell you which vendor is best for your needs. The real trick to using computers for information searching lies in knowing what you want and selecting those words or *descriptors* that will help you locate it precisely. This often involves selecting a number of synonyms and then "asking" the computer to locate information about the topics you have chosen. In *on-line* searching, you see the information you are asking about almost instantaneously, either on the computer screen or printed out by the computer's printer; in *off-line* searching, you tell the computer what kinds of information you want, and it prints out the response on a high-speed printer at the vendor's home office; then the product is mailed to you. Off-line searching is cheaper, but you have to wait for the information to arrive in the mail.

Information Resources: Published Works

The invention of the printing press ensured wide availability of information. In fact, most of us are now drowning in journal articles, books, pamphlets, project reports, and so forth. What you need to know are the sources most appropriate to your needs. Not many of the sources of information that I will describe tell you how to go about *applying* the knowledge they contain. They do, however, provide information from which you can work in developing applications suited to your particular needs and circumstances. The last part of this section suggests some ways to convert this information into practical applications that you can use. As you read, remember that high-cost items are often available for loan through some local library—public, school, college, or university learning resource center.

A System for Collecting and Retaining Information

Often, someone doing staff development has to track down a resource pertaining to a particular activity. There should be a central file in which information about that resource is kept, so that other staff members can secure it when they need it. To create such a central file, you need (1) a uniform way of recording information about the resource, (2) an easily accessed location for the file, and (3) someone assigned to keep the file up to date and to expand it continually.

A uniform record of resource contacts should include at least the following information:

1. Name of the person completing the form
2. Date the form was written
3. Category of resource—for example, Information, Equipment, and so on
4. Specific nature of the resource
5. Specific procedures involved in securing the resource—whom to call, where to go to get it, and so on
6. Description of experience in using the resource with particular attention to future prospects from that source, pitfalls to be avoided in using the resource, how well the resource filled the bill, and so on
7. Anything learned about securing resources, in relation both to the particular resource and to resource acquisitions in general

In addition, some procedure should be developed for categorizing records, so that, for example, someone looking for used audiovisual equipment does not have to read through the entire file to find what is needed. You'll need to make up a list of descriptors that are meaningful to your agency. A good source of descriptors that can be found in any library is called "The Library of Congress Subject Headings. " Of course, you can just use common sense to create your own descriptors, but by using Library of Congress (LC) descriptors, you can build a system of your own that relates to library systems in general. Since many individual records would be likely to contain references to resources that would fall under more than one category, a cross-referencing system should be developed. If you need help to do this, you should consult your local librarian—a person who knows all about systems for filing information. Once you've done that, you will have established a working link with one of your best information sources: the library.

Librarians can seem busy and unapproachable, and you may be embarrassed at not knowing your way around. Memories of school library experiences may haunt you and make you hesitant to ask for help. But professional librarians are trained to teach people to use the many resources of a library; they want to be helpful. They will explain, when asked, how to use the card catalogue, encyclopedias, almanacs, government documents, old newspaper files, projectors, microfilm readers, and so forth. In many libraries, particularly those on university and college campuses, librarians can do your computer searches for you, for a fee.

Many communities have several types of libraries. In addition to the city, county, school, college, and university libraries, some businesses or industries maintain specialized libraries that could be useful to you. If you are getting ready to look for information in libraries, it is helpful to know about all the libraries in your community. If one library cannot help you, the librarian there may know of another that can.

Finally, in addition to developing a central resource file, you should consider developing a specialized library of your own that will include journals, books, agency reports, government documents, and so forth relating to your program. Again, if you decide to establish your own library, ask a librarian to help you set it up. Or ask if he or she knows a retired librarian who might become your volunteer librarian. Remember that your library not only can be a resource to you when you want to conduct a particular staff development activity; it also can be a generally useful resource for all staff.

There is one problem to overcome in creating such a file: getting staff to complete and turn in the resource file record forms. If staff members agree to develop such a file, however, and if someone is made responsible for it, it should grow. Once people begin to use it and see how valuable it can be, chances are they will be highly motivated to add to it continually.

Finally, don't overlook one of the best free sources of information available to you: the Yellow Pages of your telephone directory. For example, under the heading "Associations" can be found references to the following: Athletic Organizations, Business and Trade Organizations, Church Organizations, Fraternal Organizations, Fraternities and Sororities, Labor Organizations, Political Organizations, Professional Organizations, Social Service and Welfare Organizations, Veterans and Military Organizations, and Youth Organizations and Centers—as well as the name, address, and telephone number of every group in town that considers itself an "association," providing it has a phone. Clearly, the headings listed above all represent potential sources of resources, some of which will be discussed at various points throughout the remainder of this chapter.

Getting Money for Staff Development

Money may be the "root of all evil," but without it staff development must be limited in scope. Agency budgets may seem ironclad, but there *are* ways of acquiring dollars to do things that were not anticipated or included when the administrator made up the budget.

First, it's possible to involve staff in actual budget development, so that staff as a whole has a say in the budget priorities (including staff development activities) for the coming year. One program I've heard of used the technique of *group contracting* to negotiate a consensus on budget priorities. The administrator found that this led to improved staff commitment to the agency's goals and a keener awareness by staff of the necessary budgetary processes that go into running an agency.

If a small amount of money is needed for a specific staff development activity, you can turn to a charitable group in the community. Such groups can be found, as indicated earlier, through the Yellow Pages of your telephone book; they include church groups, fraternal organizations, veterans groups, or any other association that has charity or community service as one of its major goals.

Larger amounts of money to support some activity may be available from a granting agency or foundation. Such sources, often highly specialized in their interest, might be directly relevant to your needs. Here are some sources to look at; they're probably available at the library.

The Catalog of Federal Domestic Assistance.   This catalog explains the nature and purpose of programs. It specifies major eligibility requirements, tells where to apply, and lists printed materials available. It is indexed by subject and agency, and master indexed by program category. Descriptions include program title, nature and purpose of program, eligibility, contract, what printed information is available, authorizing legislation, and administering agency. It is available from the Superintendent of Documents, U.S. Government Printing Office, Washington, D.C. 20402, and is revised periodically.

Annual Register of Grant Support.   This source provides indexes by subject, organization name, and geographic area of private foundation and federal sources. It lists information for each entry regarding funding preferences, application deadlines, usual size of grants, form in which the application should be made, and often the name of the contact person at the organization. It is an excellent source for foundations because of the triple index and the extent of other information provided. Use of this register allows a narrowing of possible funding agencies for any specific purpose.

The Grantsmanship Center News.   Published eight times a year in a newspaper format, this source is available from the Grantsmanship Center, a nonprofit institution (1015 West Olympic Boulevard, Los Angeles, California 90015). It contains articles on how to write grant proposals, how to negotiate with government and foundation grantors, how to plan and administer grant projects, and who is funding what kinds of projects. It also includes announcements of workshops and summaries of conference proceedings on the design and management of projects supported by grants. It is a good source of ideas about how to plan and organize projects and programs, as well as news about program ideas that have been carried out under grants.

Locating and Using Services for Staff Development

At times, what you need to conduct a staff development activity is someone with particular knowledge and skill. The first place to look is your own staff. To that end, you should create a resource file of staff skills, knowledge, and experience, including foreign languages, travel abroad, audiovisual machine operating skills, and the like. To do this, send staff a questionnaire surveying their skills.

Next, expertise is often available from universities and colleges, and such institutions expect their faculty and staff to make their expertise available to the local community.

A first step in developing your central resource file might be to brainstorm a list of the kinds of resources you are likely to need, and then assign one or more people to make up the necessary record forms on potential resources relevant to those needs. Remember that there are a great many organizations in your community that are directly concerned with peoples' problems, ranging from high schools to unions, from the department of public welfare to mental health clinics. Many of these organizations employ people with special competence and experience that might prove useful to you. You should know these people, and it doesn't hurt to have this acquaintance on a first-name basis. Most human service workers develop such contacts over time in the course of their work, but usually only in reference to limited, specific needs. What is being suggested here is that you develop systematically a network of contacts that could be potentially productive, even though there is no specific need at the moment.

A good source of information about human service organizations can be found in the directories developed by organizations such as the Welfare Planning Council or United Way; some counties develop their own directories. Directories usually contain brief descriptions of each organization's program, as well as basic identifying information such as correct name, address, telephone number, and director's name.

Finding Equipment for Staff Development

Equipment "freebies," bargains, or loans are abundant, providing you know where to look. Equipment used for staff development can include audiovisual machines, bookcases (for your library), copiers, cameras, and the like.

Government auctions of all kinds can be a gold mine of inexpensive equipment and supplies. Usually such auctions are announced in the classified ads of your local newspaper and are held under city, county, state, or federal government auspices. Insurance companies and moving companies have also been known to dispose of property by auction. Newspaper ads can also provide a tip on auctions resulting from bankruptcy proceedings; look under "Legal Notices."

State and federal government surplus warehouses are open to a select population. Your agency must apply to the governmental unit in question for permission to purchase such equipment. Large universities often dispose of used equipment by quietly selling it to the public. It may take a little telephoning to locate these sources, but once you've tapped into them, you'll find it well worth the effort, especially with regard to future purchases.

Another source of equipment could be local fraternal organizations, since most of them include community service as one of their goals. Such organizations are often reluctant to provide cold cash, but through their membership are often in touch with sales, wholesale prices, or even good used personal property. In addition, such organizations could be talked into purchasing and donating specific kinds of equipment if a little placque displaying their name as donor is placed on the equipment.

Getting Volunteers Involved in Staff Development

Much of what has already been said pertains to volunteers as well. The librarian who helps you create your own agency library, the lawyer who speaks to your staff about legal aspects of their work, the local citizen who sits on your organization's advisory board—all are volunteers, providing meaningful services without pay. The tradition of volunteering to help others is a strong one in this country, one that can be drawn on if you can define clearly the tasks to be done—and if you know where to look for such volunteers.

Finding volunteers is not that difficult once you begin to look for something specific. As indicated before, social service and welfare organizations, professional associations, fraternal groups, labor unions, and so forth are all good sources of volunteers. In addition, the local United Fund or Welfare Planning Council usually has a Volunteer Bureau where people who are interested in volunteering time and skills register this interest, with agencies drawing from this pool. Finally, the key to good use of volunteers is to have something specific and "do-able" for them to do.

Some Basic Rules About Acquiring Resources

Rule 1: Always assume you can get resources free.   If you need something, begin by trying to get it donated to your office. Items donated to a nonprofit organization are tax deductible for the donor. For example, if you need a typewriter, a local business can donate a machine that it's replacing. The business can take an income tax deduction for the value of the typewriter as a charitable contribution, and you might be able to invest the several hundred dollars that a new one would have cost in helping another client.

Obviously, there is a double advantage to be gained from a donation. Not only have you acquired a resource that you needed, you have also developed a relationship with the donor—be it an individual or an organization—that could be nourished against the need for future assistance and support.

Rule 2: Sell to the resource's needs, not to yours.   Don't try to convince a lawyer to donate time for a presentation to your staff by telling him or her only how useful this will be to *your* program. Tell the lawyer how you intend to provide for his or her needs. Although lawyers feel the need to help people, it may not be their strongest need. Besides, they can provide for their need in that respect by helping a paying client. Find out as much as you can about resource people, and then sell the idea that you can help meet *their* needs while they are helping you. For example, if you meet a lawyer who is running for public office, he or she might agree to make a presentation to your staff on the legal rights of clients. Then get the local newspaper to cover the event, with a picture of a "local citizen volunteering time to help staff understand better the legal rights of clients and the legal obligations of staff." That publicity is a payoff the candidate can use.

Rule 3: Assume you've made the sale, and let the buyer make the lesser decision.   If you give prospective resources a chance to say "no," they may do so. To avoid this problem, assume the resource has already agreed to do what you asked, and proceed to a lesser decision—the way the resource is to be delivered, or the time and place at which the resource can be secured. For example, if you're calling a university professor in search of information, you'd do better to ask *when* it would be convenient to have an appointment, rather than asking *whether* or not the professor would be willing to talk with you.

Rule 4: If you can't get it (to keep) for free, borrow it.   Some potential donors simply cannot give you certain items, such as an expensive videotape recorder, but they can lend it to you. If your needs are short-range, this could be an entirely satisfactory arrangement.

PLANNING FOR STAFF DEVELOPMENT

Planning is determining in advance *what* is to be done, *how* it is to be done, *when* it is to be done, and *who* is to do it. It encompasses setting objectives, as well as making day-to-day decisions on how these objectives can best be achieved. Hence, planning involves the determination of both ends and means (Robbins, 1980, p. 128).

Planning for staff development can be thought of in terms of *time frame* (short-term, medium, or long-term); *objective* (focused on an individual, a work team, a larger subdivision of the organization, or the entire staff); and *scope* (ranging from narrow and specific to broad and general). This book presents a somewhat idealized planning model for use with any staff development activity:

1. Negotiate a contract for administrative support to initiate staff development in the organization. Subsequently, negotiate contracts with relevant parties at each stage of the staff development process.
2. Involve potential participants in planning staff development as early and as fully as possible.

3. Work toward a consensus on needs and priorities. This will provide the basis for defining the objectives of staff development in general, and for any particular staff development activity.
4. Create a written plan for achieving your objectives. Share your plan and be prepared to modify it on the basis of the feedback you receive.
5. Identify each significant event that must occur and the sequence in which events must occur if you are to achieve your objectives. Using one of the planning techniques to be described, work out a written schedule that includes these events, and use it to guide your efforts.
6. Select the method(s) you will use to achieve your objective.
7. Identify the resources you will need to use this method, and arrange to acquire these resources.
8. Build in a way of monitoring and assessing the effectiveness of staff development.
9. Implement your plan; over time, modify it as needed, using the information received from monitoring and assessing its effectiveness.

The DSS example, portions of which have been presented at various points in the text, can be reviewed in terms of the degree to which it followed the framework for planning presented above:

1. *Negotiate a contract:* Example 1 (page 28) presents a detailed discussion of the initial contract this staff developer worked out with her administrator, allowing her a comparatively free hand to begin the staff development process with a particular staff unit. Her subsequent management of the needs assessment process included a detailed contract negotiation process with the staff unit involved in this project.

2. *Involve potential participants:* Example 5 (page 71) describes a needs assessment process in which staff were encouraged to create a list of their concerns. No attempt was made to impose issues on them. After the use of several needs assessment procedures, it was decided to focus on problems associated with time management. Because of a loss of funding and a resultant cut in staff size (leading to heavier loads for each staff member), this was a meaningful concern for individual staff members. In addition, improving staff management of work assignments was a crucial need of the organization: Unless staff efficiency could be improved, the unit as a whole might well experience punitive funding cuts.

3. *Work toward a consensus:* The achievement of a staff consensus was also described in Example 5.

4. *Create a written plan:* Example 11 (page 90). The staff developer presented written objectives but gave no indication that these were shared with the participants. The objectives specified levels of desired achievement by the unit and presented them in easily measured terms. It would seem essential to the success of these plans to let staff know the details of the expected outcome.

5. *Identify each significant event:* No information was provided about any written schedule used by this staff developer to help this activity occur on time.

The more complicated a staff development activity, the more essential such a schedule becomes. There is evidence that staff were involved prior to the actual training event, by maintaining individual time logs (described in Example 14, page 111). In addition, in Example 11, a specific date was identified by which a minimal level of performance was to be achieved.

6. *Select the method(s):* Example 14 (page 111) focuses on goals for each individual participant but also includes a discussion of some of the methods used (each staff member was to keep an up-to-date daily time log, the log was to be monitored by the supervisor, time wasters were to be identified, and group problem solving was to be used to help each participant eliminate time wasters).

7. *Identify the resources:* No information was given about resources used for this activity; but, with the exception of finding a place and time to meet, no particular resources were needed to put this plan into operation.

8. *Build in assessment:* Example 14 includes reference to the monitoring activities of the unit supervisor. Generally, the objectives for the individual staff were met. Although weekly deadlines were not always met, staff worked to eliminate time wasters over a three-month period. The staff developer writes: "The success rate was outstanding, even with our resistant worker."

9. *Implement your plan:* Example 14 makes clear that the staff development activity was carried out, with good results.

In terms of planning, the chief shortcoming of the DSS examples was the failure to develop a schedule as a way of guiding this process as it unfolded. Techniques for creating such a schedule are presented next. In the discussion that follows, we will attempt to answer two questions:

1. How can you use planning techniques to (a) identify all the activities that must be put together, in sequence, to achieve your staff development goals, on time, and (b) identify potential trouble spots so you can cope with them before they are reached?
2. How can you achieve a favorable balance of payoffs and expenses when planning staff development activities?

Planning Techniques

A number of techniques have been devised to aid in the planning of complex projects. Three of the most commonly used (flow charting, Gantt charting, and PERT—Program Evaluation and Review Technique) will be discussed here. Rather than provide specific instructions for the use of these techniques, I will focus on the particular advantages and disadvantages of each. There are many sources that provide specific instructions for devising and using each technique; I will refer you to those I've found to be helpful.

Each of these techniques requires the user to break down a complex project into a network of subtasks; each technique uses a graphic format to display this network in such a way that the overall flow of the project is revealed; each display then provides a visible way of defining the tasks that must be done, and monitoring progress on each of these tasks. Let's start with flow charting.

Flow charting.   This method helps a planner to plot a series of activities, highlight the decisions that must be made about each activity, and consider alternative next steps that would follow if the decision went one way or the other—the results of a "yes" response versus the results of a "no" response. An activity (drawn in a box, using as few words as possible to save space on the page) might be: "Seek administrative approval for project." An arrow is then drawn down or across the page to a diamond that might contain the question: "Did boss give approval?" (Or, to save space: "Did boss O.K.?") In one form of flow charting, two arrows emerge from the diamond, one going down to the next activity box—the "yes" arrow, indicating a move to the next step; and one arrow going to the side—the "no" arrow, indicating a hitch in the plans and a need to do something about this exigency. The planner is expected to anticipate the steps in the entire project, in terms of both moving ahead and coping with any obstacles encountered. Anticipating decision points presumably helps the planner to develop strategies to ensure "yes" decisions, as well as considering alternative strategies when obstacles are encountered (see Gottman and Clasen, 1972, pp. 179–200, for a very good piece of programmed instruction on flow-chart construction).

Gantt charting.   This method focuses less on decisions and more on laying out, in order, the tasks that need to be done successively if the final goal is to be reached. Using graph paper, the chart attempts to display time dimensions, in scale—something that is not found in flow charting. With a Gantt chart, you can show when work on a task is to begin, and when the task should be completed. (In some cases, it is probably more correct to say *must* be completed, since other tasks cannot be begun until earlier tasks are completed; for example, you can't conduct a needs assessment of all staff until you have received administrative approval to do so.) Although the element of time is used in the Gantt chart (unlike flow charting, where time is not mentioned), the chart does not make clear which particular tasks are tied to which other tasks—which tasks cannot proceed without the completion of these earlier tasks.

In a sense, a Gantt chart is a horizontal bar graph, with each horizontal line on the chart representing a task. A time dimension, for example by weeks, runs along the top of the chart. The planned-for beginning and completion dates for each task are shown by darkening the line between the two dates for each task. Putting them all in sequence tells you when the project can reasonably be completed. You may discover (from this detailed combination of analysis and prediction) that the completion date is further away than you had supposed, leading you to consider a change in the project, a change in the finish date, or an addition of staff, in order to get the job done on time. For a fuller discussion of Gantt charting, see Burman (1972, pp. 8–9), or Lauffer (1978b, pp. 175–181).

PERT.   One of the most complete planning techniques is the Program Evaluation and Review Technique (PERT). As in Gantt charting, the planner identifies the key activities and events involved in the development of a project. In PERT, an *event* is the beginning or completion of a task, and an *activity* is the actual performance of a task. Activities take time and require the use of resources such as money, work, material, and space, but events do not require resources, since they simply represent the moment in time when something was started or completed. Events in a PERT network are indicated by circles (with a number in them to identify the event, but not necessarily in sequence of occurrence). Events are described and listed separately in a key, each next to its identifying number. Activities are indicated by lines connecting the circles. Above each line is written an estimate of the time it will take to complete the activity. One of the advantages of PERT is that it can depict the parallel activities that often go on in a complex project; for example, assuming the administrator gave approval for involving staff in a needs assessment process, one individual or subgroup may be working on developing a draft of the needs assessment questionnaire while a second individual or subgroup arranges for participation by different units of the organization in the needs assessment process. Still another person or group may make arrangements with the secretarial pool so that the needs assessment questionnaire, when ready, can be typed, duplicated, and distributed to the entire staff. These are parallel activities in that each can move forward whether or not progress is being made on the others. Although the chart can become very complicated, PERT at least makes clear the chain of parallel events that must take place for the project to reach completion, and the points at which each set of events combines with the next set.

PERT is one of several planning techniques that can be used to identify the *critical path* in a project—that is, the particular set of successive events that add up to the longest path through the network. In other words, some tasks can be accomplished quickly, while others take longer, but the critical path indicates that the entire project cannot be completed before a particular date. In other words, any delay along the critical path will delay the entire project. PERT also makes it possible to determine where in the project there is slack time—which events can be started later than initially scheduled without in any way delaying the overall project. Knowing where there is slack time might allow a planner to deploy personnel who have little to do for the moment, to other tasks in the project.

Typically, planners have a particular completion date in mind, a date set on the basis of a number of considerations. For example, a particular conference might be set for a particular date because that is when you were able to secure the conference facilities (and you had to make the reservations two years in advance to guarantee that these dates would be yours). Given that date, you work backward over the PERT network, adding estimated times as you go. The critical path is your irreducible minimum. You may discover, when you analyze the project in this way, that you would have had to start it three months ago in order to bring it to completion on time. At this point you can decide to add additional staff so that certain tasks can be done more quickly, or to delete some part of the project, or to look for more efficient ways of completing certain tasks. You might also consider a change in the projected finish date, but in many situations that is out of the question. Two sources are useful with regard to the use of PERT: One is a piece of programmed instruction put out by the Federal Electric Corporation in 1967, and the other is the book on precedence networks by Burman (1972).

To summarize:

1. All three techniques (flow charting, Gantt charting, and PERT) use a graphic display that enables a planner to look at the flow of a project over time and to see the connection between completion of early and later tasks.
2. All three techniques require the planner to break a project into its successive component tasks.
3. Flow charting is particularly useful for anticipating decision points in a project, and for anticipating what to do if the decision made goes this way, or that way.
4. Gantt charting does not deal with alternative options (ones that depend on which decision is made), but it does introduce time as a measure that can be used in monitoring progress toward reaching an established completion date.
5. PERT is particularly useful for displaying parallel activities and for identifying the critical path in a complex project that includes many parallel activities. The critical path is the chain of events that cannot be reduced with respect to the time required to complete it. Any delay in the critical path will delay the entire project. PERT can also be used to identify slack time—those points in the network where work on a particular task or set of tasks can be delayed without delaying the overall project.
6. Gantt charting and PERT can be used to monitor progress during work on a project. If certain tasks take longer to complete than was estimated, each technique can be used to consider alternative ways to complete the project on time, such as investigating the possibility of a change in completion date, seeking better ways of completing certain tasks more quickly than planned, adding personnel, or considering a change in the project's overall design or goals.

Clearly, PERT is the most complex of the three planning procedures described, but it also provides the most information about a complex project. Each approach has its value; it is up to you to decide which is most helpful for your purpose.

Illustration of Planning Techniques

To illustrate these three planning techniques, a hypothetical staff development project will be presented, demonstrating the use of flow charting, Gantt charting, and PERT. Assume that you, as a lone staff developer, or as part of a staff development committee, have been examining the staff development program in your organization and have decided that your orientation program is too hit-or-miss, lacking any clear sense of purpose and direction. It is your opinion as a staff developer (or as a committee) that staff who are not given good support in their new jobs get the impression that the organization (viewed in the abstract) doesn't really care that much about them, with a resultant negative impact on their sense of commitment to their work. What follows is a breakdown of the project into its component tasks, and a sample of each of the three techniques in relation to some of these tasks, to give you a feel for their use.

Flow charting.   First, list activities in order:

1. Consider several staff development projects, and select "an improved orientation program" as a possible high-priority need.
2. Request administrative support for conducting a needs assessment with regard to an improved orientation program.
3. Tabulate staff responses to the needs assessment process regarding an improved orientation program (along with other possible staff development needs).
4. Prepare a written report on staff response and deliver a copy to your administrator.
5. Assuming that the needs assessment process indicates that staff see "an improved orientation program" as a high-priority need, prepare for a staff meeting in which the results of the needs assessment process are reported, and staff involvement is solicited in helping to develop an improved orientation program.

If you want real staff involvement in the planning process, you probably cannot go much further in your planning without overcontrolling the development of the project, but you could come to the meeting with some prethinking about ways to go about improving orientation:

1. Devise a pre- and posttest that could be given to new staff who would participate in the orientation program, to measure its effectiveness.
2. Conduct visits to other agencies working with a similar client population to learn how they orient their staff.
3. Assemble or create a collection of written documents for an orientation manual, based in part on what was learned from visits to other agencies.
4. Create a plan in which new staff are assigned to a staff "buddy" who will guide them through their early days on the job. Included in this plan would be the creation of procedures for the recruitment and training of staff who have been on the job awhile to serve as buddies to new staff members.

Note that items 1–4 are all major tasks, each of which must be broken into component subtasks. Note, too, that each of these tasks can go forward fairly independent of the other three. There are some connections, however:

- Pre- and posttests might include a focus on some of the manual's content, and would therefore have to wait in part until the manual's contents have been determined.
- As indicated, the manual could be informed by what other agencies do for their orientation. Nevertheless, the manual would be likely also to include policies and procedures that are unique to this organization, regardless of what other organizations do.
- Training of staff who agree to play the buddy role will, in part, be influenced by what is done about tasks 1–3. This all suggests another activity that has to be built into the plans: a systematic way for individuals or subgroups to share routinely what they have learned and what they are doing. (This assumes that this project should not be the sole responsibility of one person.)

Our samples (for flow charting and Gantt charting) will focus on the early needs assessment stages of the project. The discussion of other major tasks and their interconnectedness is meant to be suggestive of the overall process. In order to demonstrate PERT's particular usefulness in handling parallel activities, the PERT chart will display the entire project.

Next, (for the flow chart) you would identify the major decision points:

1.   After activity #1, you or the staff development committee decide whether or not to seek approval for conducting a needs assessment at this time, focused on "an improved orientation program."
2.   After activity #2, administrator(s) decide(s) whether or not to approve an assessment of staff needs at this time, with particular attention to work on an improved orientation program.
3.   After activity #3, staff decides whether or not to support the development of an improved orientation program.
4.   After activity #4, administrator(s) decide(s) whether or not to approve the plan for going ahead with a staff meeting focused on involving staff in planning for an improved orientation program.

Obviously, planning would continue past this point, but this should be sufficient for our flow-charting sample (see Figure 7–1).

Gantt charting.   To develop a Gantt chart for the same set of needs assessment–related activities, time factors would need to be added. Although you would not identify decision points for a Gantt chart, you would need to recognize that decision making often takes time, and to build this element of time into your chart. In the Gantt chart shown in Figure 7–2, time estimates have been included for the entire project, projecting it out for fourteen weeks.

PERT.   Building on the task breakdown already described, a PERT chart could be constructed by adding a list of *events* to be depicted. (Remember that the numbers used to identify events have no particular relationship to the order in which events occur; they are merely used to identify each event.)

Event #1:   You, or the staff development committee, complete plans to approach the administrator with a request for approval of conducting a needs assessment process, with particular attention to improving the orientation program.

Event #2:   Administrator(s) approval received (to conduct needs assessment).

Event #3:   Results of needs assessment completed, indicating that "an improved orientation program" is perceived by staff as a high-priority need.

Event #4:   Administrator(s) approval received (to conduct a staff meeting in which an attempt will be made to involve staff in helping to develop an improved orientation program).

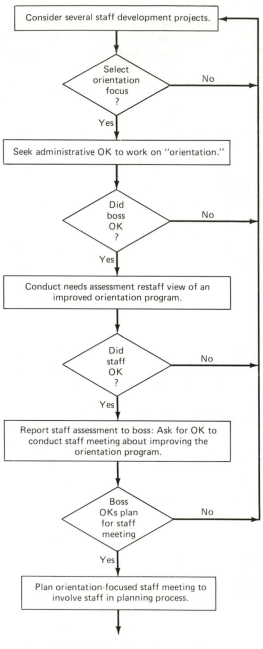

FIGURE 7-1 Flow chart sample

188

WEEKS

PROJECT TASKS	1	2	3	4	5	6	7	8	9	10	11	12	13	14
Obtain boss's approval to do needs assessment recommendation	↔													
Conduct staff needs assessment re orientation	←→													
Report to boss on results of staff needs assessment		←→												
Schedule staff meeting to recruit staff assistance			←——→											
SUBCOMMITTEES														
1. Write pre and post test				←————————→									
2. Write orientation manual				←——————————————→									
3. Visit to agencies to view their orientation				←————→									
4. Recruit "buddies" for buddy system				←——→									
Schedule Staff meeting to coordinate plans												←——→		
Begin orientation program														→

FIGURE 7-2   Gantt chart sample

It should be clear that PERT is not particularly useful, as compared to a Gantt chart, if a project proceeds as this one has up to this point—that is, with each event depending on the immediately preceding event before it can occur. It is only when a project involves a number of parallel tasks that PERT becomes particularly useful. For this reason, the entire PERT chart for this project has been presented, including a depiction of the critical path. All the events in this network follow:

Event #5:   Staff meeting to plan orientation program ends.

Event #6:   Agency-visiting subcommittee's first meeting ends.

Event #7:   Selection of agencies to be visited completed.

Event #8:   Schedule of visits to agencies completed.

Event #9:   Visits to agencies completed.

Event #10:   Written report of visits completed and sent to orientation manual subcommittee.

Event #11:   Manual subcommittee's first meeting ends—members of the pre-/ posttest subcommittee sit in, to get a sense of what manual will be about.

Event #12:   Writing of drafts of manual begun.

Event #13:   Drafts of manual sections completed.

Event #14:   Feedback (from one another) on drafts of manual sections received by authors.

Event #15:   Rewrites of drafts of manual sections (based on feedback) completed.

Event #16:   Assembled manual completed, duplicated.

Event #17:   Buddy system subcommittee's first meeting ends.

Event #18:   Buddy system subcommittee completes job description of "buddy," and its plans for recruiting buddies are accepted.

Event #19:   Recruitment of buddies completed.

Event #20:   Report of plan for buddy system completed.

Event #21:   Pre-/posttest subcommittee completes first meeting.

Event #22:   Drafts of pre- and posttest completed.

Event #23:   Field tests of pre- and posttests completed.

Event #24:   Copies of revised pre- and posttests distributed to all staff.

Event #25:   Meeting to coordinate "improvement of orientation program" project components completed.

Event #26:   Orientation program ready for implementation.

See Figure 7–3 for a sample of the PERT chart that would be constructed.

Payoff/Expense Analysis

In these days of tight budgets, it is not uncommon for organizations to create budgets with little or no money set aside for staff development. Of course, many of the activities that I have defined as falling under the umbrella of staff development—supervision, consultation, training students, and the like—are either covered by the salaries of persons doing staff development or are not identified explicitly as staff development. Nevertheless, it helps to have money specifically earmarked for staff development. For one thing, it signals the organization's recognition that staff development is an essential component of organizational operation. For

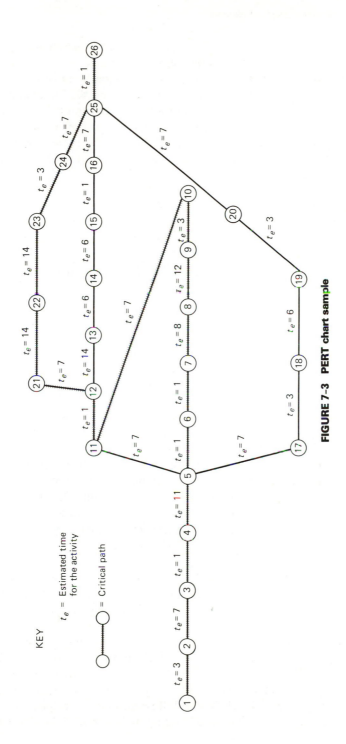

FIGURE 7-3 PERT chart sample

KEY

t_e = Estimated time for the activity

⊙—⊙ = Critical path

191

another, it is helpful to be able to make plans that could entail financial outlay in the knowledge that there is a budget with which to work.

As with other topics in this book, it is not possible here to discuss the budgeting process in depth. For a fuller discussion of that topic, see Vinter and Kish (1984). The techniques involved in cost-benefit analysis are complicated and lie far outside the domain of this book. Computing just the *cost* of one staff development project would, for example, require information about the salary of the staff developer and the percentage of that person's time that went into the project; it would also need to include the costs of secretarial services used by the staff developer, overhead costs such as electricity to operate equipment used by the staff developer, the cost of supplies consumed by the staff developer's project, and so forth. Accordingly, I have used the term *payoff* instead of *benefit,* so that it's clear that I'm not trying to discuss cost-benefit analysis; for the same reason, I have used the term *expense* instead of *cost.*

Payoffs are the expected or realized desirable outcomes of an activity. Some payoffs are *tangible*—a completed orientation manual, or a list of potential buddies to help orient new staff. Others are *intangible*—good feelings, cooperative interactions among staff members, opportunities gained.

Expenses can be defined as the tangible and intangible resources that must be used to carry out an activity that is designed to reach a goal. Some *tangible* expenses include such things as the staff developer's salary, or the amount of time that staff devote to staff development instead of carrying out tasks directly related to service delivery. *Intangible* expenses could be exemplified by staff members' feelings of disappointment when they think that staff development is not designed to meet their felt needs, or their sense that the agency does not care about them very much when it provides a poorly managed orientation program.

Identifying intangible payoffs and expenses can be difficult—an *intangible* is, by definition, "something that cannot be touched"—yet intangibles can be important in the same sense that morale is important. One way to identify the intangible payoffs and expenses of any staff development activity is to list all the people who are likely to be affected by the activity, and then to ask yourself how each person on your list would be likely to respond to that activity. For example, if administrators are likely to view an activity as helpful to them in handling a difficult problem, their resultant support could be viewed as an intangible payoff. Members of the maintenance staff, however, might see the activity only in terms of the extra work it would entail, and might become generally less cooperative as a result—an intangible expense.

The following exercise should help you clarify these concepts:

Suppose you drive to the market to shop for the week's groceries. You fill your shopping cart and proceed to the checkout stand. While standing in line, you talk to a neighbor who tells you some of the recent events in your neighborhood.

In this incident, which of the following items is a tangible expense? an intangible expense? a tangible payoff? an intangible payoff? Write the appropriate term in the blank to the right of the item. (Don't look at the answers until you're done!)

1. The groceries you bring home: _____

2. The money you paid for the groceries: _____

3. The information you picked up from your neighbor: _____

4. Finding a sale on an item that was on your shopping list: _____

5. The other work around the house that didn't get done because you went to the market:

_____

The correct answers are as follows:

1. *Tangible payoff:* You achieved your objective of getting needed food.
2. *Tangible expense:* The cost of the food.
3. *Intangible payoff:* It's difficult to attach a dollar value to information, but it's nice to know what's going on.
4. *Tangible payoff:* The payoff here (saving money by buying something that's on sale) is the greater number of things you can buy for the same amount of money.
5. *Intangible expense:* You can't attach a dollar value to the annoyance of knowing that there are a host of household tasks awaiting your return.

In staff development, you are looking for the most favorable balance you can achieve of payoffs over expenses. This involves some computation, so you can compare the payoffs and expenses—tangible and intangible—of different approaches to a project. Tangible expenses are probably easiest to compute: An external consultant wants a fee plus expenses; renting a particular training film costs a particular amount, and so forth. In addition, many expenses, such as the percentage of the staff developer's time (and salary), can be easily computed; for example, two hours a week out of a forty-hour week is equal to 5 percent. The staff developer's salary is known, and 5 percent of one week's salary can be computed. Computing tangible payoffs may be more difficult, depending on the goals of the project.

There is a way to calculate the *intangible* payoffs.[1] First, develop a list of the intangible payoffs you hope to achieve: If a group is working on the project, they could brainstorm such a list. Then decide on the importance of each item on the list, using a scale from 1 (least important) to 7 (most important). If a group is working on the project, have each person make these ratings in private, then share and average the results.

Let's assume you are comparing two or three ways to carry out the project. Decide whether each way will or will not provide each of the intangible payoffs

[1] I am indebted to Rand Anderson for this procedure.

on the list. If it looks as if that way will contribute to the achievement of a particular intangible payoff on the list, that payoff's score is given as a *plus* for the alternative being considered. If it neither contributes nor detracts, a *zero* score is given. If it detracts from achieving a desired payoff, the value for the payoff is a *minus* for that alternative.

Suppose you have decided you need to replace your old car. You have three alternatives: (1) buy a new car, (2) buy a used car, or (3) lease a car. The desired intangible payoffs are: (1) that the car handles easily, (2) that the car is available today, (3) that the car is comfortable, (4) that the car looks good, (5) that the car will please your spouse, and (6) that the car is safe. A group of your friends helps you by privately rating the degree to which each of these payoffs is important, in the long run, on a scale of 1 to 7 (these ratings will be averaged below as the "average score"). The plus, zero, or minus is assigned in relation to whether or not the item will, in your view, provide the desired intangible payoff. For example, a new car handles easily (+) but has to be ordered, so it is not available today (−). It's comfortable (+) and looks good (+), but it doesn't please your spouse (−) because it costs so much. However, it *is* safe (+). Adding the pluses and minuses together (see Table 7–1, the "New Car" column), we get a total of +13.2 (5.8+3.2+3.2+1.0) and −7.4 (−5.0 and −2.4). Combining +13.2 with −7.4, we get +5.8. Table 7–1 represents the way in which each alternative relates to the desired intangible payoff.

It looks as if the leased car is the best alternative in terms of achieving your intangible payoffs. However, when comparing tangible losses—purchase price versus monthly leasing cost, finance charge if the car is bought on time, insurance, maintenance, and standard repairs—all losses that will vary depending on which alternative (new, leased, or used car) you are considering, the net cost of the leased car is highest, and that of the used car is lowest. In other words, this procedure does not automatically provide a clear-cut decision for you—only a basis on which to make a decision.

TABLE 7–1. Replacing Your Old Car

DESIRABLE INTANGIBLE PAYOFFS	AVERAGE SCORE	ALTERNATIVES		
		NEW CAR	USED CAR	LEASED CAR
Handles easily	5.8	+5.8	−5.8	+5.8
Available today	5.0	−5.0	+5.0	+5.0
Comfortable	3.2	+3.2	−3.2	+3.2
Looks good	3.2	+3.2	0	+3.2
Pleases spouse*	2.4	−2.4	+2.4	−2.4
Is safe	1.0	+1.0	−1.0	+1.0
Total .		5.8	2.6	15.8

*A very frugal spouse.

Let's apply this procedure to planning for an orientation program project. For purposes of this exercise, let's assume we're trying to decide whether to rely on a manual *alone*, or a buddy system *alone*. Which provides the largest payoff for the smallest expense? First, we compare these two alternatives for intangible payoffs, beginning with a list of the intangible payoffs *we want to achieve*. Again, as a way of testing your ability to use this content, why not carry out your own assessment of the payoff/expense comparison, and then compare it with mine?

DESIRED INTANGIBLE PAYOFFS

Satisfying to new employees
Low demand on staff energy
Minimum error rate of new staff
Accurate information
Easy to administer
Easy communication about this agency's orientation program to other agencies for public relations purposes
Quick and efficient movement of new staff into carrying full job load

Next, rate each of these items on a scale of 1 (least important) to 7 (most important). My ratings follow:

DESIRED INTANGIBLE PAYOFFS*	RATING	BUDDY SYSTEM	ORIENTATION MANUAL
Satisfying	7	+7	−7
Low demand	2*	−2	+2
Minimum error	5	+5	−5
Accurate	6	−6	+6
Easy to administer	2*	−2	+2
Easy to explain	1	−1	+1
Quick movement	4	+4	−4
		+5	−5

*I rated "low demand" and "easy to administer" as being of equal importance to demonstrate how you would handle a tie. In this case, you show two ratings of "2," skip "3" and go next to "4."

I based my ratings[2] on the following:

"Satisfying."   I believe that a new staff member would find it more gratifying to have a fellow staff member to turn to than an impersonal manual, which, although it can provide needed information, cannot provide support and encouragement. In a crisis, it could prove very unsatisfying to be told to "look it up in the manual." So the buddy system gets a plus, the manual a "minus."

[2]Note that, to avoid confusion, I have not rearranged the list. If I had, the order would be "satisfying" (7), "accurate" (6), "minimum error" (5), "quick movement" (4), "low demand" (2), "easy to administer" (2), and "easy to explain" (1).

"Low demand."   Once the manual is done, little staff time will be needed to make it useful, beyond explaining what might prove momentarily obscure. A buddy system, however, would put continuous if intermittent time demands on staff. So—buddy system, minus; manual, plus.

"Minimum error."   If a buddy system is easily available, the new staff member can avoid making errors; with a manual, the new staff member still has to interpret the written page into an action. So—buddy system, plus; manual, minus.

"Accurate."   A manual that has been worked on by several staff members and an administrator is likely to be correct, but individual staff, acting as buddies, may make mistakes or give inaccurate interpretations of policies and procedures. So—buddy system, minus; manual, plus.

"Easy to administer."   For a buddy system to work, many different people, acting independently, must be available to many new staff members, which may be hard to track, because requests for help are intermittent and unpredictable. A manual is easy to distribute, and therefore easier to administer. So—buddy sysem, minus; manual, plus.

"Easy to explain."   A manual is a package that can easily be given to other agencies for public relations purposes. The buddy system job description is brief and would need further explanation and examples of specific incidents to make clear how the system works. So—buddy system minus; manual, plus.

"Quick movement."   An available buddy provides a role model of performance, whereas a manual provides information but not a way to use that information. So—buddy system, plus; manual, minus.

According to these ratings, the buddy system (+5 total) seems more likely to provide *desired intangible payoffs* than would the orientation manual (−5 total). Since the orientation manual will take longer to prepare than the buddy system (and will involve more staff activity, which could be translated into tangible expenses) it might be advisable to start with the buddy system, and add the orientation manual when it is ready. In the long run, of course, the plan is to provide an orientation program that includes *both* the buddy system and the manual. My purpose here was to provide an example for comparing payoffs and expenses.

CONCLUSION

Managing staff development in ways that are both efficient and effective requires planning and coordination. This chapter has covered ways to locate resources; ways to plan for their use; and ways to consider alternative steps to a staff development goal, selecting those steps with the best balance of payoffs and expenses. The use of these procedures is predicated on a systematic assessment of staff needs and organizational needs, leading to a selection of high-priority needs and a specification of measurable objectives that are chosen to diminish or eliminate these needs through staff development. In the final chapter, I will present some ideas about ways to achieve and maintain an organizationwide staff development program that is both dynamic and productive.

chapter 8

KEEPING STAFF DEVELOPMENT ALIVE AND WELL

- What is a "good" staff development program?
- How can you determine whether or not you have a "good" program?
- How can you improve your existing program?
- What can you do to sustain a "good" staff development program?

In the first chapter of this book I gave you my definition of *staff development.* I listed and then explained a host of activities that could be viewed as staff development activities, although many of these activities have other functions to play. In subsequent chapters I have tried to draw on the accumulated knowledge, experience, and opinions of many people in presenting a set of procedures that can be used to make staff development work. In this final chapter, I want to consider staff development in general, in order to help you think about where you are, where you would like to be, and how to get there with regard to the staff development program in your organization.

WHAT IS A GOOD STAFF DEVELOPMENT PROGRAM?

Obviously, deciding whether or not something is "good" is a subjective matter, based on whatever values you hold. For some, an effective orientation program that makes it possible for people to assume a 100 percent "work-ready posture" as soon as possible after being hired, plus a one-day-a-year in-service, supplemented by informal on-the-job consultation with fellow staff members, is just fine. It costs very little and doesn't interfere with staff members' work schedules. Since you've read this far, you know that I don't think much of such a limited program. Neither do most staff members, who recognize the value of systematic opportunities to continue their professional development. Indeed, the *good* staff development program, in my view, is one that uses most, if not all, of the activities I listed in Chapter 1, and conducts those activities effectively. It's not simply a matter of providing supervision—it needs to be supervision that staff find easily available, instructive and supportive, intellectually stimulating, and generally useful.

Of course, it is pointless to evaluate the effectiveness of any staff development activity if staff development never occurs in your organization. So the first step in assessing your staff development program is to determine just how many of these activities are available in your organization.

DO YOU HAVE A GOOD STAFF DEVELOPMENT PROGRAM?

Although quantity is no guarantee of quality, it is generally accepted that people learn and grow in different ways. Accordingly, the wider the variety of staff development opportunities available, the greater the likelihood that all staff will benefit from staff development; and the more benefit staff members derive from such programs, the better the quality of service they can provide to clients. So first, let's count the number of staff development activities that are actually available to staff, and rate the degree to which each of these activities, when present, is generally available to *all* staff.

Listed here are the staff development activities I identified and described in Chapter 1. For each of them, assign a rating on the following scale:

3 = happens regularly or quite often
2 = happens occasionally
1 = rarely happens (including once-a-year activities)
0 = never happens

THE ACTIVITIES (IN NO SPECIAL ORDER)

A. Supervision with a heavy teaching emphasis
  • for individuals...3 2 1 0
  • for groups of staff 3 2 1 0
B. Consultations with a heavy teaching emphasis
  • for individuals...3 2 1 0
  • for groups of staff 3 2 1 0
C. Orientation
  • for new staff 3 2 1 0
  • for staff changing positions within the organization 3 2 1 0

D. In-service training 3   2   1   0
E. Out-service training and education 3   2   1   0
F. Full-time educational leave 3   2   1   0
G. Field trips to cooperating agencies 3   2   1   0
H. Problem-solving staff meetings 3   2   1   0
I.   Development and use of an accountability system 3   2   1   0
J.   Participation in research 3   2   1   0
K. Service as a field training site for students 3   2   1   0
L. Maintenance of an easily used staff library 3   2   1   0
M. Periodic individual evaluation 3   2   1   0
N. Informal social activities for staff 3   2   1   0
O. Other—anything not listed that you consider a staff development
     activity 3   2   1   0

Maximum total score is 51 (a rating of 3 for each of the 17 activities, unless you add activities under "other"). If you rated all of the activities at the "occasional" level, your score would be 34. A good program should score somewhere between 34 and 51. Of course, you may have rated some of the activities a 1 or a 0, in which case you would need a total of 33 on at least 11 activities in order to have an acceptably good program. In other words, this simple exercise dealing with the degree to which a range of staff development activities are in use provides a rough way to assess the program.

One could argue with some of the specifics. For example, as social workers develop more competence, they often want greater autonomy, which means less one-to-one supervision. The absence of one-to-one supervision provided on a regular basis to experienced workers might be appropriate (although it would lead to a lower score on this exercise), but even highly autonomous staff should have consultation available if and when they need it. And self-managed peer group supervision can be very helpful.

So although you might quibble with the mathematics in this exercise (which implies that anything under the magic number 34 is less than "good"), if you ended up with a score of less than 30, there is probably plenty of room for improvement, in the sense that there is simply too little going on in the way of staff development.

But, you may protest, aren't some of these activities more important than others? Couldn't a staff development program be in fine shape with just a good orientation program, good individual supervision, good in-service training, and a periodic evaluation (which, according to this scheme would total, at the most, a 12)? The answer is a qualified "yes": These four probably are the absolute necessities of any staff development program. But think how much better things would be if some of the other activities were introduced as well.

The other point this exercise makes is that those activities rated 0 or 1 deserve special attention. Let's assume that a good staff development program is characterized by a wide variety of activities and that, to some degree, the more activities the better. As mentioned earlier, however, the fact that an activity occurs does not guarantee that it occurs *effectively*. Indeed, in some organizations, staff development has a bad reputation because the activities that *do* occur in the name of staff development are poorly or unsatisfactorily managed. People are bored or annoyed at having to leave a heavy job load to waste time on an activity that they do not want or that is poorly staged. Staff may be forced to participate in activities because an administrator tells them to, even though these activities have little apparent relation to the daily demands of their job. Programs may be planned for them with little attention to what they want for themselves. For all these reasons, staff development can develop a bad reputation within an organization.

Having read this far, you should be able to develop a list of criteria for an *effective* staff development activity, or to rate all activities according to the following criteria, using the same scale as before:

3 = happens regularly or often
2 = happens occasionally
1 = rarely happens (including once a year)
0 = never happens

A. A contract for staff development is successfully negotiated with the appropriate administrator(s), and the administrator(s) then provide dependable support 3 2 1 0

B. Felt needs of staff are systematically and periodically assessed..... 3 2 1 0

C. The results of the needs assessments are publicized 3 2 1 0

D. The results of the needs assessments are used for the planning of staff development 3 2 1 0

E. Plans include ways of meeting organizational needs as well as felt needs of staff... 3 2 1 0

F. Adequate resources for staff development are located, recorded in a file, and acquired 3 2 1 0

G. Plans for staff development are made in such a way that deadlines are met 3 2 1 0

H. Participants in staff development activities agree to a contract concerning their participation in the activity 3 2 1 0

I. Entry-level skills and/or knowledge of staff participants are assessed prior to the beginning of the activity 3 2 1 0

J. Midstream evaluations of staff development activities are administered; results of the evaluations are used in planning "next steps" in the activity 3 2 1 0

K. Follow-up evaluation of staff development activities are administered; results of the evaluation are used in planning future activities 3 2 1 0

L. Participants in staff development activities rate the person(s) managing the activities as having done so skillfully.................... 3 2 1 0

A perfect score on all these criteria would be 36. If you come anywhere near that, chances are that the quality of staff development activities in your organization is excellent. A score of 24 (based on a rating of 2 for each criterion) suggests an acceptable performance, with room for improvement. Anything less suggests a considerable need for improvement. Note that a rating of 1 or 0 on any of these criteria suggests a serious deficit in the effectiveness of staff development, because *all* the criteria need to be met if the program is to be effective.

I have not included one other criterion, because it is difficult to gather information about it, but if your organization scores a 3 or even a 2 on this one, you're doing really well. Here it is:

M.   There is good evidence that staff are making regular use on the job of
       what they acquired from the staff development activity 3   2   1   0

HOW CAN YOU IMPROVE YOUR EXISTING PROGRAM?

Let's assume that the results of these rating exercises suggest that you are not doing enough in the way of staff development, or that the staff development program is not being managed effectively. How do you improve?

First, you have to develop some common concern about the quantity and quality of staff development. *Common concern* refers to a concern on the part of several staff members, regardless of their place in the organization's formal structure. To translate this concern about the shortcomings of the staff development program into some corrective action, however, probably requires the support of an administrator with the power to affect the current situation, or of some sort of staff development committee. Many organizations have such committees, with a rotating membership; if the organization is fairly large, committee members may be chosen to represent different work units within the organization.

Improving the existing program starts very much as any staff development activity should: with administrative support, using a contract to address the problem. This could be followed by a needs assessment, in which staff are enlisted (through techniques like those described earlier) to determine staff concerns. One might, for example, use the list from the first of the two preceding exercises as a Delphi list in order to determine staff priorities concerning the type of staff development they would like to see. Setting such a process in motion may be difficult enough (especially where the existing program is, according to the standards I've propounded, quite limited), but it will probably be easier than addressing a situation in which the *quality* of staff development is poor because the people managing it lack skill. For example, a supervisor might be viewed as uninterested in the educational aspects of supervision, so that on the rare occasions when she attempts to act in an educational role, she does so ineffectively. When such a supervisor is entrenched in her position and has a great deal of power, a direct challenge to her staff development performance may make her defensive. In such circumstances, it is probably advisable to tackle some other program shortcoming first in order to demonstrate the value of such corrective efforts and to build up some power that can be used later on to address the supervisor's situation.

One large child care agency I knew had an excellent reputation for the quality of care it provided. Nevertheless, administrators placed strong emphasis on individual and family work, with almost no support for any group work activities. A fair number of staff liked the group work approach but could not attract administrative support for staff development activities—group supervision, consultation, in-service training, and the like—that would support group work activities. Undaunted, group-oriented staff created an informal seminar for themselves, often meeting during their lunch hour, which in time became a highly prized form of group consultation. In other words, you don't have to confront an administration directly that is not ready to support certain staff development activities, providing some staff members are willing to join together to address their needs.

In another case, a social worker in a hospital knew that he would soon be appointed the social work representative to a new interdisciplinary team that would be holding regularly scheduled problem-solving staff meetings. He knew of two other team groups that had been created in other parts of the hospital: One had been marvelously helpful to all involved, but the other had been a total disaster, creating rather than resolving conflicts. Further, he knew that a key member of the new team was to be a supervising nurse with whom he had not gotten along in the past. He was worried that this team might also experience interpersonal problems.

As it happened, this worker was a graduate of our School of Social Work who had decided to take an off-campus staff development course I taught. During the "clinic" portion of the class, he described his concern to the class and asked their advice. Based on the class discussion that ensued, he approached the other staff members who were to be appointed to the new team and suggested they meet before the team actually began working on patient issues, so as to work out their own procedures, anticipate any communication problems, and—in effect—work on their own development as a group before they had to function as a group. He later reported that this had been highly effective. By anticipating problems in communication and power before they surfaced around patient management issues, and working out solutions to these issues before the group began its official work as a team, they were able to create a harmonious and productive team.

I have included this example to make two points: first, that the series of group development meetings that prepared the way for the team's work on patient issues was a form of staff development in that the staff group did problem solving around potential group pitfalls, thereby improving the ability of all the new team members to do their job on the team, and, second, that any staff member can take responsibility for the improvement of staff development. Improving staff development, then, can start with just one person, but usually works better when others can be enlisted in the process.

Many aspects of staff development involve an innovation (see Chapter 2 on contracting), whether in the introduction of new staff development activities, or in the introduction of new ideas about practice through an in-service training program. Over the years, considerable knowledge has been developed through research about factors associated with successful innovations. These were assembled in a comprehensive manner by Rothman and his associates (Rothman, 1974). Among their findings were the following ideas:

- Innovations are more likely to be adopted when they are linked to something people want to change.
- Innovations are more likely to be adopted if they are compatible with the organization's existing value system, and if the way in which they are introduced is compatible with the way in which the organization has introduced new ideas in the past.
- Innovations are more likely to be adopted if they are not complex and can be explained or demonstrated with ease.
- Innovations are more likely to be adopted if they can be tried out in a small way— that is, using only part of the innovation, or using it with only a portion of staff.
- Some people in an organization are what might be called "early adopters"—people who are more willing than others to try something new. Your innovation is more likely to attain widespread adoption if you try it out first with these early adopters.
- Certain staff members, regardless of their formal job position on staff, are respected by fellow staff members and serve as informal opinion leaders. An innovation is more likely to be adopted if the organization's opinion leaders can be enlisted to support it.

Rothman concludes his discussion with the following admonition:

> Let there be no misunderstanding: a practitioner cannot use the foregoing in cookbook fashion, employing recipe A to produce innovation B. We have attempted to indicate certain conditions that can facilitate or remove blocks to innovation. Just as with all of the other generalizations and guidelines [in this book], these need to be carried to fruition by a knowledgeable, dedicated, imaginative individual; a practitioner or change agent who is able to delicately fuse science and art in the interests of creating a social order more conducive to human values. (Rothman, 1974, p. 483)

I referred earlier to a *staff development committee.* In many settings, such a committee could serve an important function. The group should be representative of major constituent staff groups, preferably composed of volunteers with a strong commitment to staff development. Since the group would be representative, the members would be in a position to identify innovative work units and staff who are respected as opinion leaders. It would have members who could identify areas of discontent with regard to the quality of existing staff development, or problems caused by the lack of it. It could help to do the necessary behind-the-scenes work involved in administering needs assessment procedures. Finally, it could spread the word about staff development programs, and do so in language familiar to co-workers. In short, the committee could provide the "person power" to support effective innovation.

Many committees use a system in which one-third of the membership changes every year, and each member serves for one three-year term. The chair can be elected by the group or appointed by the administrator, but each chair's time in that office should be limited.

CONCLUSION

In concluding this book, I would like to borrow from Rothman: There are no cookbook solutions to staff development problems. Each has its own particular brand of historical, political, and technological components, and each requires a thoughtful approach. But the first ingredient is commitment to the cause of staff development—a belief that we can all improve, and that to do so, we have to commit ourselves to the process of making our agencies work better by making ourselves work better. In the interests of our clients, we can do no less.

REFERENCES

ABBLESSER, H. (1962). "Role Reversal in a Group Psychotherapy Session." *Group Psychotherapy* 15: 321–325.

ANDERSON, N. (1965). "Primary Effects in Personality Impression Formation Using a Generalized Order/Effect Paradigm." *Journal of Personality and Social Psychology* 2: 1–5.

ANDERSON, N., and BARRIOS, A. (1961). "Primary Effects in Personality Impression Formation." *Journal of Abnormal and Social Psychology* 63: 346–350.

ANDERSON, N., and HUBERT, S. (1963). "Effects of Concomitant Verbal Recall or Order Effects in Personality Impression Formation." *Journal of Verbal Learning and Verbal Behaviors* 2: 374–391.

ARONFREED, J. (1969). "The Concept of Internationalization." In D. Goglin and D. Glass, eds., *Handbook of Socialization Theory and Research.* Chicago: Rand McNally.

ASCH, S. (1946). "Forming Impressions of Personality. " *Journal of Abnormal and Social Psychology* 41: 374–391.

ATKINSON, J. (1964). *An Introduction to Motivation.* Princeton, N.J.: Van Nostrand.

AUSUBEL, D. (1960). "The Use of Advanced Organizers in the Learning of Meaningful Verbal Learning." *Journal of Educational Psychology* 51: 267–272.

BALES, R., and STRODTBECK, F. (1968). "Phases in Group Problem-Solving." In D. Cartwright and A. Zander, eds., *Group Dynamics: Research and Theory,* 3rd ed., pp. 389–398. New York: Harper and Row.

BANDURA, A. (1969). *Principles of Behavior Modification.* New York: Holt, Rinehart and Winston.

BANDURA, A., ROSS, D., and ROSS, S. (1963) "Imitation of Film-Mediated Aggressive Models." *Journal of Abnormal and Social Psychology* 66: 3–11.

BANDURA, A., and WALTERS, R. (1963). *Social Learning and Personality Development.* New York: Holt, Rinehart and Winston.

BASS, R., and VAUGHAN, J. (1966). *Training in Industry: The Management of Learning.* Belmont, Calif.: Wadsworth.

BERNARD, S. (1975, May). "Why Service Delivery Programs Fail." *Social Work* 20(3): 206–211.
BERTCHER, H. (1978, Fall). "Guidelines for the Group Worker's Use of Role Modeling." *Journal of Social Work with Groups* 3(2): 235–246.
BERTCHER, H. (1979). *Group Participation: Techniques for Leaders and Members.* Beverly Hills, Calif.: Sage Publications.
BERTCHER, H., GORDON, J., HAYES, M., and MIAL, H. (1969). *Role Modeling, Role Playing: A Manual for Vocational Development and Employment Agencies.* Ann Arbor, Mich.: Manpower Science Services, Inc.
BERTCHER, H., and MAPLE, F. (1977). *Creating Groups.* Beverly Hills, Calif.: Sage Publications.
BIDDLE, B. (1979). *Role Theory: Expectations, Identities and Behavior.* New York: Academic Press.
BIEHLER, R. (1978). *Psychology Applied to Teaching,* 3rd ed. Boston: Houghton Mifflin.
BOSTWICK, G., and KYTE, N. (1981). "Measurement." In R. Grinnel, ed., *Social Work Research and Evaluation,* pp. 93–129. Itasca, Ill.: F. E. Peacock.
BRIM, O., and WHEELER, S. (1966). *Socialization after Childhood.* New York: John Wiley and Sons.
BROPHY, J. (1979). *Advances in Teacher Effectiveness Research.* Occasional Paper No. 18. East Lansing, Mich.: Institute for Research on Teaching.
BRUNER, J. *The Process of Education.* New York: Vintage Books, 1960.
BURMAN, P. (1972). *Precedence Networks for Project Planning.* London: McGraw-Hill.
CAMERON, N. (1947). *The Psychology of Behavior Disorders.* Boston: Houghton Mifflin.
CARKHUFF, R. (1969). *Helping and Human Relations.* Vol. I: *Selection and Training.* New York: Holt, Rinehart and Winston.
CARTWRIGHT, D., and ZANDER, A. (1968). *Group Dynamics: Research and Theory,* 3rd ed. New York: Harper and Row.
CAUDILL. W. (1958). *The Psychiatric Hospital As A Small Society.* Cambridge: Harvard University Press.
CHASE, S. (1938). *The Tyranny of Words.* New York: Harcourt, Brace and Company.
CHERNISS, G. (n.d.). "Recent Research and Theory on Job Stress and Burnout in Helping Professions." Mimeographed.
CLEMMER, D. (1940). *The Prison Community.* Boston: The Christopher Publishing House.
COFER, C., and APPLEY, M. (1967). *Motivation: Theory and Research.* New York: John Wiley and Sons.
COSER, L. (1956). *The Functions of Social Conflict.* New York: The Free Press.
CROXTON, T. (1974). "The Therapeutic Contract in Social Treatment." In P. Glasser, R. Sarri, and R. Vinter, eds., *Individual Change Through Small Groups.* pp. 169–185. New York: The Free Press.
DIVESTA, F., MEYER, D., and MILLS, J. (1964). "Confidence in an Expert as a Function of His Judgments." *Human Relations* 17: 235–242.
DUCHASTEL, P., and MERRILL, P. (1973). "The Effects of Behavioral Objectives on Learning: A Review of Empirical Studies." *Merrill-Palmer Quarterly of Behavior and Development* 10(3).
ELLIS, H. (1965). *The Transfer of Learning.* New York: Macmillan.
ETZIONI, A. (1964). *Modern Organization.* Englewood Cliffs, N.J.: Prentice-Hall, Inc.
FEAGIN, J. (1965, September). "Prejudice, Orthodoxy and the Social Situation," *Social Forces* 44(1): 46–57.
FEDERAL ELECTRIC CORPORATION. (1967). *A Programmed Introduction to PERT: Program Evaluation and Review Technique.* New York: John Wiley and Sons.
FESTINGER, L., SCHACTER, S., and BACK, K. (1950). *Social Pressures in Informal Groups.* New York: Harper.
FINE, S., and WILEY, W. (1971). *An Introduction to Functional Job Analysis: A Scaling of Selected Tasks from the Social Welfare Field.* Kalamazoo, Mich.: W. C. Upjohn Institute for Employment Research.
FLANDERS, J. (1968). "A Review of Research on Imitative Behavior." *Psychological Bulletin* 69: 316–337.
FREEDMAN, J. (1965). "Long Term Behavioral Effects of Cognitive Dissonance." *Journal of Personality and Social Psychology* 1: 145–155.
FRENCH, J., and RAVEN, B. (1968). "The Bases of Social Power." In D. Cartwright and A. Zander, eds., *Group Dynamics: Research and Theory,* 3rd ed., pp. 259–269. New York: Harper and Row.
FREUDENBERGER, H. (1974). "Staff Burn-out." *Journal of Social Issues* 30: 159–165.

GALL, J. (1975). *Systemantics: How Systems Work and Especially How They Fail.* New York: Quadrangle/New York Times.

GAMBRILL, E. (1978). *Behavior Modification: Handbook of Assessment, Intervention and Evaluation.* San Francisco: Jossey-Bass.

GOTTMAN, J., and CLASEN, R. (1972). *Evaluation in Education: A Practitioner's Guide.* Itasca, Ill.: F. E. Peacock.

GOULDNER, A. (1965). *Studies in Leadership: Leadership and Democratic Action.* New York: Russel and Russel.

GRINNELL, R. (1981). *Social Work Research and Evaluation.* Itasca, Ill.: F. E. Peacock.

HAGE, J., and AIKEN, M. (1967). "Relationship of Centralization to Other Structural Properties." *Administrative Science Quarterly.* 12: 72–79.

HALL, R. (1972). *Organizations: Structure and Process.* Englewood Cliffs, N.J.: Prentice-Hall, Inc.

HAMOVITCH, M. (1963). Class Lecture, University of Southern California, School of Social Work, Fall.

HARVEY, O., and RUTHERFORD, J. (1960). "Status in the Informal Group: Influence and Influencability at Differing Age Levels." *Child Development.* 31: 377–385.

HASENFELD, Y. (1974). "People Processing Organizations: An Exchange Approach." In Y. Hasenfeld and R. English, eds., *Human Service Organizations, pp. 60–71.* Ann Arbor: The University of Michigan Press.

HASENFELD, Y. and ENGLISH, R., eds. (1974). *Human Service Organizations.* Ann Arbor: The University of Michigan Press.

HAYAKAWA, S. (1962). *The Use and Misuse of Language.* Greenwich, Conn.: Fawcett.

HJELLE, L., and ZIEGLER, D. (1981). *Personality Theories: Basic Assumptions, Research and Applications,* 2nd ed. New York: McGraw Hill.

HOPPE, F. (1930). "Erflog und Misserflog." *Psychologische Forschung* 14: 1–62.

HORN, ROBERT, ed. (1977). *The Guide to Simulations/Games and Training,* 3rd ed. Cranford, N.J.: Didactic Systems, Inc.

INGALLS, J. (1973). *A Trainer's Guide to Andragogy: Its Concepts, Experience and Application,* rev. ed. Washington, D.C.: U.S. Department of Health, Education and Welfare, Social and Rehabilitation Services.

IVEY, A. (1983). *Intentional Interviewing and Counseling.* Monterey, Calif.: Brooks/Cole.

JAYARATNE, S., and LEVY, R. (1979). *Empirical Clinical Practice.* New York: Columbia University Press.

JOHNSON, R. (1975). "Meaning in Complex Learning." *Review of Educational Research* 45(3): 425–454.

JONES, E., and ANESHANSEL, J. (1956). "The Learning and Utilization of Contravaluant Material." *Journal of Abnormal and Social Psychology* 53: 27–34.

JONES, E., and GERARD, H. (1967). *Foundations of Social Psychology.* New York: J. W. Ley and Sons.

JONES, E., and KOHLER, R. (1958). "The Effects of Plausibility on the Learning of Controversial Statements." *Journal of Abnormal and Social Psychology* 57: 315–320.

JOYCE, B., and SHOWERS, B. (1980, February). "Improving Inservice Training: The Messages of Research." *Educational Leadership* 37. pp. 379–385.

JOYCE, B., and SHOWERS, B. (1983). *Power in Staff Development through Research in Training.* Arlington, Va.: Association for Supervision and Curriculum Development.

KATZ, D., and KAHN, R. (1966). *The Social Psychology of Organizations.* New York: John Wiley and Sons.

KELLEY, H., and WOODRUFF, C. (1956). "Members' Reactions to Apparent Group Approval of a Counternorm Communication." *Journal of Abnormal and Social Psychology* 52: 67–74.

KOZMA, R., and BERTCHER, H. (1974). "Evaluation of a Self-Instructional Mini-Course on Empathic Responding." Paper presented at the American Education Research Association, Chicago, April 15.

LABOVITZ, S., and HAGERDORN, R. (1981). *Introduction to Social Research.* 3rd ed. New York: McGraw-Hill.

LAUFFER, A. (1973). *The Aim of the Game.* New York: Gamed Simulations, Inc.

LAUFFER, A. (1978a). *Doing Continuing Education and Staff Development.* New York: McGraw-Hill.

LAUFFER, A. (1978b). *Social Planning at the Community Level.* Englewood Cliffs, N.J.: Prentice-Hall.

LAWRENCE, G. (1974). *Patterns of Effective Inservice Education: A State of the Art Summary of Research on Materials and Procedures for Changing Teacher Behaviors in Inservice Education.* Tallahassee, Fla.: State Department of Education.

LINSTONE, H., and MURRAY, T. (1975). *The Delphi Method: Techniques and Applications.* Reading, Massachusetts: Addison-Wesley Publishing Company.

LOUCKS, S., and MELLE, M. (1982, April). "Evaluation of Staff Development: How Do They Know It Took?" *The Journal of Staff Development* 13(1):

LUCHINS, A. (1957). "Experimental Attempts to Minimize the Impact of First Impressions." In C. Hovland, ed., *The Order of Presentation in Persuasion,* pp. 63–75. New Haven: Yale University Press.

MacBRIDE, P. (1984). "An Inservice Education Program: Effects on the Professional Knowledge, Attitudes and Behaviors of Classroom Teachers." Unpublished doctoral dissertation, University of Michigan, School of Education.

MacCOBY, E. (1961). "The Choice of Variables in the Study of Socialization." *Sociometry* 24: 357–371.

MacDONALD, R. (1981, September). "Assessing the Impact of Staff Development on People: How Do You Know It Is Making a Difference?" *Inservice* (National Council of States on Inservice Education).

MAGER, R. (1975). *Preparing Instructional Objectives,* 2nd ed. Belmont, Calif.: Fearon.

MARCH, J., and SIMON, H. (1958). *Organizations.* New York: Wiley and Sons.

MASLACH, C. (1976). "Burned Out." *Human Behavior* 3: 16–32.

MASLACH, C. (1982). *Burnout: The Cost of Caring.* Englewood Cliffs, N.J.: Prentice-Hall.

MAYER, J., and TIMMS, N. (1970). *The Client Speaks: Working Class Impressions of Casework.* New York: Atherton Press.

McCLELLAND, D. (1965). "Toward a Theory of Motive Acquisition." *American Psychologist* 20: 321–333.

McKEACHIE, W. (1969). *Teaching Tips: A Guidebook for the Beginning College Teacher,* 6th ed. Lexington, Mass.: D. C. Heath and Company.

MILKOVICH, G., and GLUECK, W. (1985). *Personnel/Human Resource Management: A Diagnostic Approach,* 4th ed. Plano, Tex.: Business Publications, Inc.

MILLER, G. (1956). "The Magical Number, Plus or Minus Two: Some Limits on Our Capacity for Processing Information." *Psychological Review* 63: 81–97.

MILLER, I. (1971). "Supervision in Social Work." *Encyclopedia of Social Work,* 16th issue. New York: National Association of Social Workers.

MILLER, N., and DOLLARD, J. (1941). *Social Learning and Imitation.* New Haven: Yale University Press.

MILNES, J., and BERTCHER, H. (1980). *Communicating Empathy.* San Diego: University Associates, Inc.

MOOS, R. (1974). *Evaluating Treatment Environments.* New York: John Wiley and Sons.

MORENO, J. L. (1952). "Psychodramatic Production Techniques." *Group Psychotherapy* 4: 243–273.

MORENO, Z. (1951). "Psychodrama in a Well Baby Clinic." *Group Psychotherapy* 2: 100–106.

MURDOCK, B. (1961). "The Retention of Individual Items." *Journal of Experimental Psychology* 62: 618–625.

NAPIER, R., and GERSHENFELD, M. (1981). *Groups: Theory and Experience,* 2nd ed. Boston: Houghton Mifflin.

NATFULIN, D., DONNELLY, F., and WARE, J. (1973, July). "The Doctor Fox Lecture: A Paradigm of Educational Seduction." *Journal of Medical Education* 48(7): 630–635.

NICHOLSON, A., JOYCE, B., PARKER, D., and WATERMAN, F. (1977). *The Literature on Inservice Teacher Education: An Analytic Review.* ISTE Report III. Syracuse, N.Y.: The National Dissemination Center.

NYBELL, L., MORTON, T., RUBY, P., BERTCHER, H., and GAUNT, R. (1977). *Staff Development for Supervisors.* Ann Arbor: University of Michigan, School of Social Work.

OJEMANN, R. (1968). "Should Educational Objectives Be Stated in Behavioral Terms?" *Elementary School Journal* 68(5): 223–231.

OVERTON, A. (1960, April). "Taking Help from Our Clients." *Social Work* 5(2): 42–50.

PAWLAK, E. (1976). "Organizational Tinkering." *Social Work* 21: 376–380.

PERROW, C. (1970). *Complex Organizations: A Critical Essay.* Glenview, Ill.: Scott, Foresman.

PETERSON, L. (1963). "Immediate Memory: Data and Theory." In C. Cofer and B. Musgrave, eds., *Verbal Behavior and Learning: Problems and Processes,* pp. 336–373. New York: McGraw-Hill.

PFEIFFER, J., and JONES, J. (1965–1975). *Structured Experiences for Human Relations Training,* vols. I–V. LaJolla, Calif.: University Associates.

POLANSKY, N., Ed. (1975). *Social Work Research: Methods for the Helping Profession,* rev. ed. Chicago: University of Chicago Press.

POLLACK, I., and JOHNSON, L. (1965). "Memory Span with Efficient Coding Procedures." *American Journal of Psychology* 78: 609–614.

PUGH, D., HICKSON, D., HININGS, C., and TURNER, C. (1968). "Dimensions of Organizational Structure." *Administrative Science Quarterly* 13: 65–105.

REED, B. (1981, August). "Gender Issues in Training Group Leaders." *The Journal for Specialists in Group Work* 6(3): 161–170.

ROBBINS, S. (1976). *The Administrative Process.* Englewood Cliffs, N.J.: Prentice-Hall, Inc.

ROBBINS, S. (1980). *The Administrative Process,* 2nd ed. Englewood Cliffs, N.J.: Prentice-Hall, Inc.

ROSENKRANS, M. (1967). "Imitation in Children as a Function of Perceived Similarity to a Social Model and Vicarious Reinforcement." *Journal of Personality and Social Psychology* 7: 307–315.

ROTHMAN, J. (1974). *Planning and Organizing for Social Change.* New York: Columbia University Press.

ROYSTER, E. (1972). "Black Supervisors: Problems of Race and Role." In F. Kaslow, ed., *Issues in Human Services,* pp. 72–84. San Francisco: Jossey-Bass.

SAYLES, L., and STRAUSS, G. (1980). *Human Problems of Mangement,* 4th ed. Englewood Cliffs, N.J.: Prentice-Hall.

SCHECTER, D., and O'FARRELL, T. (1970). *Training and Continuing Education: A Handbook for Health Care Institutions.* Chicago: Hospital Research and Educational Trust.

SCHMUCK, R., RUNKEL, P., SATUREN, S., MARTELL, R., and DERR, C. (1972). *Handbook of Organization Development in Schools.* Center for the Advanced Study of Educational Administration; University of Oregon: National Press Books.

SCOTT, J. (1958). *Animal Behavior.* Chicago: University of Chicago Press.

SEARS, P. (1940). "Levels of Aspiration in Academically Successful and Unsuccessful Children." *Journal of Abnormal and Social Psychology* 35: 495–536.

SHAW, M. (1981). *Group Dynamics: The Psychology of Small Group Behavior,* 3rd ed. New York: McGraw-Hill.

SIMON, S. (1972). *Values Clarification.* New York: Hart Publications.

SKINNER, B. (1968). *The Technology of Teaching.* New York: Appleton-Century-Crofts.

STANTON, A., and SCHWARTZ, M. (1954). *The Mental Hospital.* New York: Basic Books.

STROTHER, D., Ed. "Practical Applications of Research." *Newsletter of Phi Delta Kappa's Center on Evaluation, Development, and Research,* Vol. 5, No. 3. (March, 1983), p. 2.

SUCHMAN, J. (1965). "Inquiry and Education." In J. Gallagher, ed., *Teaching Gifted Students: A Book of Readings,* pp. 193–209. Boston: Allyn and Bacon. ·

TAFT, R. (1954). "Selective Recall and Memory Distortion of Favorable and Unfavorable Material." *Journal of Abnormal and Social Psychology* 46: 23–29.

THOMAS, E., and FELDMAN, R. (1967). "Concepts of Role Theory." In E. Thomas, ed., *Behavioral Science for Social Workers,* pp. 17–50. New York: The Free Press.

THOMAS, E., and McLEOD, D. (1960). *In-Service Training and Reduced Work Loads.* New York: Russell Sage Foundation.

THOMAS, E., and McLEOD, D. (1967). "A Research Evaluation of In-Service Training Reduced Workloads in Aid to Dependent Children." In E. Thomas, ed., *Behavioral Science for Social Workers,* pp. 341–349. New York: The Free Press.

TWAIN, M. (n.d.) From the record *Hal Holbrook in Mark Twain Tonight.* Columbia Masterworks OL 5440.

VINTER, R. (1963). "Analysis of Treatment Organizations." *Social Work* 8 (July): 3–15.

VINTER, R., and KISH, R. (1984). *Budgeting for Not-for-Profit Organizations.* New York: The Free Press.

WALTER, G., and MARKS, S. (1981). *Experiential Learning and Change: Theory, Design and Practice.* New York: John Wiley and Sons.

WEBER, M. (1947). *Theory of Social and Economic Organizations.* Translated by K. Morris. New York: Harper and Row Publishers.

YERKES, R., and MORGULIS, S. (1909). "The Method of Pavlov in Animal Psychology." *Psychological Bulletin* 6: 257–273.

ZIMMERMAN, C., and BAUER, R. (1956). "The Effect of an Audience upon What Is Remembered." *Public Opinion Quarterly* 20: 238–248.

INDEX